Eight Seconds of Grace

Also by Thad Beery

"The Rodeo Road"

Eight Seconds of Grace

The Stories of John McBeth

Thad Beery

Foreword by Bob Tallman

Stockport Publishing, LLC
Stockport, Ohio, 2014

Cover: Original Portrait of John McBeth on KO Sundown, by Mark Storm, 1974. From the John McBeth Collection.

Library of Congress Control Number: 2014935038

ISBN-13: 978-0-9916482-0-7

For anyone who has ever dreamed of being a cowboy.

CONTENTS

FOREWORD

Memories . . . are the greatest bank account you can have if your life has been full of friends, family and travel. I am truly rich. I remember watching John McBeth riding at the Cow Palace in San Francisco before I ever met him. He had a manner about him, the way he walked, the way he stood with his hands on his hips, and the way he would listen to people when he talked to them. At the same time he was very assertive and sure of himself—and then he proved it when he strapped a bronc saddle on one of those bucking horses.

I remember even back then, before he'd won the world, he had a manner and character about him that said, "World Champion." He was different. He was taking care of business. He had a plan! He wasn't afraid to go home and work.

One of the reasons he has been successful is because of his work ethic. Yet, I remember that in spite of his businesslike manner in the arena, in his shop and at home, he always had a quick smile. His smile is not wide—but very deep. I don't know why he decided to be friends with me, but I always counted it a privilege.

I remember John McBeth at Yukon, Oklahoma, when it was about fifteen degrees with the snow blowing sideways during the NFR. He got on about ten bucking horses at the bucking horse sale held in conjunction with the finals there, and then went over to the rodeo, shook out his chaps, and got on his bronc. I think they paid those guys twenty bucks a head to get on them, too. But that's just the way it was back then. That was the way all those guys were. And you never showed a sign of weakness either or they'd get on you, bad. There were no trainers: There was no Justin Sports Medicine like today. If you had some tape you might tape yourself up, but if not you just gritted your teeth and got through it. That's a lost era.

I've watched John ride at Denver, Fort Worth, Houston, San Antonio, and the Cow Palace. I've watched him at Salinas, and Reno, and the big Canadian rodeos, and he didn't always win first, but he was a businessman about it, and if it was a two-header or a three-header he'd place strong in that average every time.

As time went on we kind of got separated a little bit, and then when he came back around after he'd quit riding, I found it very flattering that he'd followed who I was, where I was going, and what I'd done. When a guy like that takes notice of you and sincerely discusses what you're doing that's a mentoring you can't write a prescription for. You can't hire that. That's big, BIG. I've tried to do it for younger guys like he did it for me.

I remember when John did the TV telecasts for Hesston. The Hesston Corporation and their telecasts were the biggest thing that had ever happened to rodeo back then. John's on-air descriptions were so vivid, more than you usually see on TV. I liked it because when he'd do a replay he could get me to riding a bucking horse just sitting in the office on a swivel chair. Another unusual thing he could do as the world champion saddle bronc rider, he could talk about the calf roping. He has a very well-rounded background and is a great lover of good horse flesh.

Sometimes he'll call up with a question and ask me what I think about one thing or another, and I'll tell him what I think. If I don't think it's any good I tell him, and if I need to think about it I'll tell him that, and he'll say, "Bob, we're not as young as we used to be. Don't wait too long." The guys of John's era were "equipped" with quips, one-liners, phraseology, and they let me adopt it and adapt it to fit my nature. It served me well in my career as an announcer.

Later in life when I was going 130 miles an hour and they were slowing down a little bit, we might not always have had time to visit but they'd always raise their head to me as we passed by and kind of nod as if to say, "Go on with it, lift and spur!" And the acceptance of those men of that era is a memory I have that makes me rich.

The 1970's were a special time in rodeo. The business side of rodeo grew in the '70's. It was a time of the first sponsors, Coca-Cola, Coors. And those cowboys of that era were the characters that really made the business shine. They made business decisions that are still being thought of today as the right thing to do, the right way to do it. They didn't care if they ever got recognized for it or not. They knew that they were doing something without management, without legal assistance. They were doing something that would create a place for our kids, and now our grandkids, to live and operate and to raise the next generation in. Everything they won, everything they made, they put back in to it.

A group of us sat down in Plymouth, California, one day and formulated a plan for the Circuit System in play today in the PRCA. The next day Larry Jordan caught a plane for the head office with our written plan and I mailed out the information about what we were going to do. We knew it was a slam dunk. John was a part of that group and was appointed secretary of the Prairie Circuit. The Circuit System was a way for more regional cowboys to get some local publicity and more money in their pockets. John's biggest contribution to the sport was the business side of it. Being a world champion he did not try to parlay that into fame and fortune; what he did parlay it into was business. He used it to further the rodeo business and his livelihood.

One other thing about me and McBeth, something we had in common. We both married over our heads. I've been married to Kristen for 45 years and John and Francie have been together for over 50.

I was asked during the preparation of this foreword, "Why is this book important?" It's important because the stories of those days are hero stories. That's what those guys were. And by telling these stories John is opening up that bank account I talked about earlier and sharing his memories with all of us. Yet even as we are enriched, the balance in that account never drops.

Bob Tallman

PREFACE

I first met John McBeth at a pro rodeo in Grinnell, Iowa, in the summer of 1973—the year before he won the saddle bronc riding world championship. It was my first pro rodeo. I was an eighteen year old kid enrolled in John's bronc school that started the next day in Onida, South Dakota. I thought hitting Grinnell was a good idea; it was on the way to the school and would give me a chance to win some money to help pay for the trip. John thought the same thing.

I drew the horse to win on that day. About three jumps into the arena he turned back and spun to the left. He was slow and deliberate and jumped in that air and hung there as he came around. I got an intense rush riding that big hairy creampuff as he floated three feet off the ground with no power at all! He was tailor-made for spurring. I was a green kid who missed every chance he gave me to score points. I spent most of the ride spurring the cantle instead of the bronc, a starry-eyed kid distracted by his first exposure to the big time. I even remember thinking, "Wow! I'm riding in my first pro rodeo . . ." as I was riding in my first pro rodeo.

When the pickup man put me back on the ground I was sitting third. John was the next bronc rider to go. He had drawn considerably worse than I had. His horse kicked to its belly once or twice and ran down the middle of the arena. His lack of anything even resembling a buck made him incredibly hard to spur and nearly impossible to place on. Yet, John spurred him every jump, where no jumps actually were; he imposed a rhythm on that bronc, where no rhythm existed.

When the horse got to the end of the arena he jumped

away from the fence, reversing direction to gas 'em back toward the chutes. It was the first move he made that was anything close to a good jump. John was sitting up with an arch in his back as the horse came off the fence—side-on to me. He was leaned back with his feet stuck in the front end, lifting on his rein, with his toes turned out and his free arm shot straight in the air. He had his chin tucked into his chest as he sighted down his rein arm. He spurred that bronc in the neck like it was the tenth round at the National Finals Rodeo, beating me by a point, dropping me to fourth.

At the stripping chute after the riding I introduced myself. He sized me up in an instant. I told him I was headed for his school. He slipped into mentor-mode and critiqued my ride as only the guy who is fixing to win the world can. I knew then I had the right teacher. He was all business. There was no attitude or talking "down to the rookie." All his attitude was reserved for the broncs. It pumped me up, talking cowboy to cowboy with the best. When I jumped in the car to head for Onida I knew I was a better bronc rider than when I'd got up that morning, and I learned more at the stripping chute than in the arena that day!

At the school I made my first good ride, and John got on one to show us how it was done. He *had* to ride good because he'd been telling us how to do it for several days. You could see how excited he was. He chapped up and hefted his saddle over, and he was twitchy—that's all. Just twitchy. He said to the pickup man over his shoulder as he stepped aboard, "You sure don't want to screw it up after telling these boys how to do it all week."

Yeah, the pressure was on.

He hopped in the saddle, put his feet in the stirrups, gripped his swells and looked over the back of the chute at all ten of us, clustered about. He said, "I won a second on this bronc at San Antone!" And he lifted his rein and nodded.

The bronc was a beautiful paint horse that bucked *good* for six seconds before he cracked it back to the left and spun, really getting rank. McBeth was perfect. We all screamed our heads off when we saw that. We had to. It was moving. It was inspirational. It was what we all came for.

I saw John ride eight or ten times after that when our paths crossed at some rodeo or another over the next few years. I never saw him anywhere close to bucked off—never even out of shape. I never saw him miss a lick. Every jump was an exact copy of every other jump and they were all perfect, no matter what the horse did. McBeth was consistent, he was methodical, he was flawless.

He told us at the school, "If one of these top cowboys tells you he can walk over and lift the corner of those bucking chutes you better not bet against him." And I believed it! No, I mean I *literally* believed it. That's the impact his presence had on me, and lots of other people too. The rodeo world is filled with John McBeth advocates. People he has helped, guided, and inspired to go farther and accomplish more than they thought they could. You will meet some of them in the pages of this book.

So, when the opportunity to collaborate with John on this book project presented itself I jumped at the chance. I found that the name of McBeth knocked down doors in the rodeo world like a Kansas tornado tearing through a board shack. What could be a tight-knit, close-mouthed fraternity under different circumstances opened up at the sound of his name. It set up a line of communication to the movers and shakers in the world of pro rodeo. Everywhere I went and everyone I talked to stood a little bit straighter and smiled a little bit easier when I mentioned John. They jumped at the chance to help—elated at seeing him get a little bit of his due. They said things like, "Anything for John," or "I sure owe him a lot," or "I'm glad you're doing this project because he sure deserves the recognition." The stories they told prove that John has about done it all in this world. They told me about John as the competitor, businessman, friend and mentor. The picture they draw is of an exceptional person with an unconquerable spirit that in anything he chose, would have labeled him a champion.

I also discovered through many conversations with John that if he weren't the world champion bronc rider he could have gone a long way as a story teller. He's that good. That's what cowboys do during a long night's drive from Grand Junction to Reno to get on another'n—they tell stories, one after another, each one meant to top the other. It's an acquired skill, like sleeping sitting up, or smiling at the sight of your own blood. These stories, then, offer a glimpse of the Kansas cowboy who made himself a world champion. Some of the stories were told to me by John directly. Some are the result of interviews with the people that know John the best: His friends and family. Still other stories are the bits and pieces gathered from John's students and fellow cowboys, woven back together through my own interpretation. A few of the names and places have been changed, fictionalized, to protect the innocent—those that *are* named.

When I asked John what he wanted in the book, he said, "I'd like for it to be fun to read with some laughter, some serious parts, and maybe even a few tears." It's hard to describe something as complex as a human being, perhaps more so a champion, especially when these stories have been filtered through four decades of time and the imperfect memory of the human mind. Often the author's job is to combine several disparate tales describing the same event and toss in a dash of that special writer's dust picked up in an arena of his own. The trick then is to make all the different versions ring true for those that remember.

Luckily, the immutable truths about the values that matter—what we believe, who we are, who John is, and the meaning of cowboy—come through unvarnished. The rest is just in the details.

So here lie the recollections of all of us, about the way it was and the way it should be. And it's probably—for the most part—true.

ACKNOWLEDGEMENTS

The first thank you I have to say is to the man himself, John McBeth. The opportunity to write this book has been a blessing for one who has always followed the sport of rodeo, admired rodeo cowboys above all other professional athletes, movie stars and millionaires, and even rodeoed a little bit himself back in the day. The name of John McBeth has granted me access to the Who's Who of rodeo. Those contestants, administrators, judges, announcers, bullfighters and rodeo producers—cowboys all—have graciously accepted me at face value, opened up their heart and mind to my questions, and offered whatever assistance they could to this book project. It is remarkable not only that such accomplished, successful, and incredibly busy people responded in such a positive way to help with John's project, but that *anyone, anywhere,* has such devoted friends. So let me add my voice to all those others still sounding in my ears and thank John for the help when I needed it most.

The next to be acknowledged is Shellie McBeth, John's daughter-in-law, Blake's wife. Shellie came up with the title for this book while John and I were struggling for one that fit. When she suggested "Eight Seconds of Grace" I thought first of how gracefully John always rode a bucking horse—with smooth precision. Then it occurred to me how much grace he always showed those people around him, like me at the Hall of Fame (the last story in the book), and I thought the title really fit who he was. Then when Shellie said she hadn't thought of that, but, "It was by the grace of God that he did what he did for all those years and came away unscathed," the title hit the trifecta, and Shellie hit the mark.

In no particular order let me thank Hadley Barrett, National Cowboy & Western Heritage Museum and ProRodeo Hall of Fame rodeo announcer and the voice of the sport in my ears. Hadley gave me an inside look at the Prairie Circuit Finals Rodeo produced by John when he was that circuit's secretary and the secretaries were the entire administration of every circuit in the PRCA. He drew pictures of the long history between John and the great bucking horse Jesse James, and contributed mightily to the story by that title under this cover. Hadley also told the story about the "Perfect Score" and his recollections formed the basis of "TV Cowboys."

Thanks to Ivan Daines, the great Canadian Hall of Fame bronc rider, for living the "Perfect Score" story that Hadley told. Three people were witness to this story and all three agreed on its details exactly.

Thanks to the Blackwell family, Rex and his boys, Jace and Jade, bronc riders all. The story of their friendship with John, spanning generations, is encapsulated in the story "McMentor."

Thanks to Robert Etbauer, the two-time world champion saddle bronc rider. Robert spoke of all the cowboys he knew of that John had helped. He talked about John's bronc school and what it had meant to him when he was starting out and ". . . didn't even know about binds in a saddle . . ." and sure didn't have any. He also described—as only one who has been there can—the greatest bronc ride he ever saw John make at the indoor rodeo in Kansas City. His impressions run strong throughout much of the book.

Another world champion, Tom Reeves, had a special relationship with John, living in the McBeth home at an impressionable time during his last year of high school. His relationship with the McBeths and his rise to the status of world champion bronc rider are chronicled in the story "One Defining Moment."

Roland "Butch" Tirelli, who I will always think of as the "Brooklyn Bronc Rider" and a man who John said ". . . could ride about anything if he only knew it . . . ," shared the details of a story John told me about a Wild West Show produced by Butch in Caracas, Venezuela. Their trip to foreign shores together and the challenges they faced are chronicled in "International Cowboy."

Thanks to Derek Clark, fifteen-time NFR saddle bronc rider and by extension his grandmother, Imogene Veach Beals, for checking a couple of historical facts concerning the book. Their family has a tremendous archive of rodeo history. Thanks also to Derek for his recollections in "Science Project."

Thanks to Larry and Reneé Clayman for the story entitled "Monkeyshines" written about the most civilized animal in pro rodeo, Todo.

Tom Miller helped tremendously by painting a verbal picture of John as an instructor and friend. His impressions of John are evident throughout the book. Tom won the average in the bronc riding at the National Finals Rodeo three of the six times he went—an unbelievable accomplishment.

A debt of gratitude is owed to Jim Sutton, of Sutton Rodeo, Inc., one of the truly great stock contractors and bucking stock breeders of our time. Jim allowed us to have some fun portraying his "other" impressive skills—aside from running one of the most successful rodeo production companies, managing a ranch, and raising and training the fifth generation of Suttons to be involved in the sport—in the story "All Around Cowboy."

Thanks to John Willemsma for the view of John McBeth he contributes in the story "Hall of Fame." An incredibly accomplished artisan and saddle maker, "Long" John credits The Cowboy Shop in Burden, Kansas, and John McBeth with helping him get started.

Thanks to Bob Tallman, the National Cowboy &

Western Heritage Museum and ProRodeo Hall of Fame Inductee, who delivered the most amazing interview under the most trying of circumstances. Bob's words in the foreword to this book prove that his success was meant to be, as John saw so clearly some 40 years ago and recounted in "Friends in High Places."

In the same story, Cotton Rosser demonstrates his versatility as a rodeo producer, showman and pilot. If you throw in contestant and service on the board of directors there is no aspect of the business that Cotton did not excel at.

Thanks to the McBeth family for their hospitality during the Hall of Fame induction ceremonies. They welcomed me into their clan and made me feel at home.

John's wife, Francie, is a part of every story here, as she is a part of John. One's accomplishments cannot be separated from the other. She told me about their life together in and out of rodeo. Her career resumé is a match for John's. She detailed an unbelievable streak where she earned sixteen pink Cadillacs working for Mary Kay Cosmetics, one every two years, which served as the genesis for our story "Pink Cadillac." She talked about a family meeting after the Houston rodeo in 1974 when she and John sat down with the boys and decided to go for it and try to win the world. The results of that meeting are chronicled in "Championship Run." On the other end of the spectrum she also discussed "A Bad Day" and shrugged off the disappointment she felt at that time as John would a sub-par performance.

Bart McBeth, John's oldest son, told an unusual story about him and John hitting the rodeo road together in the aptly titled story "Father and Son." Francie and her daughter-in-law, Eunice, Bart's wife, had a unique experience: They were spectators at the Prairie Circuit Finals rodeo where John and Bart competed against each other in the saddle bronc riding—a very rare if not unprecedented occurrence in the event.

Blake McBeth, the younger son, shared his special memories of growing up around rodeo in "Untold Stories," and coincidentally, it was through conversation with his wife Shellie that the story—like the book—got its title.

They say a picture is worth a thousand words. A few more pictures, then, and I could have saved myself a *lot* of work. The photographs in this book are remarkable and add to the stories as no number of words could. I'd like to thank in no special order those people that provided photographs: Joe Ownbey, Brenda Allen, David Jennings, Chuck Korte, Larry and Reneé Clayman, Derek Clark, Butch Tirelli, Jim Svoboda, Al Long, Bern Gregory, DeVere Helfrich, Ferrell Butler, D. R. Fox, Bart McBeth, John and Francie McBeth, and Jerry Gustafson.

Thanks also to the artists, Keith W. Avery and Mark Storm, for their portraits of John McBeth aboard Sage Hen and Sundown, respectively.

A special thanks to Brian Gauck, Photography Coordinator at PRCA Properties, Inc. and Gerianne Schaad, Director of the National Cowboy & Western Heritage Museum for their assistance with photos from their respective archives.

Thanks to my editors Sterling Bobbitt and Lynne and Maren Beery for proofreading the manuscript and making suggestions. They were always right and the book was much improved through their efforts. Special thanks to my wife Lynne who has been supportive and patient throughout.

Most important of all, thanks to the readers of this book for their support of rodeo and John McBeth and this effort. It is your involvement that gives this project its purpose.

". . . he was a cowboy's cowboy, and that's what I wanna be."

Tater Decker

A Note To The Reader

A "Glossary Of Rodeo Terms" has been included with this volume to help anyone not familiar with rodeo cowboy jargon or "saddle and tack" terms. The glossary begins on page 238 and will prove invaluable to most readers.

CHAMPIONSHIP RUN

*An eminently respected hall of fame cowboy, former
president of the Professional Rodeo Cowboys
Association, and U.S. Congressman from Oklahoma,
Clem McSpadden, said to John McBeth: "I've been
in the rodeo business for 50 years. I've never seen
anybody so graciously dominate an event like you
did."*

In the month of March, 1974, John McBeth took the
lead in the world saddle bronc riding standings. He had
been a dominant force in saddle bronc riding for a decade,
qualifying for the nine previous National Finals Rodeos by
virtue of finishing in the top 15 money winners at the end
of the regular season. But, thus far, he had fallen short of
winning the world.

It was anybody's race from March to September during
the big summer rodeo runs when so many of the rodeo
dollars are won. There were some future champions
nipping at his heels: Joe Marvel, Bobby Berger, Monty
Henson, J.C. Bonine; and some former champions in the
event seeking a return to glory, Bill Smith, Dennis Reiners,
Mel Hyland; yet, John held them off through the spring and
summer. Barely.

Right after Labor Day the race was still tight, with a
group of talented bronc riders hot on his case. With the
homestretch in sight—three months left in the season and
the NFR looming ever closer in early December—John
knew he had to get it in gear. His good friend, Bobby
Berger, had an airplane. So together they flew out of
Newton, Kansas, to Spencer, Iowa, where they competed
on a Thursday night.

Behind the chutes, before the bronc riding in Spencer,

The top fifteen saddle bronc riders in the world competing at the National Finals Rodeo, 1974. Back row, left to right, Joe Marvel, Melvin Coleman, Sammie Groves, Mike Marvel, Bill Smith. Middle row, Dennis Reiners, Shawn Davis, Jim Kelts, Mel Hyland, Bobby Brown. Front row, Wayne Harris, Monty Henson, Bobby Berger, J.C. Bonine, and John McBeth. Photo by Al Long, PRCA Archives.

John was talking to some of the boys and they were asking him where all he was entered that week. Maybe they were searching for an edge, thinking they'd have to out-travel him to catch him in the standings, since catching him in the arena was problematic. When he gave them a quick run-down of his itinerary over the next week and a half they couldn't believe it. They literally thought he was pulling their leg.

"You entered Memphis, Omaha, and Albuquerque along with Pendleton, Oregon, and Puyallup, Washington?" they asked, with jaws slack in disbelief. "And you're traveling alone?"

John didn't show much reaction to that.

2

"You get five head at Puyallup," one guy said. "How you gonna do that??"

John set his jaw in that way he does when he means business, and said, "Well, hide your head and watch me!"

Both Berger and McBeth earned scores that placed them deep in the bronc riding that night at Spencer, with John winning a third when all was said and done. They got a room in town that night and John got the last good sleep he would enjoy for more than a week.

The next morning they left Iowa in a dense fog that blanketed most of the Midwest. They flew to Wichita, Kansas, through heavy cloud cover under instrument flight conditions. As they approached the spot where they figured the airport ought to be, after covering some five hundred miles and never once seeing the ground, relying only upon the plane's instruments and their own navigational abilities, the runway suddenly appeared from out of the mist ten feet below the plane as they touched down.

John said a quick thank you to Bobby Berger (and the Big Man above), and grabbing his gear, hustled into the terminal to catch a noon flight to Las Vegas. When he got to Vegas he rented a car and drove the 120 miles to St. George, Utah, where he had a horse called Hyrum Special in the Friday night performance.

St. George has a reputation for putting on a great rodeo. They add a significant amount of sponsorship money to the pot and draw a slew of contestants from all over the country, including many of those top money-winning bronc riders who were breathing down John's neck. Hyrum Special was a good draw to have. He was one of those broncs that you dream about, but seldom get. He was a big strong sorrel with no dips or dives in his routine; he just flat tried to buck you off. He was a horse that you should win on if you rode him right, and if you didn't you were liable to be getting up off the ground. He was regularly voted into the stock pen at the NFR by the top bronc riders in the world. The combination of Hyrum Special and John McBeth proved lethal to every other bronc rider's aspirations of winning at St. George. Although he didn't know it yet, John's score would hold through the final perf of the rodeo the next day and by Monday morning a check would be in the mail to McBeth's Kansas address for first place money.

He drove back to Las Vegas and turned in the rent-a-car. After booking an 11:00 A.M. flight to Pendleton, Oregon, (the only flight available that morning) John realized he wouldn't be there in time for the start of the 1:00 P.M. performance. But, luckily, at the Pendleton Round-Up, the saddle bronc riding was run in two sections. The first section of bronc riding was held right after the rodeo started, shortly after one o'clock, with the second section held just before the rodeo ended at about three. He figured he could make it there for the second section, so he put in a phone call to Bobby Brown at the Severe Brothers Saddlery bunkhouse in Pendleton where many of the cowboys stayed while competing at the Round-Up.

"Hey, Bobby," he said when he got him to the bunkhouse phone. "I need you to do something for me."

"Name it."

"I need you to make sure Gangster doesn't get loaded in the chutes for the first section of the bronc riding. I'm gonna be flying in late, and there's no way I'll be there in time for the first section."

"That'll probably cost you a quart of whiskey," Bobby said, and John could tell he was grinning even over the phone line.

"No problem."

"You need a ride from the airport?" Bobby asked.

"That'd be great. It'd save me from having to rent a car."

So, Bobby was behind the chutes when the bareback

riding concluded that afternoon. He had taken a good look at Gangster previously to be sure he'd recognize him quickly when they ran him in the chutes. And sure enough, when a cowboy swung open the gate to the bronc pen and pushed the broncs charging and snorting down the alleyway toward the chutes, Gangster was in the lead. Murphy's Law. Bobby hopped off the fence and blocked the alleyway in front of the herd. He waved his hat back and forth over his head emitting a, "Whoa, boy . . . whoa," as he turned the herd, and over the profane protests of the chute help he drove them back to the far end of the alleyway where they'd come from. As the herd turned at the end of the alley and under the prompting of the angry cowboy headed back toward the chutes for the second time, Gangster was left at the tail end of the line where he wouldn't make the first section to be loaded.

Satisfied with the situation at the bucking chutes, Bobby hopped in his car and picked up John at the airport. As they hurried out of the airport parking lot, squealing the tires turning on to the main drag, hustling to get to the arena in time for the second section of broncs, Bobby said from behind the wheel, "Ol' Gangster went back in the hole, John. But this'll probably cost you *two* quarts of whiskey. I had to drive the whole herd right back over the guy loading the broncs in the chutes when Gangster came first. So, that guy probably deserves a quart of whiskey, too."

"That's a deal," John grinned.

When he rode Gangster that afternoon John felt a debt of gratitude to his friend, and, ironically, his competitor, for the opportunity. As happens so often in rodeo, John had to do the work—make the ride—but without a lot of help from a lot of people he'd have never had the chance.

After Pendleton, John needed a ride to Puyallup, Washington, where he was entered in the Washington State Fair. Puyallup was the five-head affair, and he was up that night and the next afternoon, back to back, in the first two go-rounds. He hooked up with a couple of bareback riders in Pendleton who were going his way, with the agreement that John would do the bulk of the driving. They'd, ". . . been hittin' it pretty hard . . ." and wanted to get some rest. So, he added his gear to the pile in their trunk, jumped behind the wheel of their car, and they hit the road squealing the tires again for the five hour sprint over the mountains to Puyallup. They had to get there in time for the bareback riding in that evening's performance—the first event. John put the pedal down and drove like he meant it with the two bareback riders blissfully nodding off asleep against the windows. Hours later, when they got to Puyallup, John was in a wrung out state and the other two boys were refreshed.

A couple of cups of concessionaire coffee at the fairgrounds, and the knowledge that he'd drawn well in the first two rounds were enough to re-energize John. His first bronc was a big black that reared out of the chute and bucked in a tight circle to the left, turning back right in front of the judges who got a close look at John's spurs setting sharply in the neck of the big bronc and an earful of his squeaking rosin. One go-round down and John was leading by a mile.

The bronc he rode the next afternoon wasn't as strong, but he still placed in the round by belly punching him with his right foot after marking him out to make him take a lead and help get him going, and giving him his head so he wouldn't weaken.

He traveled to Othello, Washington, that night. He was so tired he never could remember how he got there, who he rode with. He was behind the chutes prepping his gear when Droopy (Doug Brown) walked up, took one look at him and said, "What's wrong with you, John? It seems like I can see right through you."

John said, "I am so tired. I haven't slept in days."

"Where are you going after here?" Doug asked.

"I've got to be in Albuquerque, tomorrow night," John told him.

"How are you gonna get there?"

"I have no idea."

"Well, Cook and I are going," Doug said. "But we're not up until the next night."

"I've got to be there tomorrow."

"Well, I tell you what," Droopy said, doing a quick mental calculation. "We can get you to Boise tonight, and you can catch a flight from there to Albuquerque."

So, after the rodeo at Othello, John caught a couple of hours of sleep on the floor of their van on the way to Boise. All he remembered the next day was waking up underneath the portico at the airport in Boise and dragging his rigging bag and saddle and the little suitcase he always traveled with into the terminal. He was as tired as he ever remembered being in his life. But he thought of his family back home, his wife and two sons, and the support they needed. He thought of all the long years he'd beat down the road from rodeo to rodeo, always winning more than his share, but, as of yet, no world championship. This was his chance. He was leading the world standings with the home stretch of the season in sight. And he was on such a run—in the midst of a hot streak, drawing and riding, like no other he'd ever had. It brought a pounding to his pulse, a spring to his step, a smile to his lips, and he was energized. Hell, he could sleep when he got old.

He drew bad at Albuquerque and finished out of the money.

That night John called his wife Francie.

"Hello, Francie," he said.

"Hey stranger!" she answered.

"How are you?"

"I'm fine."

"How are the boys?"

"They're fine, too," she said. "Where are you?"

"Albuquerque."

"Where all have you been?" she wanted to know.

And that started a *long* conversation.

Francie lived under a shadow of worry about the miles John traveled. The broncs never bothered her. She didn't believe he would ever get hurt riding. But the highway was another story. She would worry about the travel and pray he was safe. She had no way to call him when her woman's intuition said she should. It was always a relief when his voice came over the wire from a payphone . . . somewhere.

"I am so tired," he said.

"We knew it would be hard," she said. "When we sat down in that hotel in Houston last February and had our family meeting, remember?"

"I remember."

"And we talked it over and decided that this was the time for you to go for it because you were having such a good winter."

John had won Houston and Fort Worth and placed at Denver and San Antonio during the run of big winter rodeos in January and February. He was leading the race for the world championship almost from the get-go.

"I remember," he said.

He remembered the support she'd shown sitting in that hotel room in Houston. The grind of ten long years with a husband on the road most of the time and the stress of keeping the home and family together day to day sounded in her voice as she encouraged him to hit it again.

"We'll make up for lost time after the finals . . . ," he said into the phone. ". . . and I'll get some sleep." He laughed.

"I can't think beyond this week," Francie confessed. "I'm so focused on what we're trying to do. I'm really going day to day. I have been all year. I just tell myself,

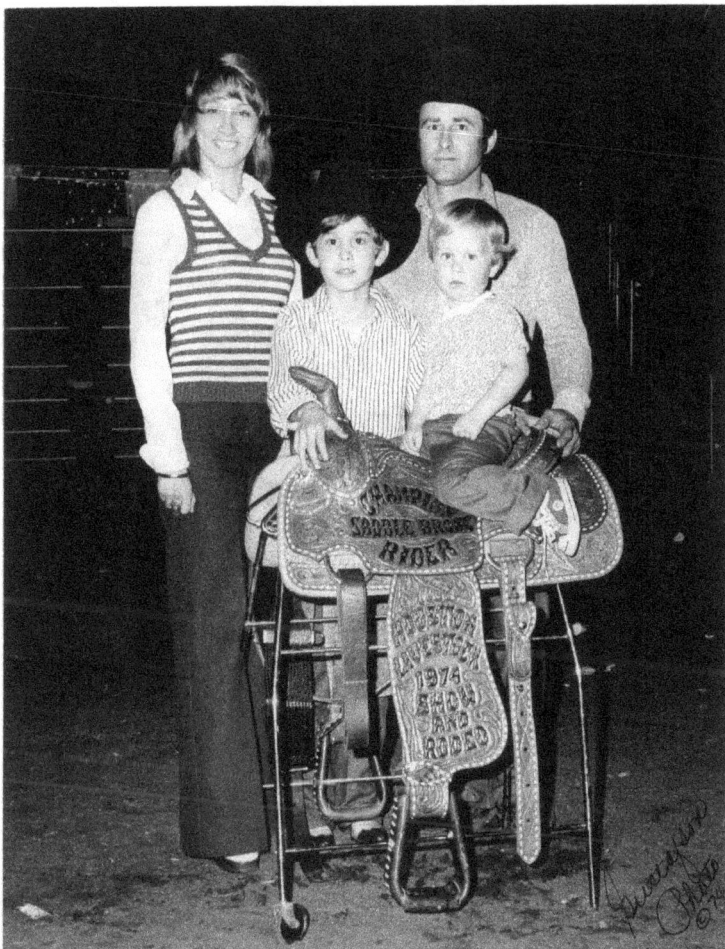

The family that decided to go for the championship in 1974 after winning the Houston Livestock Show and Rodeo in March. From the left are Francie, Bart, Blake and John McBeth. Gustafson Photo.

'Get through this week. Get through this week.'"

"Me too."

John flew back to Puyallup for the third and fourth go-rounds. He was set up in back to back evening/afternoon performances once again. He drew well again at Puyallup and was deep in the zone with his riding. It seemed like forever since he'd been bucked off or missed a horse out;

John got off to a hot start at the big winter rodeos in his championship year, 1974. Shown here winning Fort Worth aboard Arthur Raymond. Gustafson Photo.

he was spurring the hair off everything they ran under him. He was in the thick of the average race when he left the next day.

He and John McDonald caught a ride to Kamloops, British Columbia, with a couple of bulldoggers who were traveling in a pickup truck pulling a horse trailer. He and McDonald rode all night over the mountains from Puyallup to Kamloops in the nose of the trailer, in the "tackroom" area, sitting on a pop crate playing gin. McBeth wanted to lie down on the trailer floor, prop his head up on his gear bag and sleep, but his competitive nature got the best of him, so through the long night he beat McDonald out of forty dollars at cards instead.

The rodeo at Kamloops was held in a cozy little building with a small arena. John won the bronc riding on a sharp little bay horse that jumped in the air and floated, coming around in a tight circle to the right.

He flew to Omaha the next day and won the rodeo at Aksarben (Nebraska spelled backward). He had a stocky bay horse called Jewel that he was unfamiliar with, but would not soon forget. Jewel was muscled and sleek and had what was probably some Morgan blood in him. He reared out nice and veered off to the right side of the arena, bucking down along the fence in front of the packed-house crowd. He had a lot of extension in his kick, but not a lot of front end drop, making him nice to ride. John put the iron to him, setting his feet in the mane. He was standing up almost vertically when he charged, the horse was kicking so high. The ride thrilled the crowd who were right on top of the action. Clods of arena dirt tossed up by the bronc's hooves landed in the first few rows of the bleachers. It was good for the win at Omaha.

The next morning he caught a plane back to Puyallup for the final go-round. It was a long flight and a costly ticket, but he had to do it. He was sitting in second after four rounds and had to go for the average win—the big payout in a multiple go-round riding. He drew a rank one in that fifth round; what they call an eliminator. A horse that you can be a lot of points on if you go wild and stick a ride on, but one that's liable to throw you off if you try it. John was faced with a choice: ride conservatively to hold onto his second place ranking or go for broke and risk bucking off and dropping out of the average altogether. About all he needed to do was make the whistle to assure himself of a nice payday. The prudent move might have been to ride conservatively, be sure to get a score for the average. So, of course, he went for broke instead, and spurred his way to the fifth go-round win as he fell one point short of winning the average.

Before the bronc riding that day a cowboy had been bemoaning the long five-head competition. "I feel like I've been here all month, instead of all week," he complained.

"I can't wait to get down the road to anywhere else. I'm so tired of this town." John just shook his head. He hadn't even seen the town.

He flew from Puyallup to Memphis, Tennessee, the next day, for the Mid-South Fair. Another long flight, another expensive ticket.

After twelve days, nine rodeos, and thirteen broncs, he had placed six times for over $10,000 dollars. It turned out to be the icing on the cake. The bronc riders who had been chasing him all year never came close to catching him after that. That twelve-day run effectively sewed up the championship. John went into the National Finals Rodeo with enough money won to guarantee him the world title. No one could mathematically catch him, even if they won the NFR. He won just shy of $37,000 in 1974 and set a new record for yearly winnings in the bronc riding. But the money was insignificant just a few years later—because a few years later, "If you didn't win that much money just at the finals . . . you drew bad."

STATUE IN BRONZE

I asked John what inspired him to become a bronc rider. What person or event or experience moved him in that direction? This is the story he told.

Thad Beery

In 1946 my dad took me to a rodeo in Newton, Kansas. I was just a little kid about six years old. You can imagine that my eyes were wide open seeing all those cowboys and the stock and the fanfare of what was a pretty big rodeo. It must have made a big impression on me because as young as I was, I can still see it all clearly in my mind.

There was a big, bad character there, a cowboy, by the name of Hugh Ridley. Now by bad I don't mean dishonest or criminal, I mean tough, no-nonsense, and not to be messed with. Now, Hugh was a rodeo cowboy of the Old Breed, big and burly, and in his day he'd competed and won in most of the rodeo events—if not all of them. Well, on this day Hugh had brought a skinny little seventeen year old kid along with him and entered him in the saddle bronc riding. The kid was shy and didn't say much to anybody. He kind of looked down at the ground and didn't make eye contact with most of the other fellas that were there. When somebody'd speak to him he'd mumble an answer, not really looking up—polite, but kind of withdrawn. Like maybe at his young age he was a little bit uneasy just being there.

So, all the old hands, noticing this, started to razz Hugh Ridley a bit, not saying anything too inflammatory, you know, because they sure didn't want to get ol' Hugh too riled. But, they were telling him that the kid's first draw in the two-header—a big bay horse with white socks that I can still see to this day—was gonna eat that kid up. Hugh just smiled a tight little smile like he was gritting his teeth, just tolerating their comments.

It became a pretty big deal even before they ran the broncs in the chutes. I think all the other cowboys wanted to see Hugh taken down a notch and figured the kid getting splattered would fill the bill nicely. Now, understand, nobody was malicious about it, nobody wanted to see the kid get hurt or anything, but that's just the sense of humor those old timers had. If the kid got bucked off and lost the entry fee Hugh had paid, it'd tickle the fancy of all those boys who couldn't prod Hugh any other way.

Well, when they ran the bay in the chute, there was a pretty good crowd gathered around Hugh and the kid. Hugh acted like he didn't notice all the attention, helping the kid halter and saddle the bronc and holding the horse's head while the boy measured his rein. The kid, meantime, went in to action. With a spry step he vaulted up on that chute and balanced on the top rail as he swung his saddle over the gate and set it down on the bronc's back. He worked quick and smooth setting his gear, like he'd done it a thousand times before, exhibiting a confidence with the bronc that he'd never shown around the men. Still, he never looked up, never looked around, like he was concentrating on his business, shutting the world out.

When the bronc riding started and it was the kid's turn to go, you could see he was a little bit nervous or excited. There was a twitchiness about his face and in his hands. As he slipped into his saddle and was getting his feet in the stirrups the horse got a bit broncy, throwing his head up and down and rattling back and forth in the box. From his place on the back of the chute, Hugh firmly took a hold of his halter and spoke to him in low tones to distract him from the kid. I heard a few snickers of anticipation from the cowboys clustered around watching. I looked up into my dad's face at that moment and saw the intent look he wore as he watched Hugh and the kid, as if he were studying the action to learn a trick he might use.

The bronc reared up when they cracked the gate, and the kid spurred him in the neck, marking him out. The bronc looked so big and the kid looked so small it seemed like an uneven match. The kid's ten-gallon hat looked bigger than he did, like he could crawl under it and hide if it started to rain. Yet, jump after jump that big bay cracked 'em hard and the kid beat him to the ground every time, setting his feet in the front end before the horse gave him the jerk.

I could sense the emotions in the group of cowboys surrounding us as they changed from an expectation of the kid's crash, to hoping for any kind of a buck off, to almost a desperate longing for vindication of their earlier estimate of the situation as the kid stuck a ride on the bay with more than a modicum of style. The excuses started before the kid reached the pickup man.

"Aw, that horse had an off day!"

"The kid was just lucky!"

"No way he could do that again in a million years!"

And the grumbling only intensified when they realized that the kid had won the first go-round.

By that evening the kid had gained somewhat of a celebrity status locally. And like the notice accorded most celebrities, a lot of the public wanted to see the kid fall on his face. In fact, a lot of cowboys were betting on it at the local watering hole in town that night.

Like the kid, I was too young to visit the tavern, but I overheard a cowboy talking to my dad the next morning and he said that, "The boys were sure gettin' on Hugh last night. They were tellin' him they'd never seen such 'Luck of the Draw' as in that first round, and they were challenging him to put his money where his mouth was and place a bet with them on the outcome of today's riding."

Well, I don't know if Hugh bet with them or not, but he didn't have much to say when the broncs were run in the chutes for the second round of the bronc riding. He and the kid just went about their business like they did the first day. The naysayers behind the chutes, meanwhile, were more vocal and boisterous than ever, like they had more riding on today's outcome than yesterday's (which as I explained earlier, some of them did).

I heard the scuttlebutt before the bronc riding from where dad and I sat on the top rail of the stock pen behind the chutes.

"It's gonna be a different story today!" one cowboy said.

"He's got old Baldy today!" said another. "And he's no cupcake like the horse he rode yesterday!" And they pretty much all agreed.

My dad had that introspective look on his face again, like he was studying for a test.

Baldy was ranker than the bay. He about kicked the chute apart when they ran him in. He had to be tied with a halter rope to be saddled and mounted. The kid handled it just like the day before. He went through his routine quick and smooth like this was the one thousandth and *first* time he'd been through it all. He looked to be a little bit nervous or excited with the same twitchiness to his hands and face I'd noticed the day before. But in spite of all the attention he was drawing, and all the pressure that must have been on him from the other cowboys, from Hugh, from the bronc— who was a pistol for goodness sake—and from his own inner desire to succeed, he was still concentrating on his business, shutting out the world and doing his job.

Baldy dashed in to the arena when they cracked the gate and did an immediate left that would've dumped more than half of the bronc riders there, I'm sure. He swooped and dived and jumped and kicked and jerked his head up and down trying to give the kid the slip. Finally, after four or five seconds of the dirtiest trip you ever saw, he got pissed that the kid was still anchored on his back and drilling holes in him with his spurs, and he took his head and flat out bucked as hard as he was able. The kid had him right where he wanted him at that point, and he put an exclamation point on every lick he threw. He extended his rein arm out straight and lifted on his rein. He threw his free hand out behind him. He turned his toes out and set his feet in the front end a split second ahead of the horse's timing. As on the day before, I could sense the emotion in the group of cowboys around me, only now I was getting vibrations of surprise and maybe . . . awe. The naysayers were suddenly rooting *for* the kid.

When he'd made it back to the chutes and it was announced that he'd won both go-rounds *and* the average, and he'd accepted the congratulations, the back-slapping and handshakes of all the cowboys there, I walked up behind him, reached up and tugged at the hip pocket on his jeans. He turned around and looked down at this little tot tugging on his pants, and smiled at me.

"I w . . . w . . . wanted to ask you . . . ," I stammered. "What's your name?"

"Casey," he answered.

And to this day, I don't believe I could've found a better hero to inspire me in my career. 'Cause there's a big old bronze statue at the Prorodeo Hall of Fame today, dedicated to Casey Tibbs.

TOPSY TURVY

*"I never had a mentor. I learned by watching and
listening and trying different things. Sometimes it's just
a little tip that makes all the difference."*
John McBeth

Back in the day, a lot of the rodeos didn't have saddle
bronc riding. There just weren't that many bronc riders
around. A rodeo producer would rather not include the
event at all if he was going to end up with just three or four
entries because it didn't make for much of a contest, the
purse was small, and it didn't impress the paying public
when they were given a "short" program. Rodeos typically
had a full slate of bareback and bull riding, but bronc riders
were at a premium.

Not so in Strong City, Kansas, in 1961. Rodeo was
starting to really kick in about that time, and it had been a
big deal in Strong City for years. In fact, that year the
rodeo filled two separate saddle bronc riding events:
amateur and pro. Many of the top pros were entered
because the rodeo had a good reputation, excellent stock
and a healthy purse. It also drew almost all of the amateur
bronc riders from around the region for the same reasons.
If you were a saddle bronc rider, Strong City was the place
to be.

John McBeth entered the amateur bronc riding that year.
As he carried his gear bag and saddle behind the chutes that
day, he noticed some of the pro bronc riders were kind of
giving him the eye. He didn't think much about it; he just
figured it was because he was an amateur and didn't know
many of them, personally, so he went about his business
checking the binds in his saddle and rosining up his chaps

and swells. It did start to get on his mind a little bit, however, when he noticed a couple of the top riders looking right at him as they whispered back and forth with big grins on their faces.

"What's goin' on," John said out loud, but talking to himself. "Is my fly open or something?" he mumbled, looking down.

"What are you talking about?" V. A. Palmer asked, looking up from his own gear a few feet away.

"Oh nothin', V. A. I've just been getting some funny stares since I got here is all . . . like I forgot my pants or something."

"They probably just want to remember you the way you look now," V. A. said.

"What do you mean?"

"Well, you know what you have, don't you?"

"Well, no. It's just another old horse."

"I'll tell you, John," V. A. said with a conspiratorial look on his face, like he was divulging a secret. "They don't like to have that horse in the bronc riding. He's generally a bareback horse. His name is Topsy Turvy and he's real light-headed, and if you ever pull on that rein, he will flip over backward on you."

"He'll Turvy?"

"He'll Turvy. I'm sure that's how he got his name. In the bronc riding he spends a lot of time upside down."

"Thanks, V. A. Good to know."

As might be expected considering his reputation, the bronc proved to be head shy in the chute. He tossed his head up when John moved to halter him, and then stuck his head down between his front feet trying to avoid the halter altogether. Quite a few of the pro bronc riders, whose event came later in the program, were gathered around the chute watching, some smiling, some smirking. The bronc had a great reputation as a bareback horse. He would get in the air and wild horse it, leaving the ground off all fours,

19

jumping with his head up and get light in the front end—almost rearing up as he bucked. The bareback riders could really lay back and gap out on him, scoring a ton of points. But the saddle bronc riders who clustered around the chute at Strong City that day wanted nothing to do with Topsy Turvy. Most of them would turn him out if they drew him and live to ride another day. They knew from reputation or experience that about the time the ride reached its hairiest point, with the bronc lunging in the air with his head up and his front end higher than his rear, right at the point where a bronc rider needs his rein most of all—to give it a tug and pull himself forward in the saddle underneath his swells—this bronc would flip. No, the only thing any sane saddle bronc rider wanted to do with Topsy Turvy was to watch some other fella get lunched. And they were watching.

When his saddle was set and pulled and it was time to go, John very delicately took the slack out of his rein, laying it over his swells to measure its length. And just that slight action on the rein was enough to trip the bronc's trigger. In a heartbeat he flipped over backward and slammed the saddle against the back of the box. The bystanders loved the action.

By the time the bronc came back down on all fours one second later, John had laid his plan. He slipped out about a foot more rein than what the horse measured through his hand, slid into his saddle and got his stirrups on his feet. In about two seconds flat he had a bite of the swells between his thighs and was nodding for the gate, having not so much as lifted on his rein. In fact, his rein hand never moved until the bronc broke from the chute and John spurred him out, lifting the rein out of the way at that point to avoid spurring over it.

All the other hands came to the fence or climbed up on the back of the chutes to watch, anticipating a wreck. The bronc went into his usual routine, blowing in the air, head up, light in the front end. John was cantleboarding, using his stirrups to press himself forward in his seat, then snapping off his binds and grabbing a hold above the horse's shoulders before the horse launched himself each jump. He was leaning back, even as the horse adopted his front-end-high mode of bucking, letting the cantle surround him and carry him forward with the impetus of the bronc. Not once did he pull on his rein. In fact it dangled loose, the extra foot of length he'd measured off flapping between his outstretched hand and the horse's neck. He was riding without using his rein at all!

The bronc riders who watched knew this couldn't last. They knew this kid, this amateur, would get jerked loose on one of those high-flying jumps and slip back out from under his swells. Then he'd have to use the rein to pull himself forward, or lift on it, at least, to lever himself down tighter against the cantle. But John did none of the above. The snap of his binds when he spurred back and the jump forward when he charged the front end were enough to keep him forward in his saddle, under his swells. The clamp he put on the bronc's front end with his spurs every jump never weakened, carrying him aloft, tight in his saddle. He kept reaching out with his rein hand each jump, giving the bronc the slack in the rein. He could have thrown the rein away.

Not having his head tugged on made Topsy Turvy happy to buck rather than fight his head. He was free to have the same dramatic trip in the bronc riding the bareback riders had been enjoying for his entire career. The result was that the crowd that day was treated to an exciting wild-horse ride, the stock contractor was tickled pink to see his good horse excel in the saddle bronc riding, and the other bronc riders got a lesson in horsemanship. John won the amateur portion of the bronc riding at Strong City that year with a score that was high enough to place him third if he'd been entered in the pro event.

Through the years McBeth became noted for riding with

an exceptionally long rein. He always extended his rein hand out straight and lifted, never pulling on the rein. This style gave the horses their head and allowed them to buck to the best of their ability. John always seemed to be able to get the best out of a bronc.

"Thanks for the insight," John said, when V. A. Palmer congratulated him on his win.

"Oh, I didn't do nothing," V. A. said. "You did the riding!"

"Yeah," John agreed. "But I never could have done it without the tip you gave me."

TWENTY SEVEN HEAD

"The more I practice the luckier I get."
Unknown Golfer

I've put on bronc schools that were a couple of days long, others that ran for a week. After just a day or two I'd start to see some guys getting sore, some of them *real* sore after mounting three or four bucking horses a day. Those were usually the boys that didn't ride too well. Let's face it; *one* horse can beat you up if you're not riding right. A cantleboard meeting your tailbone with a thousand pounds behind it, or the swells of your saddle barked across a shin or a knee, or the ground rising up to meet your shoulder or the back of your neck at twenty miles an hour can leave you with a seven-day hurt—no matter your age or state of tune. You'd see those guys struggle to get out of their car at the arena in the morning. They'd do the "double-hump" to rise up off the seat, where they'd put their feet out the car door, lean forward and start to stand, then fall back on the seat, rock once, and throw themselves forward again, using their momentum to lift themselves up like an eighty-year-old getting out of a deep sofa. Sometimes their first few steps as they headed over to the bucking chutes were reminiscent of Walter Brennan in the old TV show "The Real McCoys" where he'd pump his arms and kind of fall forward to get going when he couldn't push off of sore legs. You'd hear them talking behind the chutes about how stiff and sore they were, and watch them gingerly slip into their saddles to check their binds and warm up their rosin, every point of contact between hard leather and soft cowboy bringing out a quiet hiss between clenched teeth. If they refused to give in to the pain and fought their way

23

through it, they would get better. In the short run their muscles would loosen up, their bruises would become pliable and less sensitive and their mind would start operating on a plane above the merely physical. This would happen in a heartbeat, as soon as they saddled their first bronc of the day. In the long run, over the course of weeks or months, their body would become rodeo tough—their muscles would work without pulling and they could take a hit without bruising. Anyone who has been active in a physical way will recognize this phenomenon—the way the body adapts, gets into shape. Whether it's the pounding a football player endures, the stress of a weight lifter or the agony of a long-distance runner, the pain dissipates over time, through repetition, and is replaced by sheer toughness.

Of course, along with the physiological changes that occur invisibly, seemingly magically, in the tissues and organs, a fellow starts to ride better, too. He learns to avoid that cantleboard and those swells and get to the ground on his feet, upright, substantially reducing the pain he endures.

It was with an understanding of these processes, both physical and mental, that I went to a bronc riding in Strong City, Kansas, one day. It was in the springtime when Emmett and Ken Roberts would buck out their whole string to see what they had in preparation for the upcoming season. They'd buck out all their old proven broncs to see if they still had it, any new horses they'd acquired over the winter, and their young colts to see what they were made of. Invites went out to all the top hands in the region; they wanted cowboys who could darn sure challenge their stock, make them show their mettle. They were also paying seven dollars and fifty cents a head mount money and wanted to get their money's worth. Most of the bronc riders there were pros. I was one of only a couple of amateurs there that day. This was early in my career and it was kind of an honor to be invited.

I got on every kind and description of horse that day: big ones, little ones, rank ones and relatively tame ones; horses that bucked like the devil and some that ran off. I slipped into a zone. I'd been riding a lot and I was in good shape. I was young and didn't have an ache or a pain—no complaints. I didn't get tired. I didn't get sore. I just craved broncs. More broncs.

At some point I decided to get on every horse there that day and ride them all. So when I'd get off of one bronc I'd go straight to the stripping chute, grab my saddle, and head right back over to the bucking chutes. That wore me out as much as anything—it wasn't riding the bucking horses—it was that walk from the stripping chute to the bucking chutes toting my gear, time and time again, to saddle all those horses. The pickup men started helping me out after a while when they snagged me off a bronc, dropping me off at the stripping chute gate instead of out in the arena, saving me that much of a walk. They even made a joke out of hauling me and my saddle back over to the bucking chutes when they had the time between bronc rides to do it, laughing about how they'd save me some boot leather even though I'd probably wear through the seat of my pants. A lot of that day is a blur in my memory. Like I say, I was in a zone—operating on impulse, reflexively. I never did get on *every* horse there, but I do remember a couple of memorable rides.

I'd been going along riding bronc after bronc, most of them your average jump-and-kick-for-eight-or-ten-seconds-then-weaken type of animal, and then I slapped my saddle on a little dun colored horse. I think he was new to the herd because nobody expected what happened when that chute gate opened. It was like this little dude grew three feet taller when he jumped into the arena. He turned back at the end of the chute gate with a squeal and spun like a bull. He was getting in the air and cracking his hocks over his shoulder every jump. I marked him out hard and spurred him good when he turned back. I'm sure it made him mad—madder than he already was to begin with—because he got stronger the more I spurred; and I got stronger the more he bucked. It was one of those rides where time just stops. Your frame of reference becomes so skewed by intense concentration that eight seconds stretches to seem like a minute, or longer. Back on the ground you feel like you've lived a lifetime since you saddled that bronc.

The whole day went that way: I felt I was living a lifetime that afternoon. I grabbed a quick drink of water and noticed I was huffing and puffing. I had to swallow between breaths. Sweat soaked the band of my hat. My muscles were twitchy, and if I had sat down they would have trembled, I'm sure. If I had taken a break I know I would have felt tired. Instead, I grabbed my wood and tossed it on a big black that obviously had a lot of draft breed in him. He was heavy and tall, with a long shaggy mane and tail and pie-sized feet. My adrenalin took over and I felt charged to ride this big hairy . . . sasquatch.

The smell of the Kansas prairie, the bronc, leather, the rosin on my saddle and the dust of the arena filled my nostrils. It combined with the smooth feel of my leggings, the muscles under the black's coat and the chute rail beneath my feet to lift my spirits above tired or sore. I had no idea how many broncs I'd mounted that day and didn't care . . . didn't even wonder. I just knew I wanted one more, always one more.

With pounding heart I crawled over the chute gate to slip into my saddle. When the black lifted his head, looked into the arena and snorted, I felt a surge of power come into me like I could tear that chute down with my bare hands if I wanted to. I was so primed, so thrilled, so ready for him—my senses were so clear, my reflexes so quick and my muscles so strong—that I could have spurred that big-foot twice before he hit the ground when he reared out of the box.

He was incredibly strong. Big, deliberate and strong. And for that one memorable moment—that could have been eight seconds or a lifetime—I was perfect. He took these huge showy jumps. He would hit the ground with a clomp on those pies for feet and then launch himself skyward kicking his big long legs up behind me. His track was as straight as an arrow. I got ahead of him and set my feet in that big strong neck. All his power passed through me, down my spine, through my hips, down my legs and into the bottoms of my feet where they were buried in my stirrups. I could feel the surge of every one of his fifteen hundred pounds like they were my own. I was leaping. I was flying. I was untamed.

I didn't know how many broncs I'd mounted out that day when, eventually, everybody quit and started for home. The stock was tired. The chute help was tired. The cowboys were tired and sore. The secretary wrote me a check for two hundred two dollars and fifty cents for twenty seven head. I was glad they made me quit when they did. I was tired that night. The next day I got my saddle out just to sit in it, and I noticed right off that every point of contact between hard leather and soft cowboy brought out a quiet hiss between my clenched teeth.

FINDING OUT

*"You always believe you can ride 'em all, and if you do
things the right way there's no reason you should fall off
of one."*

John McBeth

Cheyenne Frontier Days, "The Daddy of 'Em All!" is
always a spectacle. The arena is so big, the entry list so
full, and the action so brisk that often broncs and bulls are
bucked one after another with little or no time between
rides to run them out of the arena. So it's not unusual that
three or four animals at a time might be bunched down at
the far end of the arena by a couple of cowboys on
horseback whose job it is to run them through the out gate
when given the chance. On occasion that bunch can grow
to a half dozen head or more and it can get real western
when a bronc tries to merge in with the crowd and a
cowboy finds himself riding his draw through a herd of
wild horses scattering in front of him with the pickup men
in hot pursuit.

Through the years the rodeo has sponsored events
rarely—if ever—seen elsewhere: The Chuckwagon Races
where "Cowboy Chariots" (heavy wooden wagons) charge
around the dirt track at breakneck speeds, wheel to wheel,
propelled by a four horse hitch; the Wild Horse Race where
3-man teams mug, saddle and then ride a wild horse in a
chaotic race to the finish line; and the Rookie Saddle Bronc
Riding where amateurs get a taste of pro rodeo at a world
class venue and a shot at a large purse competing against
their peers.

Ralph Maynard and John McBeth were entered in the
Rookie Bronc Riding. In the first go-round of the two-head

competition Maynard drew a wild horse that blew in the air with a squeal and tossed his head and shook his body like he had a mountain lion on his back. Maynard sat up and made a stylish ride fairly easily as the bronc lost all his power while he was floating in the air. But it looked dramatic and he was a lot of points. McBeth, meanwhile, also drew well, and might have made the ride of the day except that the judges got him at the gate as he missed his horse out. But their efforts, which were clearly the class of the event, had drawn the attention of a tall, lanky, middle-aged cowboy with leathery skin and big raw-boned hands who had made quite a name for himself in the previous decade riding all three rough-stock events and had since taken up contracting rodeos.

When they returned for their second head, the situation with Maynard and McBeth was somewhat reversed. McBeth won the second go-round by a mile on the showier bronc, with Maynard finishing a few places lower on a nice jumper-kicker. All-in-all they won a big piece of the rookie bronc riding pot. Maynard won the first go-round and the average, getting a nice gold buckle and a big fat check. Although they got McBeth at the gate on his first one, he put a good check in his jeans as well for the second go-round win.

As they were packing up their gear to leave, the lanky cowboy who had been watching them with such interest moseyed over followed by a little tyke who had obviously been poured from a quarter-scale version of the same mold. The boy wore the same jeans and hat as his elder and had the same style of boots on his quarter-scale feet. He used the same stride and gait as the lanky cowboy he followed, albeit in the abbreviated version. You could see from the tan sticking out below his wide-brim hat that he was already working at developing the same leathery exterior as the larger copy he followed, and if heredity means anything he would undoubtedly develop the same raw-boned

John McBeth aboard Drizzle, Cheyenne Frontier Days 1965. DeVere Helfrich Photo, Dickinson Research Center, National Cowboy & Western Heritage Museum, Oklahoma City, Oklahoma.

appearance in his middle years. As they approached, the full-grown version introduced himself to Maynard and McBeth.

"Hey boys, Jackson Blake," he said, and shook hands with them both. "Got me a little rodeo at Broken Bow, Oklahoma, next weekend. Come on down. I always need bronc riders. We'll pay your fees . . . take good care a ya."

"Sounds good to me," McBeth said. "We'll be there."

"So I can plan on ya then?"

"Yep, we'll be there," McBeth and Maynard nodded.

Broken Bow is located at the foothills of the Kiamichi Mountains in the transition zone between the Red River and the Ouachita Mountain Range. When you drive into the town out of the breaks the streets start out real low and go up the hill. There's a retaining wall on the side of the road with a stairway going up to the sidewalk, so where you park may be several feet below the sidewalk.

Maynard and McBeth drove up and down the hill a couple of times looking for the rodeo office—a building with a whole bunch of sheets of paper taped in the front windows, the judge's draw sheets listing the stock and the position for each contestant. Finally, they spotted the office and parked the car and ambled up the steps to the sidewalk.

There was a little boy in a cowboy hat playing in the middle of the sidewalk in front of the rodeo office. They both recognized him as the pint-sized version of Jackson Blake, the benefactor who had invited them down from Cheyenne and paid their fees. They stepped around the boy and walked over to the window to get a look at what they'd drawn.

"Holy cow!" John said to Ralph after a quick look at the draw sheets. "We've drawn all the good ones, Ralph. We've got Cool Water, One-Eyed Jack, Hammer Head . . . every good one he's got!"

Overhearing their conversation the little kid perked up. He stopped what he was doing and looked up at them from where he sat in the middle of the sidewalk. He recognized them from Cheyenne and was putting their names to their faces. "You must be Maynard and McBeth!" he said.

Somewhat surprised by the kid's comment, John and Ralph looked at each other before John answered, "Yeah, that's right. . . ."

The boy fixed them with a steely gaze no less intimidating than when placed on his elder copy and exclaimed, "M . . . m . . . my daddy says we're gonna find out if you sons-a-bitches can ride!"

TICKET TO RIDE

*"In my youth I had the bull by the horns. I lived in
the middle part of the United States, and I could go to
50 or 60 rodeos a year in a seasonal type of situation
and make a good living and never get more than 300
miles from the house."*
John McBeth

Francis Brewer married John McBeth in 1962 when he
was an amateur cowboy who went to mainly local rodeos.
They had their first son, Bart, and when he was very young
the rodeo business started to perk up. The tips that John
picked up from guys like Clyde Frost and V.A. Palmer
started to fall in place about that time as well. He started to
get real comfortable in the bronc riding. You could call it
opportunity knocking if you were alert enough to hear it.

John filled his permit at Ponca City, Oklahoma, in the
fall of 1963. Before he had a chance to call the association
office and buy his membership card, a bronc and bull rider
that he knew, Lee Wheaton, said to John, "I want you to go
to Texarkana with me. Jerry Hart and I are going down
there. I'll bring you home when we're done."

John talked to Francie and she said, "That'd be okay."

So, they loaded up Jerry Hart's car and headed south for
the Four States Fair. Texarkana had a new sound system
installed for the rodeo arena that year, the grandstands were
newly painted and the parking lot was improved, providing
evidence that the rodeo business was indeed perking up.

The rodeo that year was a two-head affair. John got on
his first one and made a good ride on an average horse but
didn't win anything. The next day he was in the motel
room packing the little suitcase that he always traveled with

In 1963 John McBeth was also riding bareback horses. Shown here aboard Red Bird at Ponca City, Oklahoma, where he filled his permit. Ferrell Butler Photo, Dickinson Research Center, National Cowboy & Western Heritage Museum, Oklahoma City, Oklahoma.

when Lee Wheaton walked in and saw what he was doing and asked, "Where you going?"

"I'm going to catch a bus up to Peoria, Illinois," John told him. "Jim Shoulders has the stock there and I know all his horses. I'm gonna go up there and see if I can win something."

"Well, you can't do that," Lee said.

"Why can't I?"

"'Cause you've got So-Long for your second one here, and he's the best horse in the herd. And then . . . I've already entered you at Memphis."

"You did?"

"Yep. You're gonna get eight head over there. So you're goin' over there and get on your first three. I'm goin' with you. I'm up over there, too. Now when you get off that third one I'm gonna take you to the airport there in Memphis and you're coming back here to Texarkana and you'll get on your second one here 'cause you've still got a shot at the average. Then you don't have to be back to Memphis until the next day, so Jerry'll take you back over there in his car after he's done here." Lee paused to see if John was going along with what he was saying. "Okay?" he asked.

"Okay," John answered.

"And I'm gonna be perfectly honest and tell you what I did . . . ," Lee went on. "I forgot to tell them there was a 'P' in front of your number when I entered you over there . . . and they don't take permits at Memphis." John said nothing. "So when you get off, you leave. You don't hang around that rodeo. You don't spend any time talking to those guys. You hear me?"

John figured that was opportunity knocking—loudly—so he gave up the idea of going to Peoria and headed for the Mid-South Fair in Memphis along with Lee instead. They caught a ride with a couple of fellas Lee knew and got a room in Memphis that night. John placed in two of the first three go-rounds there and Lee put him on that plane to fly back to Texarkana. Jerry met him at the airport and took him back to the motel room where he had been living for most of the week. They played cards that evening just to relax. While dealing the umpteenth hand of pitch Jerry told John about So-Long—the bronc he had drawn for the next day.

"He's sure a good one," he said. "He's a big thoroughbred-looking sorrel that takes about an average rein. There's really nothing shifty or dishonest about him; he just bucks, classy. He has a lot of power, though, so you sure want to get ahead of him. I've seen him throw off some pretty fair bronc riders."

John's average rein would be a fairly long one for most of the other guys. So in typical style for him, his rein hand was extended straight out about shoulder high when So-Long bucked out of the chute the next afternoon. He did get ahead of the horse, setting his feet in the front end before the bronc kicked each jump. He lifted on his rein so that he was in no danger of spurring over it even though he set his feet way up near the mane-line each jump. With his shoulders set square and a nice arch in his back he leaned back and let the cantle carry him along. Many of the "Old Pros" who were there that day were getting their first look at the newcomer and had mixed emotions. On the one hand they were mighty impressed with the kid's composure and style as he stroked So-Long to the second go-round win; on the other hand they were disappointed that earning a living at their chosen profession just got a lot tougher as they waved goodbye to their entry fees.

John was feeling pretty good about himself as he and Jerry pulled out of Texarkana after the rodeo that day. It was satisfying that things had gone pretty much as he had expected. Jerry was feeling pretty good, too, after placing in the bull riding. They drove well into the night to make the three hundred miles to Memphis. The happy glow that surrounded them made the miles easy ones to travel.

When Lee let them into the motel room in Memphis about midnight that night, Jerry came through the door and announced, "John took third in the average over at Texarkana! You shoulda seen him drill So-Long."

"He's placing in the average here, too," Lee put in, "so far." They were talking about him like he wasn't even there, which kind of embarrassed John.

"Maybe we got somethin' goin' on here," Lee said. "Seems like maybe we've created a monster."

"A spurring monster."

"A money monster."

They laughed.

Lee decided that he must be a pretty good judge of saddle bronc riding talent when the kid he'd chosen to back started placing and winning right out of the box and never even blinked an eye at the professional competition.

John took care of business in Memphis and tried to keep a low profile around the arena—which proved to be quite a challenge since his riding was attracting the attention of the judges, the stock contractor, the spectators and, especially, the other contestants. But he took Lee's warning to heart and hung around the car in the parking lot until it was nearly time for the bronc riding, only scurrying over to the bucking chutes with his saddle and gear bag when he saw the saddle broncs being loaded into the chutes. He slipped off into the back row of the grandstand as soon as he was done riding and hid himself among the locals the best he could and watched the rest of the rodeo from there. Between performances he wandered the alleyways of the stock barns and watched the livestock judging. He was an astute observer and became the number one spectator at the Mid-South Fair as he watched, alone, day after day. He learned the name of every cow at the fair by the name on their tag; he knew what every cowboy had won by watching every event of every performance from his perch high in the grandstand. Still, when he finished the week second in the average, everyone knew who he was.

The next morning he got in the back seat of the car with his winnings padding his hip pocket, with Lee and Jerry in the front, thinking he was heading home to Atlanta, Kansas, and Francie, when suddenly two cowboys jumped in the back seat on either side of him pinning him in the middle. He knew Kurly Hebb, the fellow on his right pretty well. He was a bronc rider who lived no more than sixty miles from John back in his home country of Kansas. He'd qualified for the NFR before and was making a name for himself in pro rodeo. They'd run into each other more than a few times at one rodeo or another and become fairly well acquainted. The cowboy on his left he knew only by sight and reputation: That was Jim Busch, a bareback rider and bulldogger from Rapid City, South Dakota, and ironically, Vice President of the association. Nobody said anything as the car pulled away—least of all John. He'd been avoiding a direct face to face with any of the pro cowboys all week, hiding the fact that he was illegitimately entered on a permit. He especially avoided anyone connected with the administration of the association. And now he found himself pressed between two of the biggies and sensed that something was up. They drove straight to the nearest Western Union office where Lee and Jerry took John out of the back seat by the ears and led him inside.

"Now you wire fifty dollars to Denver to the association office," Lee told John as they made their way to the counter, "To buy your membership."

John liked the feel of that wad of cash in his jeans and was reluctant to part with any of it so quickly. "Well, why do I have to do it right now?" he wanted to know.

"Because we entered you in Little Rock," Lee said. "You're up Tuesday night. And they don't take permits either. And you're not gonna do this again!"

"I didn't do it this time . . . ," John rightly pointed out. "You entered me."

"Wire the money!" Lee said as Jim and Kurly came through the door behind them to ensure that he did just that.

So he wired the money to the satisfaction of Jim Busch and the association office. They dropped Jim and Kurly off back in town and headed for Little Rock. For the first time John was a full-fledged member of the Rodeo Cowboys Association—soon to be a card carrying member when the mail delivered his card from the association office to his home. There's no way he could have known what a seminal moment that was in his life and career. There's no way any of us can clearly see and predict the chain of events, some planned some random, that conspire to deliver us to our future. But we can assume that he felt a strong sense of accomplishment that accompanies a goal attained.

He must have seen that even as rodeo was picking up and taking off, offering opportunity for those willing to pursue it, his career was taking off as well, gaining momentum in the under-current of the sport.

Tuesday night in Little Rock, Arkansas, John was the first contestant to walk into the arena, headed for the gate leading behind the chutes. He was carrying his bronc saddle and gear bag and was as nervous as a cat on a hot tin roof. He had Sage Hen drawn. Sage Hen was a big, rank, Morgan crossbred mare that stood in the class with the best bucking horses for most of her career. Three years previously, in 1960, she was voted the runner-up to the bucking horse of the year, Jake, by the top bronc riders in the world. John was concentrating on her, going over the moves he would need to make to get her rode as he walked past a big, tall, raw-boned cowboy standing in front of the chutes.

"Hey!" the guy said in a deep baritone. "Your name Mack-Beth? Come here."

"Yeah," John admitted, turning to face the fellow.

The big man reached in his hip pocket, pulled out a piece of paper in his ham-sized hand and slapped it into John's chest with a loud "WHAP" about knocking the wind out of him.

"My name's Bill Linderman," he said. "Sign this damn thing and go spur the shit out of that mare. And don't be entering any more rodeos you're not supposed to be in from now on!"

That was John's welcome to the RCA. He didn't know at the time that Bill was the Secretary/Treasurer of the association, but he signed his membership application and handed it back.

Sage Hen lived up to her reputation that night. All the rough-stock cowboys clambered up on the back of the chutes or jumped into the arena to watch her initiate the rookie bronc rider. Even the timed-event boys down at

John McBeth aboard Sage Hen. Original Portrait by Keith W. Avery, 1974. From the John McBeth Collection.

their end of the arena knew something special was up when her name was called, and they lined the fence to watch her buck. Dry-mouthed, nervous and sweating, John lowered himself into his saddle with something to prove to himself and all those who watched. It was a special time in his career, a special competition that he had been preparing for . . . forever, it seemed like.

Sage Hen didn't disappoint anyone. She started rank and then got stronger as the ride progressed. She circled over to the left fence and came around, throwing her head in the air every jump. That was the characteristic that made her so hard for the average bronc rider to handle: They couldn't pull on her head and get anything out of their rein. The power riders who relied on their rein to pull themselves down under their swells were out of luck. With her head up high, a strong pull on the rein would lever a rider out over the front end. But she was tailor-made for McBeth.

He rode on balance and timing, giving a horse its head. The snap off his saddle's binds as he spurred back and the jump to the front end as he spurred forward worked with the action of the bronc to anchor him in his seat. He gave her all the rein she wanted and she appreciated it, putting on a show.

John was up to the challenge, but maybe his nerves cost him on that first jump, in a lack of concentration before he got into his spurring rhythm. Yet, there wasn't a person there that night that wasn't impressed with the way he handled the mare. The ride built his reputation right from the start with all the people who saw it. He rode her right, the way he wanted to. Only problem was, he missed her out.

TURK

Thurkel (Turk) Greenough:

The first saddle bronc rider to win the Pendleton Round-Up, the Calgary Stampede and the Cheyenne Frontier Days Rodeo. The Big Three.

John McBeth and Joe Marvel were recruited to do a radio interview as part of a promotion for the bronc riding Match Of Champions held in Wolf Point, Montana. A bronc riding match is just that—saddle bronc riding only—no bull riding or roping or any of the other rodeo events, just the bronc riding. The match was held on the Fort Peck Indian Reservation in Northeastern Montana and as such received mainly word-of-mouth advertisement. But in the rodeo world it is a big deal. Only the top 50 saddle bronc riders are allowed to enter, and then by invitation only. The stock is provided by several of the top producers in that very competitive part of the country. They pool their animals to provide one of the rankest pens of broncs found anywhere, with the possible exception of the National Finals Rodeo.

The event's promoter lined up the radio interview and arranged for a car to pick up John and Joe and take them to the radio station over in Glasgow. When they hopped in the back seat of the car they found that they weren't the only celebrities going to the promotion. The Guest of Honor for the Match Riding was also in the car.

"This is Turk Greenough," the driver said by way of introduction, indicating the grizzled old cowboy sharing the front seat with him. Turk twisted around and reached in to the back seat to shake hands with both bronc riders.

"Pleasure to meet cha boys," he said with a friendly smile as they clasped hands all around.

"You ever heard of him?" the driver asked.

"You bet!" John said.

"Yep," Joe agreed.

"You were one of the first Big-Time bronc riders," John said.

"And a stunt man, and a movie star, and who knows what all else. . . ." Joe added. "You're famous!"

"Oh . . . ha, ha!" Turk said. "There's famous people wherever you go. You usually just don't know it. All I ever wanted to be was a cowboy, like you fellas."

"Well, you're certainly that," John said. "You won the world a couple of times, didn't you."

"Yep," Turk admitted and actually blushed. He was becoming uncomfortable with where the conversation was going, so he changed the subject. "Where are you from Joe? Down in Nevada isn't it?"

"Battle Mountain," Joe told him.

"I know that country," Turk mused. "Do you know ol' Bill Chambers . . . used to live ten or twelve miles west of there?"

"Well, yeah," Joe said. "They're our neighbors."

"How about the Beckley family."

"Yep, I know them, too." Joe said.

"Well, small world, isn't it?" Turk observed. "I guess *they're* pretty famous, too, then. I'm surprised we never met before, Joe . . . we know the same people." And they both smiled.

Then Turk turned to John and said, "Now, where are you from?"

"I'm from Kansas," John told him.

"Anywhere near Kingman, Kansas? We used to go to a rodeo in Kingman, Kansas, when we traveled between Dewey, Oklahoma, and Cheyenne back in the day. That was a real nice place, but one of the hottest damn places on earth. They used to have a rodeo down in a park, between two rivers."

"Yep, I know Kingman," John said. He grew up in Kingman, Kansas.

"You know, in my day," Turk continued, "A lot of people in a lot of places didn't like to see the rodeo come to town. The cowboys were usually pretty self-contained; they liked to have a little fun. But every little town always had a tough guy or two who thought they could make a name for themself by whipping themselves a cowboy. It usually didn't work too well, but it almost always happened. But Kingman was a little different," Turk explained. "They really liked to have the rodeo come to town. They liked cowboys. And they put on quite a party for us. And those old ranchers and farmers came out and we all got together and had a great time.

"Of course this was in the '20's and nobody had electricity. So the rodeo was always in the afternoon. Then in the evening, those cowboys, and everybody else, I guess, were always looking for something to do. And this was during the prohibition era so you couldn't get any liquor or do any drinkin'. Well, they sent us cowboys out east of town about a mile or so one evening to a big ol' "Chicken House," a big place. It was all shut up, you know, and dark from the outside. You had to knock on the door to be let in. Well this big ol' deputy sheriff opens the door and just stands there in the doorway. You had to squeeze past him to get in the place.

"'You got a cowboy hat on,' he says to me. 'You can come on in, you're welcome.' Well, I was sure glad to hear it because that deputy was a big ol' boy. I mean big! I stand about six-foot tall and he towered over me by a head at least.

"There was a second doorway inside the first one and you could really hear the music coming through it. There was some kind of jazz band playing in there. Then when you got through that second door the sound really hit you in the face. That and the light. The place was lit up bright with lantern light, although none of the light was showing outside as the windows were covered.

"There was a nice big bar made out of some kind of dark heavy wood that stretched clear down the side wall of the place. It had a big mirror hung up behind it, like you see in the old cowboy movies. There were several guys behind the bar serving drinks as fast as they could to a crowd of ladies and men, standing three and four deep, in front of it.

"There was a small dance band set up against the back wall of the place and four or five guys were playing on some horns, a piano and a set of drums. The lead singer had the crowd wound up and the dance floor was full of people who were all doing those 'new' dances that were so popular back then, like the Charleston and the Hop. The women, who were pretty new to saloon halls in those days, were all dressed in those real flashy styles that showed off more woman than what they used to do. Not being interested in a drink at the moment, I moved over to the far wall opposite the bar, trying to kind of skirt the crowd. Somebody had set up some tables over there loaded with food that was free for the taking. I guess it was there to draw the rodeo crowd into the place, either that or they regularly feed their customers to keep 'em happy. Anyway, I hadn't eaten that day so I moved over there to put on the feed bag.

"It was mighty satisfying, sitting there filling my belly, watching all those people having such a good time. And the girls . . . well, there's nothing I'd rather watch. So, after a couple of plates of good food, I was starting to feel about half human and I moved on over to the bar to see if I could get a beer to wash that supper down with. It took me a few minutes to move up to the bar through the crush of people. There were a lot of men and women—locals I presume—all in their fancy duds, pressed right up around the bar stools. There were some ranchers and farmers, too, and a couple of groups of cowboys from the rodeo all intermingled. They were gettin' along fine and having fun, talking to each other at almost a full-on yell to be heard over the band in the background, when all of a sudden hard feelings broke out between the local tough I alluded to before—the one wantin' to build a reputation—and one of the rodeo bunch, a friend of mine and a good bronc rider. I don't know what it was about, probably one of them bumped into the other one in the congestion around the bar or something stupid like that.

"The local guy was a lot bigger than the cowboy, and that difference had a few of the other cowboys ready to back the little guy up. And that, of course, had the locals ready to back up their guy. You could see that it was about to get real ugly in that place.

"Just then, that big deputy steps in to the middle of it. You could tell neither one of the fighters wanted anything to do with him because they both kind of backed off and gave him room while sizing each other up. The band saw what was happening and stopped playing. Suddenly it was quieter than it'd been all night in that place.

"'What's it all about, Bob?' The deputy asks the local guy who he evidently knows—probably from all the other scrapes he'd been in in the place. The tough muttered some drunken accusation you couldn't even understand toward the cowboy, when this well dressed young guy in a silky looking vest stepped in. He was about five nine and a hundred and seventy pounds but really built. He had a fighter's chin and prominent cheek bones to go with a thick nose and a bushy head of healthy hair. He gave the deputy a look and pointed to the door with his thumb like he was hitchin' a ride.

"The deputy took that as a sign and immediately shuffled the tough bodily out the front door of the place. The guy in the vest looked around at the crowd, which had separated to avoid the hostilities and give the fighters room, and he said, 'Please folks, don't let one drunk spoil the fun.' He signaled to the band to resume playing and signaled to the bartenders to pour some more drinks and order was restored that quick.

"When the bartender brought me my beer, I found out my money was no good. He said, 'It's on the house pardner. Tonight cowboys drink for free.' Well, now I *know* these Kansas folks are special, free supper *and* free drinks, and no whuppin' put on anybody. So I held up the bar with my elbow for awhile and sipped on my beer and watched the crowd gyrate on the dance floor.

"When I'd finished my beer I walked over toward the door where the deputy was back on guard duty. 'Say,' I said to him. 'Back in Montana where I come from, when somebody shows you some good hospitality it's considered polite to thank them personally. So could you tell me who I should thank for the food and the drink this evening? I'd sure like to show my appreciation.'

"He looks over the crowd for a second and then points to the guy in the vest who had eighty-sixed the drunk earlier. I thanked him for the information and then asked him, 'Who is the guy anyway? What's his name? I should at least address him properly while thankin' him.'

"He looked at me like I was from Mars. Then he said, 'You mean you don't *know* Pretty Boy Floyd?'"

YOU BE THE JUDGE

*"John McBeth made bronc riding look so easy it
probably cost him a lot of money."*
Anonymous Cowboy

Bobby Berger called John McBeth on the phone and
asked, "Are you goin' to Ft. Madison?"

"Yeah," John answered.

"Can I ride with ya."

"Sure."

"I gotta be there first perf," Bobby said.

"It doesn't matter," John answered. "We can go
whenever. I'm gonna go and stay . . . I'm not gonna enter
anywhere else."

"Well, good," Bobby said. "I'm thinking we oughta
room together when we get there. I got a broke leg."

John asked, "Well, uh, how come yer goin'?"

"I'm judging."

"Oh. Well, I'm not so sure I'm takin' you or not, then.
People'll think I'm packing you around so I can win
something."

"Ah . . . ," Bobby said. "If you don't have it coming,
you ain't gonna get it."

"Well, I know that. Okay, you can go."

When it was time to head for the rodeo, John drove by
Bobby's house to pick him up. Bobby came out of the
house on a pair of crutches with a little suitcase in his hand.
He did a little Tennessee two-step as he walked, trying to
use a crutch and hold onto the suitcase in one hand while
swinging several pounds of plaster at the end of his other
leg. He got in the car and got himself as comfortably
situated as possible, his casted leg propped up in the corner

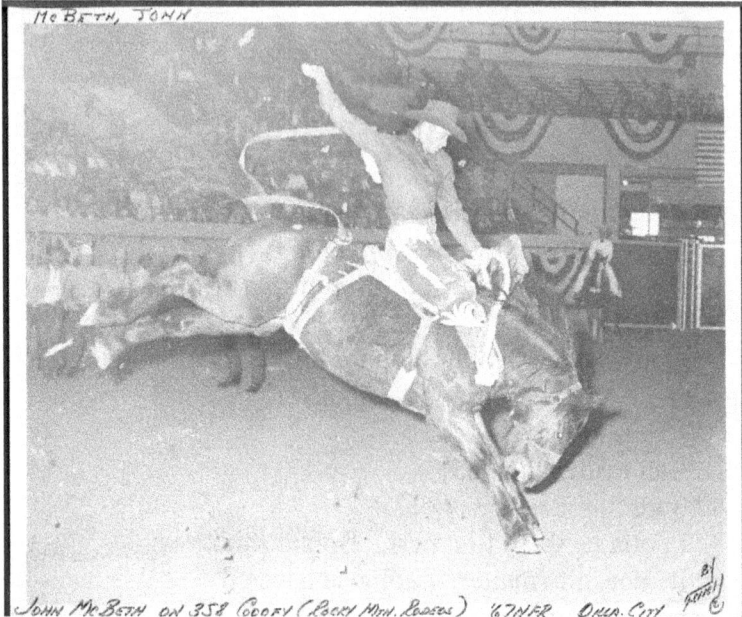

John McBeth making it ". . . look so easy . . ." aboard Goofy at the 1967 National Finals Rodeo. Ferrell Butler photo, Dickinson Research Center, National Cowboy & Western Heritage Museum, Oklahoma City, Oklahoma.

of the dash. After two or three seconds the subject finally got around to the bronc riding.

"So, what'd you draw?" Bobby asked.

"I got Bar-16 for my first one," John said. "She's just another old horse. For my second one, I've got Jake."

"Tell me about Jake," Bobby said. He was remembering the holy terror he had seen dump so many of the top bronc riders by taking a strong run to the middle of the arena with his head up, and then, when he had them worked loose in their saddle, exploding unexpectedly, and taking his head at the same time, jerking them out over the front end. "You're the only foolish guy I know that actually wants that sucker. He's too much work—if you can ride him— and he ain't any fun to ride, but you get along with him fine. I ain't ever seen him throw you off."

"Yeah, he's never thrown me off."

"Well, what do you do? He don't buck with you like he does with everybody else."

"Yeah, I know. I've rode him a time or two for nothing because people don't think he bucks when I've got him. But when I've got him I can tell you *exactly* what he's gonna do."

"What's that?"

"I'm gonna spur him out and let him run for two or three steps. Then I'm gonna drum him in the right rib and bring it back, and hit him again, on the way forward—and then get a hold of something! Because I know he's going to break right then when I jab him instead of when *he* decides to do it. And I give him way more rein than you guys give him because I don't want him setting me up for that deal. I just want him to pull my hand down when he takes his head, not my body. So, when I drum him he breaks every time. And he'll throw his head back like that . . . ," John twitched his head and neck back and to the left as he spoke, ". . . and come right around into a tight little circle to the left. And if he don't getcha right there he ain't goin' to. After he breaks, you and me could both ride him, double— and you've got a broke leg! So then you just jump up out of your saddle and spur the sucker."

"Aw, shoot," Bobby said. "I'll bet you were out of yer rabid-ass mind the first time you tried that!"

"No, the first time I tried it, it was an accident," John said, laughing. "He jerked a foot of rein out of my hand and I was grabbing whatever I could to keep from falling off and drummed him by chance."

"And it worked?"

"And it worked. He comes around to the left in that little circle—duck soup."

"Well, I ride right handed," Bobby said. "You think I'd have to spur him on the left?"

"Well, I don't know. Some people you just can't help.

You might have to change hands," McBeth grinned.

"Some people have no sense of humor at all," Bobby concluded.

Bobby Berger is known for being a man of few words. If he can say two or three words and stop, and have you guessing what he meant he is tickled to death. That makes him compatible with a lot of people. So, he and John moved into a motel room in Fort Madison and settled in comfortably for a couple of days. At night they would get a bite to eat and then go back to the room and watch a little TV, or play cards, with Bobby sitting with his leg elevated on a chair.

When it was time to rodeo, John would drive to the arena where Bobby would get out of the car and hobble over to the rodeo office on his crutches wearing the judge's vest he'd been given. He would pick up his judge's score sheets on the clipboard he was issued and hobble into the arena for three hours of work. Sometimes he thought it was easier riding broncs and bulls than judging. It was impossible to please everybody, and everybody saw everything differently. There was always somebody griping about the judging afterward, whether legitimately or just trying to save face for their own lackluster performance. Luckily, it was a pro rodeo, and that helped. The better the contestants, the better the stock, the better the rodeo producer and his secretary and timers, the better the rodeo committee, the chute help, and everybody else involved, the easier it made Bobby's job. It was a big help when everybody around you was a professional. Still, there were always complaints. And Bobby wasn't one for long explanations.

Fort Madison, Iowa, puts on a good rodeo. They have a nice facility. They add a lot of money to the purse through sponsorship donations and, consequently, they draw a lot of top, nationally ranked, cowboys. There were a couple of carloads of saddle bronc riding "Toughs" from up in the

Northwest section of the country entered, so it wasn't too surprising when John rode Bar-16, and rode her right, but finished out of the money in the first go-round. So far, nobody was complaining about Berger and McBeth being buddies.

John wasn't up on Jake in the second go-round until the last performance, Sunday afternoon. By then the first go-round had long since been paid, and a lot of the bronc riders had had their two head and knew their total and average scores. A lot of them were hanging around the chutes with their winnings already calculated, ready to watch the last perf and see if their scores got bumped, costing them some money. But there were ten broncs yet to be ridden, so anything could still happen.

Jake was the very definition of a bronc that day. He came stomping and snorting into the chute ready for work. John spoke to him in low tones as he slipped the halter over his head. Their familiarity with each other seemed like an advantage. The cowboy was cool and confident, remembering the many successes they'd shared in the past. He worked smoothly, setting his saddle. The bronc seemed tuned in to the routine too, settling down under John's calm hand.

The stock contractor saved Jake until last that day, featuring him in the last bronc riding slot in the last performance of the rodeo. All the other bronc riders were now done. Their scores recorded on the judge's sheets. The only thing that could change the rankings now, affect the money won, was John McBeth and Jake. So, with his competitors lined up on the back of the chutes, and along the arena fence, watching with rapt attention, John slipped down on Jake's back.

The announcer had a lot to talk about as he hyped the ride. "We have a special treat for you folks today!" he promised. "We've got the two-time bucking horse of the year next to go. This is Jake! And trust me, this is a horse that nobody wants to see written beside their name on the draw sheet. He has a reputation for bucking off more than his share of top-notch cowboys."

Doing double duty, the announcer had to hurry to get in his build-up for John, as well, since his repute was the equal of Jake's. "But ol' Jake's got his hands full today, folks," he said, "as he'll be tried by John McBeth of Burden, Kansas. John is a perennial top fifteen bronc rider and one of the hardest cowboys to unseat in the game...."

At that, the chute gate flew open with a crack. Jake lunged into the arena with John spurring him in the neck with a death grip. John's rein was longer than most, too long for most of the other guys to ride with. He held it up high, taking up the slack, lifting, his elbow locked out straight. Jake took three or four big lunges toward the center of the arena, trying to jerk the bronc rider loose from the lock he held on his swells and over the horse's shoulders. He was setting John up for his patented trap where he would get the rider jiggled loose, and then explode while changing direction, leaving the rider hung out to dry. But before he could spring his trap, John jerked his right foot out of Jake's neck and rammed it in the bronc's right rib cage on its way back to the cantleboard where it hit and snapped forward off the quarter bind, drumming the bronc in the rib cage a second time on one "jump" as the foot snapped back to the bronc's neck. All while the left foot stayed planted in the front end.

Jake blew up. He kicked high and hard, jerking down on the swells of the saddle as he turned left, away from the offending spur in his ribs. He took his head right down, trying to pull the bronc rider forward in his seat with the rein. He just pulled the rein down where John liked it. Where he knew it'd be. Jake had fallen into John's trap.

As the bronc turned back in that "tight little circle to the left" as John had described it to Berger while they were riding in the car, John unlocked his feet from the front end, jumped up out of his saddle and spurred the sucker. "Duck soup."

When it was announced, a few seconds later, that he had won the second go-round of the bronc riding going away, four or five disgruntled bronc riders congregated around Bobby Berger in front of the chutes, led by a couple of the Northwestern boys.

"Whatta ya mean! He ain't supposed to win nothin'! That horse didn't buck. . . ." one of them said, speaking for the whole group.

Berger said, "Yeah, he sure did! He just didn't buck like you suckers are used to seeing. John told me exactly what he was going to do; and what the horse was going to do when he did it; and it happened *exactly* like he said it would. That's control now. . . . Are there any a you guys that can tell me exactly what's gonna happen on *any* horse you get on?"

Nobody said a word. A couple of guys looked down at the ground. A couple of other guys broke eye contact with Bobby who stared them right in the face.

"No?" Bobby said. "I didn't think so. So you probably can't do *that*, can you?"

And he hobbled off on his crutches to judge the next event.

PEER PRESSURE

*"Gimme ten percent and I'll make sure you win
something!"*

Unnamed Judge

In the old days rodeo judges were found wherever you could find them. They were often locals who were members of the rodeo committee and may or may not have had any rodeo contestant or prior judging experience. They certainly lacked any sort of formalized training geared toward judging rodeo events. In the worst cases they were unknowledgeable, inexperienced, and even biased for or against one contestant or another. In the best of circumstances judging rodeo is a difficult art. The unique and always unpredictable behavior of the stock combined with the necessarily subjective nature of the scoring system renders rodeo knowledge a must, rodeo experience invaluable, and a fair and unbiased approach to the job as the quintessential goal of any judge.

Part 1: The Stuttering Pencil

John McBeth was trying to establish himself as a top pro. He'd had a lot of wins, some big wins. Yet, he was searching for the consistent checks that would maximize his revenue. He rolled into Mound City, Kansas, with high hopes. He drew a good one in the first round, a kind of a fat looking little sorrel mare that came around in a circle to the left jumping and kicking nice. John stuck the perfect ride on her. He spurred an inch higher each jump until he was setting his feet in the mane of the mare every time she kicked. He had his toes cranked out all the way. His rein arm he held straight out in front of him shoulder high. His free arm was extended almost straight up, topped by a closed fist. He lay back each time the mare kicked and kicked her first. He lifted on his rein and set his feet. It was a perfect ride.

So he was surprised when he came in fifth in the first round, and disappointed, as they paid four places. He needed consistent checks. Consistent wins. Luckily he was drawn up in the second round. He had Sage Hen.

John loved Sage Hen. She was his favorite bronc. She was the first horse he got on as a card carrying member of the RCA at Little Rock, Arkansas back in the fall of 1963. She was a Harry Knight horse and in 1960 was voted the runner-up to the Bucking Horse of the Year, another Harry Knight horse, Jake. "I always got along with her," John was heard to say. "I did a lot of begging and pleading and she listened well." She was a big Morgan cross mare, kind of temperamental. The way she bucked and the way John rode just seemed to mesh. Her style fit his or vice versa. She was, for John, a horse he couldn't draw often enough but was rarely lucky enough to draw.

So he was happy to slap his saddle down on Sage Hen in the second go-round. If he could win it he'd still be in fair shape for the average. And with a day money and average yet to be paid he could still salvage the trip. Of course he wasn't counting his chickens, yet. He was thinking of Sage Hen. He knew he had better be paying attention to her because he was also heard to say, "Don't stub your toe or she will throw you clear out of the county."

Sage Hen displayed her attitude that day, which was purely anti-cowboy. She also showed why she had been voted the runner-up to the Bucking Horse of the Year. She came out of the chute fast and rank, and then got stronger as the ride went on. John rode her the way he wanted to, maybe better than he ever had. So it was the second big surprise for him at this rodeo when he failed to place in the round. Not placing in either round left him disgusted after making two good rides.

After the rodeo he was carrying his gear from behind the chutes. He bumped into one of the judges making his way from the arena. The guy went out of his way to come over and talk a minute, falling in beside John. "Hey th—there, f—f—fella," he stuttered. "Y—y—you rode p—pretty good. Y—y—you s—shoulda probably wa—wa—won somethin' here."

"Well," said John, stopping for a second to set his saddle down on the ground beside him and turning to look the guy right in the eye. "You're the judge. Why didn't I?"

"W—well," said the stuttering judge apologetically, "I ow—ow—owed Bill twenty fi—five dollars, and I owed J—Jim fifty dollars and I owed Pete and Carl. . . .? And th—there just wasn't any room for you to wi—win anything!"

John was struck speechless. The man was looking him right in the eye and truthfully telling him why he hadn't placed. What could he say to that? He smiled an ironic smile as he picked up his saddle and headed for his pickup. He still laughs about it to this day.

Part 2: The Boot Salesman

John was traveling through the upper Midwest and drew a bad dude at a two-day rodeo. The red sorrel was the kind of horse you'd rather have at one of the big rodeos, someplace where you could win enough money to make getting on him worthwhile. He was wild and mean and unpredictable. He would fight the chute trying to hurt you in the box. He would try to foul you on the chute gate or the gate post entering the arena. He would always set a trap for you while he bucked, breaking right or left suddenly, to break your rhythm and toss you off. John got him covered to the delight of the packed grandstand who loved the wild-west style of the crazy red horse. He made a scrappy ride, altering his timing repeatedly with the ever-changing pattern of the bronc. He short stroked a couple of times, stopping his feet at the cinch and firing his spurs back to the front end as the red horse stutter-stepped, changing leads and blowing up on a complete different tack. When the whistle blew the red horse was thrashing so bad that the pickup man was unable to handle dallying up the bronc and extricating John at the same time, so he let the rein go and grabbed the bronc rider as he jumped clear. It was like a planned buck-off—the rider letting the bronc's impetus throw him to the pickup horse. The crowd went wild.

As John made his way along the arena fence back to the bucking chutes, his score was announced over the loud speaker. It put him solidly into first place. It would be a hard score to beat, and there were only a couple of horses left to go. As he got back to the chutes a big black bronc reared into the arena. John recognized him as a multi-time NFR qualifier and the most famous horse in the string. He also noticed the bronc rider missed him out badly, his feet stuck in the cinch as the horse made his first jump. John watched as the horse made a beautiful jump and kick trip down the pen. The bronc rider never unlocked his rowels from the cinch. "He'd be a great one to make a spur ride on," John thought to himself. He was surprised the kid never made an attempt to spur the big black, especially since he was so nice to ride. He figured the fella must have been satisfied just to get him rode and had set that as his goal. "What a waste," he said to himself.

He was shocked when the kid's score was announced— he was surprised there was a score at all considering he had missed the horse out. But there it was: The kid had won the bronc riding, never wiggling a foot, moving John down to second place.

After the rodeo John went over to the rodeo office and

picked up his check for second. He headed out to the parking lot to get in his pickup and there was one of the two rodeo judges sitting on his fender, waiting for him. It was a fellow he knew fairly well and thought a lot of. He was sitting on that fender looking kind of downtrodden, and he said to John as he approached, "I expect you're kind of mad at me."

John said, "Should I be?"

The judge said, "Well, you should have won the bronc riding by a long ways."

"You're the judge. Why didn't I?"

The guy gave a disgusted look and said, "You know me. I like to rodeo and I like to rope. But I'm a Tony Lama boot salesman back in this country around here and that's how I make a living. I can't win enough to go rodeoing like I want to. I have to depend on these judging jobs to get to go sometimes. And if I let you win first on that wild no-good so-and-so and that kid doesn't win first on the most famous bronc in the herd, this stock contractor will never hire me to judge another rodeo."

John could see the dilemma the man faced. He was also impressed by his honest sincerity. He took a deep breath and centered himself for a moment. Then he said, "No, I'm not mad at you. And I do know that what you say is true. And I'm right proud that you're man enough to admit it."

They shook hands and John took his second place check and headed for home.

Epilogue

In 1978 the Professional Rodeo Cowboys Association introduced the Pro Judging System. The program was expanded and renamed the Pro Officials System in 1982. Today professional judges officiate every PRCA rodeo. Professional judges are required to be members of the PRCA, preferably with contestant experience. They attend judging orientation sessions and seminars to keep up with the demands of a constantly evolving rulebook. To become approved they are tested on their knowledge of rodeo's standards and procedures.

The program intends to ensure that all individuals judging at PRCA rodeos are fluent with the rulebook, well–versed in their duties (especially as relates to proper care and handling of the livestock) and unbiased toward the contestants. Their professional reputation as a judge is built through the program and follows them throughout their career.

The judges at the National Finals Rodeo are selected by vote of the NFR contestants based upon their experience and reputation. John McBeth was twice selected to judge the NFR—the pinnacle of rodeo competition.

FRIENDS IN HIGH PLACES

Sometimes the pilot's log only tells part of the story,
even when it says 1500 hours.

It was Memorial Day weekend and the McBeths decided to take a trip together. John was entered in some rodeos so Francie accompanied him, turning it into a working vacation. The first leg of their journey was a flight from their Kansas home to the spring rodeo in Las Vegas, Nevada. That's when the Vegas rodeo was held in those days before the National Finals Rodeo moved there in 1985 and became the ten-day extravaganza at the Thomas and Mack Center on the University of Nevada, Las Vegas, campus we have come to know ever since.

In Las Vegas they rented a car and drove out to the fairgrounds. At the rodeo that evening John bumped into a friend of his, Mac Baldrige, a big-time business man from the east coast. Mac was CEO of a major corporation in Connecticut and had use of a corporate jet. Being as much a cowboy as a businessman beneath his three piece suit, Mac would frequently fly out west to enter the team roping at PRCA rodeos whenever he got the chance.

After catching up with each other for a few minutes, John said, "Say Mac, you wouldn't happen to have that airplane on this trip would you?"

"Sure do."

"When are you heading east?"

"The first of the week."

"What would the chances be of hitching a ride back to the Midwest?"

"Where about are you going?"

"Cherokee, Iowa, or Sioux City," John told him.

John and Francie McBeth pose with one million dollars in cash at Binion's Horseshoe Club in Las Vegas. Photo from the John McBeth Collection.

"That shouldn't be a problem." Mac said. "That's about where we have to stop to refuel anyway. We can't make it clear to the east coast non-stop."

"I need to tell you," John said, "I've got my wife with me, so that's two hitch-hikers."

"No problem," Mac said. "My wife's along on this trip, too, so they can have a good visit. There's plenty of room on the plane."

"I'm entered in a couple of rodeos over in California," John told him. "So where should we meet up?"

"I'm going that way, too," Mac said. "I'll be leaving out of Sacramento airport on Monday morning."

"That's fine."

John rode at Vegas that night and was winning the bronc riding when they left. His score would hold up over the next four performances of the rodeo for fourth place overall. He and Francie jumped in the rent-a-car as soon as he was through and headed for Redding, California—a pretty fair little jaunt. John drove most of the night. Francie dozed in the seat beside him, lolling against his shoulder or the passenger side door, waking every so often, too uncomfortable to get any good sleep. John was mesmerized by the white lines coming at him on the pavement ahead, his eyelids started to droop, his head nodded on his shoulders. Then he thought of the next day at Redding. He had Checkmate drawn. Checkmate! A short stout bay horse with a reputation for getting stronger as the ride progressed. Although John couldn't know it yet, Checkmate was on his way to his own championship year. He would be crowned the Bucking Horse of the Year at the National Finals Rodeo in December. He was a horse that if you didn't win the bronc riding on him when you drew him, you were probably bucked off. Just the thought of him made John's heart beat faster. He sat up straighter. He focused on the dark highway ahead. He was awake.

The first guy John bumped into at Redding the next day was his good friend "Droopy" Doug Brown.

"What are you doing here?" Doug asked with no formalities.

"Well, I've got Checkmate," John said. "I'm here to win the bronc riding."

"I know one of the guys that's judging here," Droopy said, "and he says there isn't *anybody* that can spur that horse out. They're gonna get you at the gate."

"That sounds like kind of a prejudicial deal," John said. "I guess it remains to be seen."

"No, no!" said Droopy. "It's gonna happen. They're gonna get you at the gate. And whoever's got Quicksilver is gonna slap him."

A look passed between them. Droopy's story placed a pebble of unrest in the seat of John's saddle.

Before long, the broncs were run in the chutes and John saddled Checkmate. He noticed that the guy next to him—whoever he was—had Quicksilver. They bucked Quicksilver first and John got fired up watching the other fella's ride. Quicksilver was no slouch; he was one of the best broncs in the herd, in fact in the country, and the cowboy sat up there and rode him like you're supposed to.

Sure enough. They got him for slapping the horse.

That pebble of unrest in John's saddle grew into a stone.

In a couple of minutes it was John's turn to go. Checkmate ran right down the open chute gate, trying to foul his foot and knee through the rails. John remembered what Droopy'd said, and held his feet locked in the front end until the bronc broke, and for the first couple of jumps after that. It was a risky proposition, locking in to the front end like that. A bronc with Checkmate's power can loosen a rider up in one jump and throw him off the next if he's not spurring. John got by the initial storm through the sheer strength of his lock on Checkmate's front end. He started the horse right, spurred the third jump—and every jump thereafter. As he kicked out of his stirrups at the whistle, landing like a stunt man on the back of the pickup horse, handing his rein to the pickup man, he felt like he'd made a pretty good ride.

Still, they got him at the gate, just like Droopy said.

The next day John and Francie traveled back down

toward the old gold fields in east-central California to a little town called Ione. John had the high score there in the afternoon performance and was walking back to the car with his gear slung over his shoulder when the stock contractor walked up and said, "Well, what do you think of my new announcer?"

John had noticed that the announcer was a young guy with a strong, deep voice, a good grasp of rodeo, and an easy-going personable style behind the mike.

"I've never heard of him before," John said. "But you better put him under some kind of long term contract and pay him well or he'll be going off to the big ones and you'll never get him back."

"You really think so?"

"I know so," John said. "What's his name again?"

"Tallman," the guy told him. "His name's Bob Tallman."

A while later John and Francie were getting into the car to take off and the announcer walked over and asked, "Are you John McBeth?"

"Yeah," John said.

"The boss just told me what you said, and I wanted to say thank you because that's been kind of a question here lately, and I think now he's gonna come around."

"Well, don't thank me, you deserve it," John told him as they shook hands. "You did a good job."

They went down to the Forum in Inglewood next. John had a nice old horse, ". . . a nice old timer." He did a pretty good rear out and jumped and kicked after that. John won a third there and since it was the last performance he got to pick up his check on the spot. He was in the rodeo office while the secretary was cutting the checks and got to talking to the stock contractor, Cotton Rosser. John had to turn in his car and was wondering how he was going to get to Sacramento, so he asked Cotton if he was headed that way.

"Oh, yeah, yeah!" Cotton said. "We'll go up there right away. . . . Gotta get done here. Meet you out front in a little bit."

So John and Francie turned in the rental and were standing in front of the Forum waiting. The huge parking lot was nearly empty. Suddenly, Cotton came running out the door and dashed right past them carrying a briefcase. He jumped into one of the last cars in the lot and it sped off. As it was about to peal out the exit onto the main drag it screeched to a halt. All at once it was slapped into reverse and came squealing back toward them. The car gained speed like a race car in reverse for about a block before it got close to them and started to decelerate. It screeched to a halt right in front of them and Cotton stuck his head out of the passenger's window. "Get in! Get in! Gotta go, gotta go!" he said. "I just about forgot you."

John never did know the identity of the mysterious chauffeur with the exceptional driving skills. In record time he dropped them at a nearby airport where they jumped into Cotton's plane for the flight to Sacramento.

"C'mon, c'mon, let's go," Cotton said as they loaded the plane. "You get in the right hand seat, John, and I'll get in the left. Throw your gear in the back seat there and let's go." Francie shared a grin with John as she jumped in the back seat with John's saddle. "We gotta get going," Cotton said. He was in kind of a hurry.

The plane took off with Cotton at the controls and wearing the headset, talking to the tower. Flying out of Inglewood, in the thick of L.A., you're in somebody's air space as soon as you take off. Cotton made a procedure turn to the left to follow the regulated traffic pattern out of the airport. The plane was a Beechcraft Bonanza, a pretty hot model. It had dual controls, but only one yoke and it was set on a swivel. Cotton tripped the swivel and threw the yoke over to John saying, "You fly a little, don't you? I've got a couple of rodeos next week I need to figure stock for and I've got a couple of truckloads of animals here and a couple there. . . ." He pulled open his briefcase and started pulling out stock lists as he was talking.

John looked out the window and saw that they were right over LAX, the biggest airport in L.A. He knew they were in their pattern, in what they call the zone. He had no idea what had been said over the radio, whether they had permission to be there or not. He looked over at Cotton and pointed at his ear and Cotton jerked off the headset and threw it to him. John put the headset on and started searching the panel for the N registration number for the airplane. When he found it he realized that it was the number the air traffic controller in his headset was so angry with. He executed a sharp turn to get out of the jam they were in per the controller's instructions. When he had things under control a few minutes later, he said to Cotton, "Hey, where's your map?"

"Map?"

"I need a map. I need to know where I'm going."

"Well," Cotton said. "I don't have any maps. I've been flying around here for years and I just *know* where I'm going."

"Well, I don't."

"Aw, you'll figure it out." And Cotton went back to his stock manifests.

Two hours later they approached the Sacramento airport. Cotton dozed in the left hand seat while John flew the plane from the right. He had been vectored in to the airport and had permission to land. About a mile out on final approach he started feeling a little bit uneasy. He was flying an unfamiliar airplane from the right hand seat, it was a pretty hot airplane, and they were approaching a busy airport. The gear was down and locked but John started thinking the whole thing was pretty stupid.

He looked over at Cotton and saw that he was asleep, leaning against his window. He tapped him on the leg and said, "Do you want to land this thing?"

"Where are we?" Cotton asked, sitting up and looking around.

"That's the threshold at Sacramento," John told him and pointed over the plane's nose.

"I don't want to go to Sacramento!" Cotton exclaimed, and grabbed the controls. He pulled out, aborting the landing. He pulled off to the right—unfortunately it was a left control field with a left turn pattern. This time John had the headset on and heard every syllable screamed at them by the tower. John took off the headset and threw it at Cotton.

Cotton looked at him and smiled. He said, "I've got a rodeo at Marysville at six o'clock, so we'll be a little bit late."

They were already approaching Marysville on the short hop from Sacramento. At five minutes before six they were circling the arena on Cotton's place. From 100 feet elevation and at a 40 degree bank they could see the grand entry forming up to start the rodeo. Suddenly John saw hi-lines in his field of vision and with no time to say anything just threw up his hands and pointed.

"Oh, yeah," Cotton said and jerked the yoke back, yanking the plane over the lines, setting off the stall warning horn. It occurred to John that whatever the outcome of the stall they'd be on time. Cotton dipped the plane over the lines, got the gear down and set the plane down in a well-executed short field landing on a little grass strip behind the arena. He taxied the plane right up behind the grandstand amid a crowd of kids, dogs, and horses, and shut it off.

"Well, let's get the hell out of here," he said. "We've got a rodeo to put on!"

John and Francie enjoyed being spectators and sharing the rodeo like they so rarely got the chance to do. Before long John started wondering again how they were going to get to Sacramento. After the rodeo Cotton came over to them and said, "I didn't tell you before but Mac and his wife are staying here, so we're going to take you all down to the airport in Sacramento in the morning."

As they stood on the tarmac at the airport the next day saying their goodbyes to Cotton, John thought of what an icon in the business he was, and what a great personality. "There'll never be another one like him—ever," he said to himself.

They piled into Mac's company plane, John and Mac and their wives, and Mac's two pilots. With a pilot and co-pilot to handle the flight duties, they sat in the back and talked and relaxed until they were in the air. The plane was a de Havilland DH125 twin jet.

A few minutes later they were at cruising altitude when the pilot entered the cabin from the cockpit searching for a cup of coffee from the galley. He sipped from his cup as he made small talk with the passengers: They were at 40,000 feet, he told them, and cruising with a tremendous tailwind. John was happy with the time they were making; he had to get to Iowa. Mac was happy with the fuel savings the tailwind made.

"Say," John asked the pilot, "Would it be all right if I came up and looked at the panel?"

"It's okay with me," he said, and looked to Mac.

"Oh, that's right," Mac said. "You do fly, don't you, John? Sure, go ahead."

So the pilot took John into the cockpit. He told the co-pilot to go get himself a cup of coffee and ushered John into the right hand seat. They discussed the autopilot three-axis control that John was familiar with from past experience on other airplane types. The pilot explained, "This little jet is under such power thrust that if you turned the wheel with a heavy hand you might just do an aileron roll."

"That might get you in trouble with the boss," John

observed.

"Especially if nobody's belted in," the pilot grinned. "So we typically fly it on autopilot all the time and if you want to turn you just click this little knob here," he said, indicating a little black knob like a radio tuner on top of the autopilot. "Each click is one degree. So, if you want to turn two degrees to the right you just click the knob two clicks to the right, and if you want to go left you click it the other way," he explained. "Say, why don't you and I trade seats. Then you'll be able to say you sat in the pilot's seat of a corporate jet."

So they traded seats, and for the next hour they traveled some 600 miles discussing the control panel, the plane's systems and all kinds of things related to the aircraft and flying. Then the pilot said, "I believe I'll go get another cup of coffee," and he got up and left.

John was enjoying the solitude of being alone in the cockpit. He felt a kinship with the machine as he sat at the controls contemplating nearly unlimited performance at his fingertips. The parallels between flying and bronc riding were not lost on him: The power moving you through the seat of your pants; the balance between staying in the middle of a bronc and "doing an aileron roll"; and the solitude of a bronc saddle or the pilot's seat. His reverie was broken by a loud comment from the cabin that carried into the cockpit.

"Hey! Who's flying this thing anyway!" It was Mac challenging his pilots. Everyone laughed.

They set down at the airport in Sioux City—with a type rated pilot at the controls—about two and a half hours after leaving Sacramento.

It was an hour's drive by rent-a-car to Cherokee, Iowa. By the time the rodeo was over and John had collected his check for winning the bronc riding, Mac was at home in Connecticut.

That evening the McBeths boarded a flight from Sioux

City to Wichita and retrieved their car upon arrival. They were home by midnight.

By then Cotton Rosser was already asleep out in California. He'd be up early the next morning, fueling his plane to fly out of the home pasture. He had a rodeo to get to.

Epilogue

Howard Malcolm "Mac" Baldrige was a confirmed cowboy by the age of seven. He was an incredibly gifted man who was able to successfully combine rodeo competition with his other vocations. A Yale University graduate and World War II veteran, he made his mark in business starting as a foundry hand in an iron works in 1949 and became president of that company by 1960. He joined Scoville, Inc., in 1962 and served as chairman and chief executive officer while leading the company from a financially struggling brass mill to a diversified billion dollar business. President Ronald Reagan chose "Mac" to serve as Secretary of Commerce in his administration in 1981 and Baldrige performed with distinction, receiving the Presidential Medal of Freedom in 1988. Baldrige was the PRCA's Rodeo Man of the Year in 1981 and was inducted into the ProRodeo Hall of Fame in 1988. He was inducted into the National Cowboy & Western Heritage Museum in 1984. Tragically, Mac was killed in a rodeo accident on July 25, 1987 during a team roping when the horse he was riding reared over backward and hit him in the chest with the saddle horn.

Growing up in Long Beach, California, Cotton Rosser always wanted to be a cowboy. That dream was realized when Cotton competed in all of the rodeo events as a teenager and then at Cal Poly State University at San Luis Obispo. As a professional, Cotton was on his way, winning trophies and titles with the pinnacle of his career being the

All-Around title at the Grand National Rodeo in San Francisco in 1951. A ranch accident prematurely ended his competitive career and he purchased the Flying U Rodeo Company, building it into one of the most successful stock contracting businesses in the world over the ensuing decades. His tremendous showmanship, inspired by Gene Autry, combined with the many creative innovations he brought to the rodeo arena, and his "Born to Buck" livestock breeding program have made Flying U a model for other stock contracting companies to follow. A longtime member of the PRCA Board of Directors, Cotton was named the PRCA Stock Contractor of the Year in 1985 preceding his induction into the ProRodeo Hall of Fame in 1995 and the National Cowboy & Western Heritage Museum in 2009.

The young rodeo announcer John endorsed certainly found his way ". . . to the big ones. . . ." During a five decade career Bob Tallman has announced over 15,000 rodeo performances in five countries. He has become the voice of the National Finals Rodeo, having worked the NFR more than anyone else in the history of the event, calling the action live or for radio or TV since 1977. He is an eight-time PRCA Announcer of the Year and was inducted into the ProRodeo Hall of Fame in 2004 and the National Cowboy & Western Heritage Museum in 2007. Bob has been called "the greatest announcer that ever lived."

MISDIRECTION

"Gerald Roberts once told me that amateurs compete against each other, but a true professional in this business only competes against himself."
John McBeth

One time when I was trying to win the world I went to Gordon, Nebraska. When I got there I went in to the rodeo office and paid my fees, and I remember a church group had a booth set up by there where the volunteers were running a concession stand. There was a bunch of bronc riders that I knew from up in the north and the northwest country hanging around there—some really good hands. Well, it was unusual for them to be down in this part of the country at that time of the year, it was in August, the hot time of the year. I knew they didn't like the heat, so I thought it was strange. After I came out of the office I got a cup of coffee at the concession stand and went over and sat down at their table right in the middle of those guys and I asked 'em, "What are you fellas doing around here at this time of the year?"

"Well," they said. "There's a bunch of good rodeos around here right now, York, Nebraska, and Vinita and Ponca City, Oklahoma, are coming up, and we don't want you to get all the money." And they laughed, "Ha, ha!" They were giving me a pretty hard time, hinting that there were some easy pickings around this country and acting like they had it all figured out, now. So we talked for awhile and gave each other a hard time, just kidding like you do, and then after a bit I got up and went over to a phone booth by there and called Francie to tell her I'd arrived all right.

72

John McBeth sticking closer to home, riding at Ardmore, Oklahoma aboard Kinney Brothers, Red Man. Ferrell Butler Photo, Dickinson Research Center, National Cowboy & Western Heritage Museum, Oklahoma City, Oklahoma.

When I hung up the phone and went back over to the table, they all wanted to know what I'd just entered. They were really pressing me to tell 'em, too. "Well," I said, "You're all down here; I'm thinking *maybe* I'll go up to Washington and enter Kennewick, Bremmerton and Monroe. That's a nice little run . . . and there won't be anybody up there, either."

Now, I just indicated that I *might* have entered there, but I never said I did. And shoot, in two minutes all six of 'em were in that telephone booth entering those rodeos. So the next week I won Ponca City and York and placed second at Vinita. I put $2800 in my pocket and never got 300 miles from home. I don't know how those other boys came out.

73

GOING FOR TWO

In 1974 John went into the National Finals Rodeo
with enough money won to guarantee him the world
title. No one was close enough to catch him, even if
they won the NFR.

For eight days they'd been riding. It had become an endurance-fest. After eight go-rounds at the National Finals Rodeo, Joe Marvel and John McBeth were locked in a duel of wills. They were twenty points apart in the aggregate with two rounds to go. McBeth had the World Championship sewed up, sure. Marvel couldn't win enough at the NFR to top his season earnings—but John wanted to win the NFR, too. Bad. Get the double. The problem was: Joe Marvel. He led the NFR by 20 points. For McBeth to overtake the talented Marvel something drastic would have to happen. Joe would have to draw bad, or miss a horse out, or (heaven forbid) buck off! It just didn't seem likely that *anyone* could out-score Joe by twenty points in the final two rounds if they were drawing about the same. Then Joe drew Rodeo News.

Rodeo News was rank. He was the Bucking Horse of the Year in 1970, four years previously. And he had, undoubtedly, learned a few tricks since then. It was make-or-break time. It was all coming to a head. And it was all on Joe Marvel. John could only ride what he had drawn and hope for Joe to stub his toe. But Joe had to take it away.

There were those who thought the smart move, and one Joe might opt for with a 20 point bulge, was to ride safe, not expose himself too much and risk a buck off. There were even some who thought Joe would buck off of Rodeo

News, anyway, regardless of his approach.

In that deciding ninth go-round John did his part. He got everything out of his bronc he could, putting even more pressure on Joe. A good buddy of his poked him in the ribs as Joe was mounting up and said, optimistically, "Looks like you're gonna win 'em both!"

"Don't say that!" John exclaimed. "There's a lot of riding yet to do!"

Rodeo News was nasty in the chute when Joe climbed down on his back. He tried to rear over backwards and "brad" him in the back of the box, but was restrained with a halter rope. He leaned on the gate—and Joe's leg. He wouldn't stand up and give the cowboy a decent shot at marking him out. He had Joe's leg pinned between his side and the gate. A cowboy pushed the bronc one way and then pulled him the other, trying to get him untracked and standing better. Finally, the bronc reared up and hit the end of his halter rope once more. As he regained his balance, he stood on all four feet in the center of the chute for a second and Joe nodded his head.

Rodeo News crashed out of the gate and took a long run, really building up some momentum. Joe had his heels stuck in the bronc's neck well over the points of his shoulders in a perfect mark-out. He held his feet there until the bronc reached the center of the arena and blew up. Big time! Rodeo News cut back to the left and kicked out to the right, elevating and turning back as nasty as a well-trained, four-legged, 1500 pound world-class athlete in their prime is able to.

It popped Joe's feet back to the end of his binds; it threw him back to the end of his rein. As the horse came around nearly 180 degrees in that one explosive contortion, Joe tipped his head to the left and took a little jump off that rein and those binds, and stuck that bronc in the neck with his spurs. And when the whistle blew Joe was a *lot* of points.

John punched his buddy and said, "No national finals

buckle for me! And I wouldn't deserve it! Joe Marvel!
Hats off!"

PINK CADILLAC

Over a thirty-year career marketing Mary Kay
cosmetics, Francie McBeth won sixteen new
Cadillacs, one every two years, and wound up as the
National Sales Director for the company.

The Cadillac turned off the main road into the fairgrounds. It rolled slowly through the parking lot, turned right at the grandstand and made its way past a carnival of mechanized rides, concession trailers and game booths. It reached the end of the grandstand and turned left, idling across the dirt race track surrounding the arena. It drew to a halt beside a smiling parking attendant who checked the credentials of its occupants before waving the car through to the inner-sanctum of the infield parking lot. Whisper quiet, the big motor pushed the car down between rows of pickup trucks with horse trailers, motor-homes and dusty sedans. Silently, it made its way past a semi cattle-truck with the rodeo producer's B bar J brand on the door. It slid into a parking spot behind the stock pens close to the bucking chutes. The car was so long its driver was forced to execute a three-point turn to maneuver it into the empty space.

As sleek and low and as quiet and slow as the Caddy made its entrance—gravel crunching under its tires was the only sound accompanying its arrival—it could not go unnoticed, not in a hundred years, in a thousand parking lots, among a million cars. It was pink! And not just pink, but pink across the whole of its tennis court sized top, pink along its shapely side panels that extended clear from here to there, and pink down the length of its stately hood that threw up mirages out of the distance like the desert flats.

Francie McBeth with one of the Pink Cadillacs that became a fixture at Kansas rodeos. Photo from the John McBeth Collection.

No, the Caddy did not go unnoticed, ever.

Still, its arrival was not a topic of discussion among the small knots of cowboys pulling gear bags from the open trunks of their cars, the ropers and barrel racers grooming their mounts, or the stock contractor's crew working the pens—sorting stock for the upcoming performance. It was as at home in this environment as a pair of well-worn boots—provided *they* weren't pink. It might have drawn stares or a snicker years ago when a pink Cadillac was a novelty at Kansas rodeos. It doesn't stretch the imagination to envision comments like, "Elvis is in the house!" or "I smell somethin' sweet . . ." being bandied about back then. But no more. What the patently pristine pink purveyor of Mary Kay products had come to mean to the cowboys of the Kansas plains was that John McBeth had arrived. That day the only comment loud enough to hear was, "Well, boys . . . the bronc riding just toughened up!"

When the land yacht rolled to a stop, Francie stepped out of the driver's seat—after all, it was her car. She about lived in that car—and the fifteen others she won through the years—putting down countless thousands of miles before turning them in biennially for a new one. She competed in the arena of the marketplace; sales were her event, and she regularly won the world. In fact, they do give a gold buckle for sales achievement . . . only in this case it's pink.

John stepped out on the passenger's side and stretched the kinks out of his back. He pulled his gear out of the car when Francie popped the trunk. He had a good one drawn and as was his custom he hadn't had a lot to say on the drive down. He was immersed in the bronc riding, getting his head on straight for his ride.

"Do you want the keys?" Francie asked him.

"Nope, you keep 'em."

"Okay, then. Good luck," she said.

"Yep."

"I guess I'll go find a place to sit."

"Okay. See ya."

Sometimes it seemed a little bit . . . solitary . . . driving to a rodeo with John. Not lonely, because he was there, and he would respond if she spoke to him, but solitary in that he was off in his own world mentally. He was quiet and introspective. She knew that was how he got himself ready to ride, and long ago had accepted it. It was a perfectly logical way to prepare, anyhow, she thought. She counted her lucky stars that John had the temperament he did. He never got too excited about things, either too up or too down. Unlike some of the other husbands of the women she sat with at the rodeo, who would be ugly to be around if things didn't go their way in the arena, John was always on an even keel. If he had a bad performance, or just didn't win for whatever reason, he always let it go by the time he picked up his saddle at the stripping chute. He didn't let the bad vibes linger. She knew he had to remain positive to stay "up" for the next ride, whether it was coming that night, the next day or the following week. So, she could always count on him being sociable *after* the bronc riding.

Francie made her way to the contestant's grandstand— ten rows of portable bleachers set up behind the arena. John made his way to the bucking chutes, lugging his saddle and gear bag. He didn't need to ask about the bronc branded with the number one—his draw. He knew the horse well from previous experience. Several times the big buckskin gelding had taken him to the pay window and had never bucked him off.

John made small talk with some of the other bronc riders while the bareback riding was going on. They hung around on the back of the chutes watching the horses buck from the best "seats" in the house. When the bareback riding was about over they tossed their saddles down on the ground behind the chutes and sat in them, checking their binds and rosining their swells. In contrast to some of the other cowboys who became almost giddy before they rode, joking and horsing around, John had his game face on. This was business.

When the broncs were loaded in the chutes and John set his saddle on Big Buck's back he felt the excitement course through him. The buckskin always reared out of the chute as big as a horse can. He would lift his front hooves up and tuck them into his chest as he stood perfectly vertical on his rear legs. Then he would extend and stretch his body up, put a bow in his neck and look impossibly huge. To mark him out a bronc rider had to set his feet over the top of Buck's shoulders and hold on as the horse elevated. He would squeeze his saddle swells between his thighs; squeeze the bronc's neck between his heels as his feet elevated up, up and up. He'd lay back to get his feet to the front end and find himself hanging upside down by his heels off the top of this mountain of a horse, pulling his rein against that brawny bowed neck like a mountain climber hanging on a rope, and relying on his cantleboard to cradle him in the saddle.

That was the point in the ride where the crowd always made the "Awwww!" sound—a combination of all the "Ooos," the "Wows," the "Wha . . . s?" that involuntarily escaped their throats at the majesty of the beast, standing up to his full height like a great bear defying the hunter. In an instant the bronc returned to earth with a thud; immediately the other end of the horse was elevating as he kicked his hocks up and stood on his nose.

Just the thought of what was to come had John's body reacting to the images produced in his brain. His heart beat faster; his breath came deeper; his eyes grew wide as his body slipped into the zone created by his mind. His nervous system approached a heightened state where he possessed super-human strength, became impervious to pain, and time slowed ten-fold; a state that would only climax as Buck reared into the arena beneath him.

As he stood on the third rail of the chute gate pulling his cinches and measuring his rein, the flank man climbed on the back of the chute and adjusted Buck's flank strap. The announcer began his introduction of the pair, adding extra depth to his usual spiel.

"Well, folks!" he nearly hollered into his mike. "We've got a special treat for you today . . . ."

John barely heard what he was saying as he checked the tightness of his cinch.

". . . the world champion saddle bronc rider . . ." went in one ear and out the other as he tied off his latigo in a half knot.

". . . Big Buck . . . national finals bucking horse . . ." was so easy to ignore—he'd heard it, or an intro just like it, so many times before.

". . . arrived today in a *pink* Cadillac." Whoa! That broke John's concentration as he was tucking the tail of his latigo under the saddle skirt. He heard a murmuring of chuckles from the grandstand . . . and a few from behind the chutes.

"I don't know what to say about a bronc rider who drives a pink Cadillac . . ." the announcer went on as John pulled his back cinch. The laughter got louder.

"A Cadillac, I can see," the guy said. "But pink! A bronc rider in a pink Cadillac?" The gaiety was gaining momentum. Bordering on hilarity. John tuned him out as he measured his rein. Almost.

". . . not sure I could bet on a guy. . . ." More laughter.

"Shut up!" John growled under his breath as he slid down onto Big Buck's back, focusing on the bronc with all his might.

The announcer was still prattling on when John pressed his feet down into the bottom of his stirrups, took a bite of the swells between his thighs, lifted on his rein and nodded his head. His words were suddenly of no more significance to the duo of horse and rider than ants in a far off desert, the air over the South Pole, or the rings of Saturn, as Big Buck reared out of the chute.

The cackles emanating from the grandstand were cut like butter under a machete as Big Buck elicited the "Awwww!" he was noted for. He stood in the open chute gate reared up ten feet tall. His yellow coat was sleek, his black mane and tail long and flowing. He held his forefeet close to his chest like a boxer waiting to strike; his neck was bowed like a plow horse under a load. All you could see from the grandstand across the arena was his belly circumscribed by the two cinches and John's two feet set over his shoulders, the bronc rider hidden behind the rearing horse.

In an instant Big Buck pile-drived the ground with his forefeet, completing the 180 degree rotation from up to down, taking his head between his front feet and kicking his hocks to the sky. John came into view as Big Buck came down from his high dive. He hadn't moved in the saddle. He was still lifting on his rein with his spurs locked into the horse's neck, marking the bronc out.

Big Buck jumped in the air and kicked, getting great elevation for a horse of his size. John cantleboarded, spurring back, using his stirrups and the binds of his saddle to wedge himself forward under his swells. Then, in perfect time he snapped his feet back into the front end, grabbing a hold of the buckskin, absorbing his power. True to form, Big Buck started with three or four huge "big bucks" and then, bucking at a pace that couldn't be maintained, slowly lost energy so that after eight or ten more jumps—about the time the whistle blew—he was only outstanding.

John picked up his timing easily—the horse was honest and deliberate and all power. He scratched down the bronc's broad buckskin sides. Then he jumped off his binds and charged the front end ahead of the horse's kick. He got his feet higher in the bronc's neck each jump, setting his heels right in Buck's flowing mane. With his legs extended perfectly straight and the bronc's brawny neck bowed down, it looked like John would spur over his neck on every jump—but he never did.

John handed the pickup man his rein and rolled off the back of the pickup horse as the man dallied the bronc up to his saddle horn and released the flank strap. As he walked back across the arena, the announcer gave John's score and expressed surprise that a man with a pink car could be winning the saddle bronc riding.

"Oh, shut up," John said under his breath and gave the guy a look in his perch above the bucking chutes.

A little while later, after the calf roping and the barrel race, up in the announcer's booth, the announcer turned off his microphone and laid it down on the table he was using for a podium. He turned around to dig through his briefcase, looking for the crib notes he'd prepared for the bull riding. When he turned back around his microphone was gone. His moment of panic at losing the mike turned into an eternity of fear as he saw John McBeth standing in the doorway of the booth holding his mike.

John held the mike up to his mouth like he was about to put it to use.

"Don't!" the announcer said in his haste. "*Please*, don't," he amended. He looked really scared. John looked really serious. "I . . . I know I owe you an apology . . . . I shouldn't have done it," the guy stammered. John stared—and moved the mike a little closer to his lips. "I apologize. I apologize," the guy babbled.

John put the mike right up to his mouth and spoke clearly into it. "I was just wondering: What color was *your* free Cadillac?" The announcer blushed pink the instant before he realized the mike was off—and John was smiling.

GRUNDY ON A MONDY

*"Bob Barnes was quite a guy. We were right proud
that we could call him friend. . . . He had a little
different philosophy about some things, but he made
it work."*
John McBeth

The first time I ever saw Bob Barnes, Francie and Bart
and I went to Grundy Center, Iowa. It was "Grundy on a
Mondy" because it was held on a Monday every year and it
was in Grundy County. It was one day, one perf, on
Monday. Bob Barnes, the stock contractor, was on a run
where he'd roll from town to town putting on a rodeo every
day. The day after Grundy he was headed for Preston,
Minnesota.

Bob had quite an operation going. A lot of those little
Midwestern towns didn't have a rodeo arena and no place
to host a rodeo. So Bob had four metal bucking chutes on
the back of a semi along with enough porta-panels to set up
an arena fence and all the stock pens he needed. He'd pull
in to a town and hoist the chutes off the truck in a field, a
park, the fairgrounds or a parking lot—anywhere they had
dirt or could haul it in—and in a couple of hours his crew
could set up or take down the whole arena. His approach
opened up a new rodeo market where it didn't exist before,
in places where there were no rodeo arenas, no bucking
chutes. He took the show on the road like a traveling
circus, to places that had never had or thought of having a
rodeo. You could say he was selling the sport, overcoming
objections before they arose, providing all the infrastructure
and organization so that all a rodeo committee had to do
was sign on for a show and he'd handle the rest, turnkey

the production. It was revolutionary.

At Grundy that first time I met Bob, I drew Cherokee Charlie. He was one of Bob's favorites and one of the best ones he ever owned. Now that's saying a lot considering some of the great broncs Bob has had over the years. He would jump and hang in that air and you could just pick out a place and set your feet wherever you wanted to. You couldn't hardly help but win the bronc riding on him, and that's what I did.

After the rodeo that day, Francie and Bart and I were sitting around with a bunch of other people in front of the travel trailer Bob and his wife Donita lived in while they were on the road. They were drawing the stock for the next day's rodeo in Preston, Minnesota, while their crew tore down the portable arena and got it and the stock loaded on the trucks and ready to go. Back in those days the rodeo secretary did about everything as far as organizing the rodeo. Donita was Bob's secretary and she was responsible for taking the entries, drawing positions and drawing the stock with the help of the judges.

It took them awhile to draw some of the other events, so we were sitting around watching and kind of getting acquainted with them. When they got to the bronc riding Donita would call out a name off the contestant's list and one of the judges would pull a horse's number out of the hat. He'd announce the number and she'd write it down on her sheet. My name was about halfway down that list of bronc riders and when she called out my name Bob broke in and said, "Twenty two, twenty two, twenty two!" because that was the number of Cherokee Charlie—the horse I'd just had that day. It was like he was rooting for me to draw a good one. Well, the judge pulled out a number and said, "forty six!"

"Forty six!" Bob said, and looked over at me. "That's old Dark Journey, and he's a little different type of a journey. I'll guarantee you that if you spur him like you did this one here today, I'm throwing in with you, kid!" and he laughed.

Well, Bart wore that buckle I won at Preston, Minnesota, until he was about fifteen years old. And after I took that Dark Journey there wasn't a thing I could do wrong in Bob's eyes. When we'd go to a Bob Barnes rodeo there was nothing he wouldn't do for us. If we had asked him to load a horse in backwards he'd have done it. We just couldn't ask him to do it in front of anybody else because he'd be afraid of showing favoritism, and he was as ethical as he was innovative.

JESSE JAMES

I asked John if he thought Jesse James was the greatest saddle bronc of all time. "That's debatable," he said. "You've got to account for personal experience. And then there were a lot of great broncs from an earlier era that you and I never saw. But, I feel reasonably satisfied that he fits right at the top of the heap."

You can call me Jesse James. You can call me The Bucking Horse of the Year. You can call me athletic, strong and fast. But if you're a bronc rider you call me Double-Rank.

I'll never forget the seventh time I drew John McBeth. I know, I know, some people think horses can't tell one bronc rider from another. They think we can't remember who we've battled from month to month and year to year. Some people think horses came fifth in line when God said, "Come forth and get your brains." So, of course, most people think horses can't count. But I know we were deadlocked three to three when John and I got together that last time. I remember his smell and the tone of his voice, which were unique from all other men. Even his saddle— the leather, the sheepskin pad, the sweat—emitted an aura like no other. People think we don't notice. But I didn't get where I am by being simple-minded.

I can recount our history up to that deciding seventh confrontation. The first two times I won, hands down. I did it with brute power both times. I did my big bail-out of the box like I always do. It's such a rush! I just have to. If you've never seen it before I'll describe it for you:

When the bronc rider slips down on my back, I tense every muscle in my body. I squat down just a little, especially in the rear, not so you'd notice it, just enough to allow my legs some extension when I blow up. At the first rattle of the chute gate I try to jump over the sucker before the cowboys can pull it open. I never make it, I hang in the air too long and they pull the gate too fast. But that's what I'm concentrating on, blowing right out over the gate. I jump so high I'd probably clear it if they did leave it shut.

I love wiping bronc riders off on the bottom of the announcer's booth above the chutes. They never thought of that one, evidently, when they built some of these pens. They never imagined a bronc could jump that high; and until I came along they never saw one do it.

John always handled the launch. All seven times. I never got him there. I never even got him loose. He always set his spurs in my neck and squeezed, hard. It pissed me off. Always does. So I would wait for him to move—release his lock on my shoulders—then I'd give him a couple of pretty big jumps so he would think I was actually trying to throw him off at that point. He'd get in time when I did that; he'd start popping his feet off the back of the saddle and jamming his spurs back in my neck. That really got my blood up, so I'd do a little stutter step and double the power I put into that next jump, kicking almost vertically and dropping my front end at the same time—really snatching the saddle away from him. I'd pull my head down then, too, jerking the rein away from him. The first two times I did that I heard that satisfying ripping sound as he tore loose from his gear, his rosin squealing between chaps and swells. Then his saddle got real light and his stirrups flopped, empty, around my shoulders. I

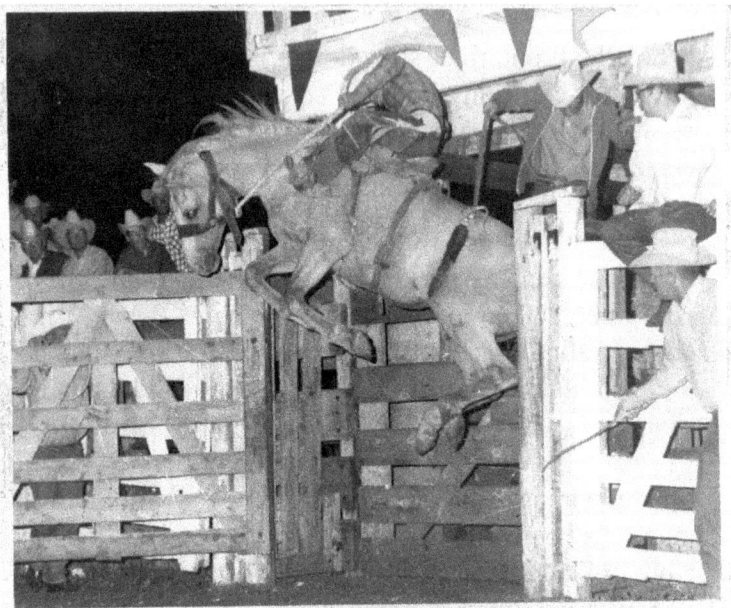

Jesse James sticking John McBeth's head into the bottom of the announcer's booth above the chutes in Burden, Kansas, 1969. Chuck Korte Photo.

tossed my head up and did my frisky buck after I threw him off, like I used to do as a colt showing off in the pasture.

It wasn't until our third match that he stayed aboard. I'd like to think I got over- confident and let it happen, but I've gained a lot of respect for his ability since then, so I'm not so sure. That third time, after my big bail-out and two jump set-up, I jerked the swells down hard and took my head when I kicked, really letting my front end drop. I started into my frisky buck, then, but to my surprise instead of a light saddle I felt iron in my neck. I realized he was still there! That made me mad and I snatched at the swells harder. When he kept spurring me instead of falling off, my anger doubled my effort. Still, he was ripping his spurs down my sides and jabbing me in the neck with every jump I took. I could hear the people starting to roar, like they usually do for me after I buck somebody off. But they were yelling for him. I didn't like that. I reached down into my big thoroughbred's heart and gave all I had—again and again, jump after jump. I was hitting the ground with a jerk and launching myself as high as I could and snatching at that saddle. I was throwing my head up when I jumped and jerking it down when I kicked. I never considered setting a trap by jumping sideways or turning back. I wanted to flat buck him off—overpower him. Then the whistle blew—too soon for me. I was just getting started. The people were roaring like they usually do, but it wasn't for me. I wasn't happy when I got back to the pen that day. It bothered me for a while. Eventually, I got over it. Every time I tossed another cowboy I felt a little bit better and the memory of that day faded.

Then he did it again! It was at one of the winter rodeos they hold inside a big building; one of the ones that lasts for days and days. When he climbed up on my chute I recognized the smell of him and his saddle, the tone of his voice, and my heart beat faster. I remembered the drumming he gave me the last time, and the old anger rose up inside me and tasted bitter. I tried to overpower him like I had done before. I blew in the air, big-time—if you're scared of heights, go find another bronc to try. From the top of my jump I jerked down on his saddle, dropping my front end, trying to snatch the swells away from him. Then late, very late in the buck, I kicked, hitting him with all my power. I was giving him a double jerk every jump, snatching down on the front of the saddle then kicking up the rear. But in spite of my performance the result was the same as the last time. He stuck a ride on me—good. He'd grab me with his feet above my shoulders before I could try to drop out from under him, and with a hold like that I couldn't get the swells away from him. Then, when I'd kick, he still had a hold of me with his feet. I could feel my kick shift his weight forward was all, down into his stirrups where he was anchored. When I heard the whistle the pickup horses came in and he jumped off on one of them. Nothing I could do. Tame horses, imagine! And helping the cowboy! I don't think much of that. John was something special that time because the people stood and yelled for a long time afterward. I was out of the arena and back in my pen and they were still yelling, like they usually do for me.

So now the score was two to two. We were dead even. He had my attention for sure. Nobody ever stuck it on me like he did on that ride in the big building. And then he did it a third time, later that same year. I'm not even going to think about that. I'm trying to forget it. It almost had me doubting myself. Almost.

Well, I didn't get where I am by being weak-hearted, so with the score standing at three to two, in *his* favor, I resolved to buck harder if I ever drew him again. That's all I could do, buck harder. And I wanted him. He was on my mind a lot. He was the twitch in my dreams. I watched everywhere I went, looking over the top rail of the bronc pen, searching the parking lot for him, scanning the faces and the saddles behind the chutes at rodeo after rodeo. In the meantime I worked on my moves. I proved myself over and over again against all the cowboys I drew. Nobody was making it to the middle of the arena on me, let alone to the whistle.

It was in that big building a year later—the building where he rode me the second time—in front of those same people, when I heard the tone in his voice again, smelled his saddle and watched him climb the back of my chute. I had never felt stronger physically. My confidence was through even that high roof. It was built up dusting bronc rider after bronc rider all year. I wasn't mad at all this time. I was cool. I was happy to have my shot at the best. That's what I had learned, that it was an honor just to get your shot. I had waited, biding my time for this opportunity, and now that it had arrived I was excited.

Now was my chance and I was ready.

I had laid my plan. So when the chute gate cracked I made to jump over it like usual. What a feeling of elation I had soaring through the air. When I hit the ground and felt him loosen his hold on my neck to spur back, I launched myself, took my head, kicked as high and hard as I could and jerked the swells away from him—as slick as that. Still, he hung with me for two or three jumps trying to scratch his way back down into the saddle, working to get back in time. I used the momentum of each jump to carry me into the next one so that I got stronger and stronger as we approached the middle of the arena. And it worked! He had no chance to recover. I heard the ripping sound of his chaps leaving the saddle and he flew straight over my head. The score was even. Three to three! Frisky buck all around the arena and down the alley to my pen! I knew the people were cheering for *me* that time.

It was a long time before our paths crossed again. I felt good after the last match. I remembered the cheers as I made my victory lap around the arena, but I kind of forgot about John and the deadlock we'd reached—and not because horses don't have a memory. I just felt satisfied to let it settle into the past. I knew I had the upper hand against any bronc rider. And then John, the deadlock, the challenge he presented, all came back to me when he climbed up on my chute in that little town near home with the grass arena.

I was excited to see him. I love a challenge. Six times through the years we'd gone head to head and we'd come out even, three each. We both knew the seventh time would decide the issue. I wanted this one bad. In the chute he talked to me more than usual, in a low soothing tone, maybe out of respect. I wouldn't be soothed. As he slipped my silver halter over my nose I snorted a challenge back at him and tossed my head a little bit, giving him the fish-eye. His eyes looked back into mine and we connected for an instant that will last my lifetime. We each saw the entity behind the eyes, the intelligence there, and sensed the purpose in our adversary. We slipped outside ourselves amid the timelessness of our competition to identify with each other. It felt like a salute.

It was a hot day, the sun bright in a clear blue sky that hung above the grassy turf of the arena. The smell of the grass, the leather saddles and halters, the other horses, filled my senses. I was fit, not a complaint from my body. My mind was clear, my purpose focused. If time had stopped right then I wouldn't have cared. For me it was always about the challenge. As soon as I'd buck off one cowboy, I'd want another, right then. I'd start thinking about the next one immediately. It was on my mind in the truck heading home, in the pasture between rodeos, while eating and drinking and waking and sleeping. It was in my blood.

It got real quiet as John climbed over the back of my chute. Everyone's attention was focused on us, as if they knew the importance of this meeting—what was between us. I broke a sweat as John slipped into his saddle. He did too. The announcer talked about me and talked about John while he got his stirrups and I got into position.

Of course I blew out of the chute. I knew it didn't bother John all that much, but I couldn't resist. I decided to give him a couple of nice jumps and kicks to make him comfortable and then I planned to erupt and throw him away. But on the second jump he jabbed me in the right ribs with a spur and then snapped his foot back into my neck. When that iron clamped down I instinctively launched into my high dive: I jumped up, snatched at his swells, and kicked. The turf was firm under my feet as I landed and I was able to pile-drive into the ground, jarring his saddle and my teeth. Then he hit me in the ribs again! I couldn't believe it; he was goosing me in the belly. Me!

I lost it. I put my head down between my front feet and kicked—angry. I built momentum as I bucked, jumping in the air and jerking my front end down off the impetus of my kick, getting stronger and stronger. I jumped here or there as I pleased. And I pleased. I snapped a kick airborne and hit the ground with a thud, delivering a sharp double-jerk. Unbelievably, he jabbed me in the neck before I kicked, and coasted through the landing! He was beating me to the punch and locking on so tight I couldn't loosen him up when I hit the ground. And I was flat out bucking. He spurred in time with me, throwing his momentum where I was going, giving no resistance for me to push against. He felt weightless. No—more than that!—he was actually nudging me along!

It never occurred to me to turn back or give a nasty swoop to unload a rider. I'd never had to. I had always been able to buck them off with brute power alone. I admit that it wasn't that unusual for a good bronc rider to make three or four, or maybe even five jumps on my back, but they rarely went farther than that. They seemed to weaken about halfway through the ride, as if they expected me to do the same. But I'd get stronger. If a cowboy was giving his all to stick with me early in the ride, he was in trouble, because I'd just keep ramping up the pressure, bucking harder and harder. Eventually we'd reach the rankest jump he could handle and then I'd exceed it on the next one. That's the thing about John that I remember the best. He was like me. He got stronger the longer the ride lasted. He spurred a little bit higher and harder every jump.

Time always slows down for me when I think about our last encounter, as it did on that day bucking out across the grass. I'd bucked like usual, getting stronger and stronger. John had matched my every move spurring better and better. Finally, I caught him in a mistake: his left foot hung in the front end for a split second. He had spurred so high he hung a spur over his rein and threw off his timing. I put so much effort into the next jump a grunt escaped from between my lips. I had him loose! He was off balance, and his feet stuck in the cinch one lick. The whistle blew as I lunged into the air again and John ripped loose from his gear. The pickup horse had already moved in under him when the pickup man saw John's feet stalled in the cinch; the guy literally plucked him out of the air.

I think I won. I bucked him off. But I got him too late. So I have to concede that he made the whistle, barely. Winning four out of seven makes McBeth the best I've ever known. Is he the greatest of all time? Well, that's debatable. You've got to account for personal experience. And then there were a lot of great bronc riders from an earlier era that I never saw. But, I feel reasonably satisfied that he fits right at the top of the heap.

INTERNATIONAL COWBOY

John McBeth told me this story. When he had finished and I asked a couple of questions about the particulars, he said, "Maybe you better talk to Tirelli. He can give you more details. His name is Roland—but don't call him that! He goes by Butch, but you just call him Tirelli."

John first met Butch Tirelli at a rodeo in North Carolina. "I'm behind the chutes getting ready to ride," John said, "When a guy walks up wearing a three piece suit and a nice pair of shoes and starts asking about the broncs. He wanted to know about C16 Wild One, I think it was. I was a little bit surprised, so I asked him why he wanted to know. He said, 'I've got him tomorrow night in the bronc riding.' It was obvious right off this guy wasn't your average bronc rider."

The two ran into each other at a rodeo here or there over the next several years and hit it off all right. Then one day John got a call from Tirelli.

"Hey John! How'd you like a South American vacation—paid!"

John laughed. He'd come to know Butch pretty well, but hadn't had any financial dealings with him before. "What kind of a vacation?" he asked.

"I'm producing a Wild West Show in Caracas, Venezuela, scheduled for December. You wanna come down and ride a few broncs?"

John laughed again—*does he want to ride a few broncs?* . . . "When in December?" he asked. "You're not doing it during the finals, I hope."

"Nope, right before Christmas."

"That'll probably work out," John said, eager to earn some extra income before the holidays.

Butch knew that having a bronc rider of John's repute would lend a lot of credibility to his project and excite the crowd in Caracas.

Butch had a history of promoting Wild West Shows. He was taught the business by people that had been part of Buffalo Bill's prototypical Wild West Show that ran from 1883 to 1913. Before long he was promoting Wild West Shows in the Caribbean on his own. Even though initially he made every mistake possible, his people always got paid and nobody got stranded in a foreign country. He never doubted that, in spite of the whippings he occasionally took, he was becoming a showman.

Wild West Shows were and are theatrical performances. Historical scenes from the settling of the west are portrayed: The famous Indian battles such as Custer's Last Stand, Indians attacking a wagon train, or bandits overtaking and looting a stagecoach are re-enacted. Trick riders and ropers are employed. Sharpshooters mystify the crowd with trick shots. Wild animals such as buffalo, elk and bear thrill the crowd, and rodeo events, bronc riding and calf roping showcase the talents of true-to-life cowboys. The promoters of these shows have tried anything and everything to sell tickets and put people in the seats.

About the first of December John received another call from Butch. "Hi John, I wanted to let you know the Venezuela show has been postponed. The promoters down there couldn't get the coliseum in Caracas reserved for the right dates."

"That's too bad, Butch. I was looking forward to it. Do you think they'll get it together eventually?"

"Oh, it's going to happen," Butch assured. "I'm just not sure when."

Several weeks later Butch called again. "John, the

show's back on," he said. "I've got eleven days to get everything together."

"Short notice," was John's reply.

"Yeah, but I told 'em, 'No problem,' when they asked if it could be done."

Butch always said, "No problem," when presented with a problem.

A few days later John called Butch back and said, "Butch, I'm really drawn up well in Houston, but I'm going to miss the flight to Venezuela because it conflicts with my schedule at the rodeo. I'll follow you down there the next day and be in Caracas in plenty of time for the show." And as it turned out he wasn't the only one to miss the flight.

It is a tradition dating back to the beginning of Wild West Shows that the Indians would always get lost for a time. They always arrived late for the show, even on Buffalo Bill's shows. The story goes that back in the old days they got part of their pay in advance to get them to the show and they would use those funds to have a good time. When the money and the whiskey ran out they would show up ready for work. Butch had hired seven Indians for his show. They were reliable non-drinkers. Yet, when he arrived in Venezuela there were no Indians. They had gotten lost! He couldn't believe it. Butch put a call through to Miami and found out that they had been in the gift shop at the airport and missed the plane. Coincidentally, they traveled to Venezuela the following day on the same flight as John.

Butch picked them all up at the airport in Maracay when their plane landed. The scene in the parking lot at the airport could easily have been adapted to the Wild West Show or a clown act at the circus as Butch supervised the loading of all their luggage and saddles and costumes on the roof of the car, a little Fiat. He loaded the seven Indians inside and then he and John pushed into both sides of the front seat of the little "clown car" for the one-hour drive over the mountains to Caracas.

John and Butch were roommates for the duration of the show. Butch hadn't cut any corners either. All the show personnel were "bunked" at the Hilton in Caracas. The close association between the two soon led to an expansion of John's duties.

"Do you know anything about black powder, John?" Butch asked as they were moving into the hotel.

"Yeah, I do."

"Can you make a nice little bang in the back of the covered wagon with lots of smoke and noise?"

"Yeah."

"Well, you're now officially our demolitions expert!" Butch said. No doubt, the cool and calm demeanor John always displayed in stressful situations contributed to that decision.

The first night the show went off without a hitch. Impressive when you consider that there was no practice run. Everybody—the bronc and bull riders, the Indians, and the cowboys driving the stagecoach and covered wagon—knew their job. The show was staffed by the best performers in the business.

The show began with a Grand Entry just like an American rodeo. The Venezuelan flag flew at the head of a long line of horses and riders following a serpentine pattern around the arena in single-file. The flag was presented in the center of the arena as the Venezuelan National Anthem was played.

With the Wild West Show being essentially a vaudevillian type of show, the performance consisted of several "acts." It was arranged to tell a story—the story of the settling of the American west.

First to come into the arena—as the west—were the Spaniards. The Pasodoble, the "double-step" music of the bullfight, rang throughout the building. Into the arena marched the bullfighter with his cape—stern, majestic, dressed in his suit of lights. The announcer introduced the "Great Luciano!" who was, in reality, Tommy Lucia, the well-known rodeo clown. The bull was released and Tommy executed a couple of Veronicas with his cape in the center of the arena. The "bull" was Tommy's trained bulldog with a set of plastic bull horns strapped on his head. He charged the cape a couple of times but failed to get a piece of the great Luciano. Eventually, the bull (dog) got a hold of the cape and snatched it away from the matador. Then he ran out of the arena trailing the cape behind him with the Great Luciano in hot pursuit. Bullfighting is a big deal in Venezuela, and the crowd ate it up.

Next came the pioneers and the inevitable Indian attack. As the natives circled around the covered wagon on their ponies, threatening to slaughter the settlers, a torch was tossed into the back of the wagon and a huge cloud of smoke erupted, simulating the wagon catching fire. Gunpowder smoke from McBeth's explosive climax to the Indian attack, drifting through the crowd and up into the rafters, left the smell of warfare in every nostril.

The stage lines came next with bandits attacking the stagecoach. They were followed by cowboys and ranch life, and the skills they developed morphed into rodeo! The bucking horses performed up to expectations, their high-flying action working the crowd into a frenzy. Butch led off the saddle bronc riding and covered an erratic horse that pitched left and right, constantly changing leads. The bronc was out of control and, when the whistle blew, shied away from the pickup horse at just the wrong time. That took Butch by surprise and upset his move for the pickup man. He banged his ribcage off the cantle of the pickup man's saddle as he rolled off his bronc. He hobbled out of the arena with the wind knocked out of him, clutching his side, unsure if he'd be able to continue the next day.

John McBeth entering the arena during the introductions at Caracas, Venezuela, 1978. Photo courtesy of Butch Tirelli.

John rode last that night, concluding the bronc riding with a thrilling ride aboard a horse that tried everything from blowing out of the chute to turning back in the arena. The crowd went wild at the way he handled the whirlwind with smooth controlled motions and a calm look on his face. They gave him an ovation.

The calf ropers and bulldoggers also performed flawlessly, impressing their South American contemporaries with their expertise. As in American rodeo, the bull riding was saved for last, and as in American rodeo it sent the crowd out through the turnstiles grinning and shaking their heads at the skill and daring of the rodeo cowboy.

Back at the hotel Butch said, "I think I cracked my ribs, John."

"Uh huh," the reply.

"Did you ever bust your ribs?" Butch asked.

"Uh huh."

"What can you do for them? Can you wrap them up or

something so they aren't so sore?"

"Nope, all you can do is grin and bear it," John said.

"I don't think I can ride this way," Butch told him.

"When you get on tomorrow the adrenalin will take over," John assured him. "You'll never feel a thing . . . until you get off." And it was so true. Butch never felt a thing.

The next morning a big-wig in the Venezuelan government wanted to talk to Butch. He had a bone of some kind to pick with the American producer about the show. A meeting was set up in his office about mid-morning, so Butch asked John to go along.

The official's gruff secretary admitted them into his office and they were seated in a couple of straight-backed chairs with no offer of coffee or tea. The bureaucrat gave them a stern look over the top of his glasses and assailed them with, "Why did your show run late last night?"

At first, John and Butch thought it was a joke and nearly laughed. Then they realized he wasn't kidding. "Uh. . . ." they apologized. "We didn't know we did."

"Oh, yes!" the guy affirmed. "This costs the government money, keeping the coliseum open late."

They smoothed things over, assuring the official that it was an oversight and would not happen again. However, the next morning, after the second night's performance, they found themselves back in the official's office once more, and he was almost apoplectic.

"Why did you cheat the Venezuelan people last night?" he demanded. "They paid for a two-hour show and your show ended ten minutes early!"

They felt like laughing once more, although this time they knew he was serious and kept a straight face.

"You are scheduled in the coliseum for two hours for your show and we give you three minutes leeway. That is all! Three minutes before the hour to three minutes after the hour." He glared at them.

They tried to gloss it over once again, only this time it required some strenuous apologies and profuse flattery to get them out of his office in one piece.

As they made their way back to the hotel, Butch said, "John, you just got a promotion and a raise."

John gave him a look, waiting for the other shoe to drop.

"You're now officially the Arena Director as well as Bronc Rider and Demolitions Expert," Butch announced with a grin, willingly sharing some of the many hats he wore as the overall head of the production with his friend.

John solved the time issue by personally introducing each act and contestant in the arena during the show. If the show was ahead of schedule the introductions were drawn out; if the show was behind, they were terse. But the show ended precisely on the hour.

Overall, the show was a rousing success: No one got hurt, everyone got paid and no one was left behind in South America. When the show was over, Butch had a lot of details to take care of. He had to get all the animals shipped back to the U.S. He also wanted to be sure his people caught their flight home. Especially the Indians! He met everybody in the hotel lobby at 6:00 A.M. the next morning to thank them for doing such a great job, wish them all a safe trip home, and watch them get on the bus to the airport. Then he went back up to his room and went back to bed.

Butch was approached by a group of Brazilian businessmen about buying the bucking chutes he'd built for the show. They wanted to start promoting bull riding "American Style" in their country. It is interesting that today many of the top Professional Bull Riders association cowboys are from Brazil. The impact one Wild West Show had on the growth of bull riding in South America is incalculable.

John had to hustle back to Houston where he was scheduled to ride in the second go-round. Arriving in

The cast and crew of the Butch Tirelli Wild West Show production in Caracas, Venezuela, February, 1978. Photo courtesy of Butch Tirelli.

Miami, he caught the plane to Houston all right, but was crunched for time and had no ride from the Houston airport to the Astrodome. If he took the time to rent a car he was afraid it might make him late. Luckily, he met a couple on the plane who lived in Houston and recognized him as the former world champ. They got to talking and the nice folks offered to drive him over to the rodeo in their car after the plane touched down.

"I arrived back in Houston by a round-about way that year," John said.

HIGH ROLL

"I went back to the finals in 1978 just to prove an old fat man could do it."

John McBeth

After he won the saddle bronc riding world championship in 1974, John McBeth went into semi-retirement. He still entered some rodeos, and his skills certainly showed no sign of deterioration, but he had decided to travel less and do some other things. Four years later in 1978 he went to a few of the big winter rodeos. He entered Denver. Then he won a round at Fort Worth. He flew back from a Wild West Show he was helping to put on in Caracas, Venezuela, to get on his second horse at the Houston Livestock Show and Rodeo in the Astrodome. He won a round at Houston and placed in another. When Houston was over he was second in the world. But he had decided to not be going to all those rodeos. He intended to stay closer to home and put in more family time, so he just entered a few local rodeos through the spring and summer. He did travel to Ardmore, Oklahoma, and North Platte, Nebraska, but that was as far as he went.

He was judging the High School National Finals in Huron, South Dakota, in early August and some people he knew from South Dakota came through there direct from the Professional Rodeo Cowboys Association Board of Directors meetings held at the Frontier Days Rodeo in Cheyenne, Wyoming. They said, "You heard what they did to the finals, didn't you?"

John answered, "Well, no, what'd they do?"

"They put all the money in the average. It's gonna pay $15,000 just to win the average."

John McBeth still riding like anything but an ". . . old fat man . . ." in 1978. Here aboard Jay Bird. Bern Gregory Rodeo Photographs, National Cowboy & Western Heritage Museum, Oklahoma City, Oklahoma.

John started thinking about that. Fifteen thousand dollars was a lot of money in those days; it was a yearly income for a lot of bronc riders, and a lot of working people, and you could win it at one rodeo. Also, the way the World Championship was awarded had been changed in 1976. The new rules declared the top money winner in the season standings as the PRCA champion—a new championship category, and the World Champion became the top money winner solely at the National Finals Rodeo. So, if you could qualify for the NFR in any position, even in the last—fifteenth—hole, you stood an equal chance at winning a $15,000 payday and the World Championship. It was enough to get the old juices flowing again.

The High School Finals ended the first weekend in August, so John started entering after that just to see if he could get back to the NFR and go for that big payoff. Of course, it was a couple of weeks after that before he actually got on one, due to the lag time between entering and the actual rodeo dates. But about the third or fourth week in August he was riding again. Right off the bat it seemed like he could do no wrong: He was drawing good and winning everywhere he went. After a blazing hot fall season, he went into the finals in December ranked 13th in the world after entering only 35 rodeos that year, an almost unheard of statistic.

In the second go-round at the NFR he drew High Roll, a notorious eliminator. It seems that the eliminators are the ones you draw over and over again—never the easy ones. John's description of the bronc all these years later says it all: "He was a notorious nasty. Nobody, I mean *nobody*, wanted on High Roll. He was cinchy, high-headed, light-headed. He could jump and whirl. I'd been on him a dozen times at least and literally hated every one of them. Most of the time it's a question of, 'Should I just turn him out? I'm not gonna win anything on him.' But in all those times I figured out what made him act that way. So this particular time at the finals I decided to try something . . . and it turned out I was right, although I didn't know it at the time.

"You see, nobody wanted to give him any rein. He'd get his head up in the air and lunge and whirl and he just wasn't any good doing that. He was horrible. So I decided I'm not even gonna touch that head. So I measured my rein about a fist from the cantle.

"Now High Roll has got a set of withers on him like a train rail. I mean that saddle's not gonna tip over sideways, there's not any way in the world it can do that. So I hobbled my front and back cinches and just pretty much conveniently forgot to pull them—either one of them.

"I also knew that the pickup men at the national finals have a designated spot and they cannot move—by law—until the whistle blows. Well, what made High Roll such a bad-ass at other rodeos was that they'd cross the pickup men in front of him and he'd get lost, he lost his lead, he lost everything. He just went a little bonkers when they did that. And the stock contractors thought that was funny. They'd get to throw somebody off or see somebody embarrass themselves, or both.

"Well, I'm gamblin', big-time. When I get to the pickup men the whistle blows. Did I make the pickup men? Nope! Did I place deep in the round? Yep! Could I feel my saddle running a foot and a half every jump? Yes! Was it scary? Terrifying! But it worked. It wouldn't work any place else except at the finals.

"Every bronc rider at the finals was just madder than an old wet hen at me. And I didn't win a penny! The go-rounds just paid points—all the money was in the average payout. They said, 'We've been trying to get rid of that sucker for ten years and here you come along and stick a ride on him! We'll never get rid of him now.'"

So, after going into the finals ranked 13th in the PRCA standings and putting that great ride on High Roll, John placed in three rounds and finished the year 9th in the world.

Not bad for ". . . an old fat man. . . ."

Epilogue

Far from getting rid of High Roll, the bronc went on to greater things in his career, winning the best saddle bronc of the NFR in 1980.

ALL AROUND COWBOY

John McBeth hosted rodeo schools at the Sutton Ranch in Onida, South Dakota, for over 40 years. He was proud to call James Sutton a friend. Through the years he built the same kind of a relationship with James Sutton Jr.

The James Sutton, Sr., Memorial Bronze is a half life-sized statue depicting John McBeth riding Sutton's Half-Velvet. The statue was commissioned by James Sutton, Jr. to honor his father. A fourteen inch sculpture of the larger piece is awarded to the outstanding saddle bronc rider at the Black Hills Stock Show Rodeo in Rapid City, South Dakota.

Sometimes a person's talents are as varied as the contributions they make to their family, to their profession, to their neighbors and community—to this life in general. Take the example of Jim Sutton Jr., for instance. He runs a ranch in Onida, South Dakota. He and his wife, Julie, raised a rodeo family and continued the tradition of contracting rodeos for five generations, providing bucking, roping and bulldogging stock from Deadwood to Las Vegas. He was instrumental in founding the Black Hills Stock Show Rodeo in Rapid City in 1978. The rodeo has been nominated for the Professional Rodeo Cowboys Association "Indoor Rodeo of the Year Award" ten times and won it twice.

Naturally, creating a huge event like a stock show, held in an urban area in downtown Rapid City, requires an understanding of the political ins and outs to bring so many diverse groups (city council, arena board, rodeo committee) to an agreement, as well as a deft hand at negotiation. And sometimes the most important skill of all is the ability to think outside the box and create a solution in an unorthodox way, where one did not seem to exist.

For example, in addition to the rodeo, the town of Rapid City has been host to a semi-professional basketball team of some repute. The team (the Thrillers) won three Continental Basketball Association championships in the 1980's and drew large crowds to the local arena. So one year when the planned dates for the Black Hills Stock Show Rodeo happened to conflict with the home game schedule for the Thrillers there was a problem. The Thrillers were a local icon, attended religiously by throngs of supportive fans, but the rodeo was the biggest single annual event in Rapid City. Something, or someone, had to give.

The principal parties gathered at the arena to negotiate a compromise in the schedule and present their respective cases. The basketball representatives pointed out that they were trying to get back to the league playoffs for another championship run. Of course their odds of winning were greater at home before a supportive home crowd than on the road facing a hostile arena. Not to mention the fact that the home gate receipts were critical to their financial bottom line. They refused to budge.

The rodeo committee, represented by Jim Sutton, among others, was in every bit as tough of a situation. Their dates fit into the PRCA schedule, and to move those dates would cause a conflict with other rodeos, affecting the number of contestants that would be expected to enter. Also, the rodeo and stock show was held at the same time every year and changing those dates would cause a ripple effect of havoc among a multitude of participants in venues from livestock production to trade shows, to dozens of vendors relying on the show for a livelihood.

After days of negotiations where basketball team representatives, the rodeo committee, the arena management team and even local politicians and chamber of commerce representatives hashed the situation over in an office in the arena building and were unable to find any common ground toward a solution, one man took the matter into his own hands.

"Well, this is getting us nowhere," Jim Sutton said. "We've been over it and over it and there is no solution that is agreeable to both parties."

"What would you suggest," countered one of the basketball people.

"I think we should shoot free throws for the right to set our own dates," Sutton responded.

The basketball representative looked shocked, as if he hadn't heard correctly. His brain slowly parsed Jim's statement and his eyes got wider. His gaze pierced that of the cowboy, rancher, and rodeo producer across from him. He couldn't believe his ears. He checked his watch.

"I've got a fella down in the arena practicing with the team right now who can shoot some free throws," he said. "Who's going to shoot for you?"

Sutton looked up and down the table. He made eye contact with every member of the rodeo committee before answering. "Well," he said, "I suppose I will."

The team rep couldn't believe what he was hearing. He appraised the raw-boned cowboy across from him for a moment. "You want to shoot free throws against my guy for the right to the disputed dates?"

"Yep," said Sutton. "The most consecutive free throws without a miss wins."

"Okay, I'm game," the rep said. "If it's acceptable to the rest of your committee."

Not seeing any other way out of the impasse and trusting to Jim's judgment, no objections were voiced by the rodeo people. Even the neutral parties, the arena manager and the politicians, said nothing—although it seemed a flip of a coin would be more fair.

So the various committees adjourned from the board room and reconvened downstairs on the arena floor itself, where a Thrillers team practice was in full swing. The team representative took the coach aside for a minute to explain the situation. As they mumbled back and forth, out of earshot of the rest of the group, the coach's eyes widened like he was seeing a pot of gold. He looked over the rep's shoulder trying to lay his eyes on the crazy cowboy who had cut such a deal. When he saw the middle-aged, cowboy-hatted Sutton, he called over one of his players—a svelte, athletic six foot six semi-pro guard.

"How do you want to do this?" the rep asked Sutton.

"You go first," Jim said. "The most consecutive free throws wins."

The coach explained the situation to his player as he handed him the ball. The player couldn't help but look Sutton up and down, either, with a look of amazement on his face. He was a dead-eye free throw shooter with nerves of steel, and he dribbled up to the line and drained his first shot touching nothing but net. Shot after shot he put through the hoop as he got into a shooter's rhythm. When he finally missed he had put down thirteen consecutive shots and the coach and the basketball team rep both looked pleased.

"Good job," said the coach to his player as he retrieved the ball and tossed it over to Sutton. "Yer up," he said.

Some of the by-standers were starting to look squeamish now. The arena manager looked down at the floor as Jim approached the line. The guys from city hall were all stifling grins. Everybody expected the first shot to clank off the rim. It swished. So did the second. When the fourteenth consecutive shot passed through the rim, the basketball guys knew they were beat and exhaled the breath they'd been holding since about shot nine.

"Go ahead," said the arena manager. "See how many you can get just for the heck of it."

No one objected. The issue was already decided, and they were all rather awe-struck by the exhibition they were watching. When Jim's twenty first shot clanked off the back of the rim they knew they'd been had. What they didn't know was that Jim Sutton had played basketball for the South Dakota State University Jackrabbits from 1955-1957. In the 1957 season he shot 92 percent of his free throws. It was a national record at the time. In 1955 and 1957 he led the North Central Conference in free throw percentage. He still holds SDSU records for free-throw percentage for a game (100 percent on 12 for 12 shooting), season (92 percent made), and career (86.3 percent). When he was drafted by the then Minneapolis Lakers in 1957 he became the first SDSU player picked by the NBA. The Lakers never cut him from their roster, but during training camp Jim went home for a horse sale and never went back to the team. Through the ensuing years he maintained a basketball goal at his home where he and his family regularly shot baskets to stay sharp.

On the disputed dates the rodeo was held in the arena and the basketball team took a road trip.

LOW 'N' SLOW

"Marital harmony trumps even the bronc riding."

Thad Beery

John McBeth had Whiskey River at Cheyenne Frontier Days. It was a great draw. Whiskey River and John would both go to the finals that year. They had combined to win a go-round at Fort Worth the previous winter. With well over a hundred bronc riders entered and enough stock to fill out the program, it was hard to get drawn up right at Cheyenne. Some cowboys entered year after year and never did get the one to win on. At a small rodeo with twenty or thirty bronc riders you could make the pay window on an average draw if a guy rode right. Not so at Cheyenne, where it took a great bronc *and* a great ride to contend. So while John wasn't counting the dollars before winning the check—he never did that—he was confident that he could win the riding.

Whiskey River loved the huge arena at Cheyenne; it's wider than most rodeo arenas and about twice as long. There's a race track running clear around the perimeter and the grandstand sits on the outside of it, so when his chute gate was flung open the bronc felt like he'd been turned out into the wide open spaces! And he bucked that way, like he was gonna toss John and lope off into the sunset unfettered by fences, cowboys and pickup horses   He was getting a lot of air. His hooves were about two feet off the ground when he dropped his front end and kicked up his rear. With no pressure on him and the whole world to play in, he bucked straight across the pen toward the distant grandstand.

John was sticking it on Whiskey River. He really

wanted this one. This was Cheyenne Frontier Days—"The Daddy of 'em All!" He'd seen the big buckles that go to the event champions. Who wouldn't want one? But he wasn't thinking about that. He was going about his business, setting his feet one inch higher in the neck each jump in that McBeth style. Seven seconds into the ride he was one jump away from grabbing that buckle when he spurred over his rein—hung his foot in the front end one jump—and stepped off before the whistle. He stood in the arena where he landed, stunned. That was all, no recriminations, no self-doubt, no posturing. It happens—it had happened—and he had to accept it and move on. He had to get to the next one with his positive attitude intact. And he didn't have any time to waste. He was entered at Aberdeen, South Dakota, that night.

So, John and Francie hustled over to the Cheyenne airport where they'd left their plane. Well, actually it wasn't their plane. It was a Cessna 182 John had borrowed from a friend of his. Luckily, the airport in Cheyenne is right behind the rodeo grounds so they got there quick. It's a general aviation airport combined with a military base so there is all kinds of traffic in and out. You can be taxiing out to take off in the company of big military aircraft. It can be a bit tricky. To add to the excitement it started to pour rain just as they were ready to go. Really *pour* rain. It was one of those high altitude summer thunderstorms that can lash out with rain, hail, strong winds—even tornadoes. The water poured down the windshield distorting their vision. Francie was a bit nervous about taking off in the downpour, and truth be told, John was too. They didn't know if it would get better or worse. If they should wait a while or just go. At the end of the runway with clearance to take off, John made his decision and pushed the throttle forward. The rain pummeled the little plane; the wind buffeted them around. It very well might have been the roughest ride John had made all day. A few miles from the airport, approaching their cruising altitude, they broke free of the clouds and the rain abruptly stopped. Francie eased her grip on her seatbelt and they both sighed with relief as the sun broke through the clouds and the air smoothed out.

John and Francie plan the logistics for one of the many trips they have taken together in 50+ years of marriage. Photo from the John McBeth Collection.

They spent a comfortable couple of hours watching the globe slowly turn beneath them from two miles up, and then Francie noticed some little things inside the cabin on the end of each wing.

"What are those?" she asked John.

"What?"

"Those little things there," she pointed.

"They're gravity fuel gauges for the wing tanks."

She nodded. It looked like she was deep in thought for a moment. She looked at the fuel level indicator on her side of the plane, looked over at the one on John's side and said, "Why do they say empty?"

"Oh, they don't work," John said.

"They don't work!"

"Nope. They're unreliable."

Francie got the contemplative look on her face again. It turned into an inquisitive one. She looked at the right fuel gauge; she looked at the left. "How do you know how much gas you've got?"

"Well, I know how much gas the engine uses at the RPM we're turning on the tachometer."

That satisfied her . . . for a couple of seconds. "What if you have a headwind?"

"That doesn't affect the fuel consumption."

She thought about that one. "Well, if we have a headwind we won't be going as fast."

"That doesn't affect the fuel consumption per hour."

She looked uneasy. She wasn't buying the explanation. "Well, if it takes us longer we'll use more fuel."

"That's true."

"Maybe you should get lower so we can land if we run out."

"If we run out, we will get lower," John smiled—and that may have been a mistake.

"If we run out!" she cried. "See! You don't know if we have enough gas or not!"

"Sure I do," he quit smiling. She was really worried.

The constant drum of the motor was the only sound for a few moments.

"What's that road down there?" Francie asked, sitting up in her seat to look over the nose of the plane. She saw an occasional car or truck moving back and forth on the highway below, appearing no larger than ants from their altitude.

"That's the highway into Aberdeen," John said, very matter-of-factly.

"We should go down there so if we run out of gas we have a place to land."

"On the road?"

"Sure, there's not much traffic."

"Well, there's heavier air down there and we'll use more fuel."

"We'll be safer if we run out of gas."

So they flew the rest of the way into Aberdeen at an altitude of two hundred feet, following the highway. When they reached the town they flew over the arena. They could see that the rodeo had already started.

"We better get a move on . . . ," John said.

The tension caused by the defective gas gauges intensified when lack of time entered the equation. They landed in Aberdeen, taxied into a parking spot and exited the plane almost before the prop quit spinning. They hustled through the terminal carrying John's equipment, his bronc saddle and gear bag, and the single suitcase they'd packed their clothes in. On the sidewalk in front of the airport their hopes for a quick ride to the rodeo took a hit when they arrived at an empty cab stand. They looked right and left to no avail—no cabs!

"I'll have to go in and make a call from a pay phone," John told Francie. "Maybe they can get a cab here quick."

As he put his gear down on the sidewalk next to their suitcase and turned to go back in the terminal, Francie said, "Here comes one now!" and pointed toward the airport entrance. Sure enough, a taxi was making the turn into the airport off the main street and slowly approached them where they stood waiting in front of the terminal— painstakingly, slowly approached.

The cabbie was a friendly sort, thin and gray headed with a Jed Clampett look about him, somewhat elderly with a friendly rural manner. "How're you folks doing?" he asked when the cab finally rolled to a stop and John stuck his head in the window to give directions.

"We're doing great," John said. "But we're in a huge hurry. We're late for the rodeo and need to get there quick."

"Well, it's not too far," Jed said, "Hop in."

"We've got some luggage we need to put in the trunk."

"Oh, I'll get that for you. Hop on in the back seat there."

John held the rear door open for Francie while she got in, but waited for Jed to come around to the rear of the car and open the trunk so he could load his saddle and gear bag himself. He figured the old fellow might strain something. He was right to be concerned. It was all the guy could do to get out of the car, stretch himself out to his full height and hobble over to open the trunk. John threw the gear in the car. He was in the back seat beside Francie growing impatient before Jed closed the trunk and made his way back to the driver's seat. Everything the fellow did was with slow deliberation: He inspected the key before replacing it in the ignition; he raised the arm on the meter like he was lifting a heavy weight; and he trolled—there's no other word for it—out of the airport onto the main road. Things got no better when the speed limit increased—as the speed of the cab didn't.

"I'm entered in the rodeo," John said, trying everything he could think of to get the guy to step on it, "and we saw that the performance was already going on when we flew over." Jed nodded that he'd heard. "I'd be glad to throw in a few dollars to augment that meter if you could get us there in a hurry." No reaction. The car still idled along shy of the speed limit. Jed had his hands locked on the wheel at ten and two o'clock and a look of deep concentration on his face. John figured maybe he *was* hurrying.

When they finally got to the fairgrounds they pulled up behind a board fence that went clear around the arena and came in on both sides of the grandstand. Francie got the suitcase and paid the cabbie as John grabbed his gear bag and saddle and ran over to the fence and tossed them over. When he followed his gear over the fence into the arena, he saw that there were two horses in the chutes, a fella was about to nod on one of them and the other one was his. When Jim Sutton, the stock contractor, saw that saddle come over the fence he knew John had arrived and he wouldn't be turning out that last bronc after all. He told the announcer to talk up the crowd, buying John a couple of minutes to get chapped up and catch his breath. The crowd was delighted by John's unorthodox arrival. It fit their conception of rodeo cowboys on the go, traveling hard and competing harder. They pulled for him all the way and were delighted when he made the winning ride.

The next morning John and Francie gassed up the plane to head for home. They verified that there had been plenty of gas left in the tanks upon their arrival and they were in no danger of running out. So John didn't have to fly home at two hundred feet.

McMENTOR

*"You feel at some point that you need to give back
some of the glorious things that have been given to
you."*

John McBeth

Over the years John put on numerous rodeo schools at
the Sutton ranch arena in Onida, South Dakota. He started
back in 1970 with the first one and was still pumping out
saddle bronc riders as recently as 2011, a span of forty one
years. John earned renown as one of the best, if not *the*
best, saddle bronc riding instructors in the world. The
Sutton family has been producing rodeos for five
generations and raises ninety percent of their own breeding
stock. With a great facility, a top instructor and the best
bucking stock available, it's no wonder John's students
have had such success. But the story goes deeper than that.

Rex Blackwell met John at the third school in 1972
where he was enrolled as a student in the saddle bronc
riding. Rex had been around horses his whole life, very
nearly being born in the saddle. He was riding by the age
of two and breaking horses with his father by nine. He
previously had qualified for the High School National
Finals Rodeo in the calf roping and bareback riding and the
National Intercollegiate Rodeo Association Finals in
bareback and bull-dogging. In 1972 he was turning pro and
specializing in the bareback and saddle bronc riding. He
knew a couple of guys that had attended John's second
school a year earlier. "That school was a week long," Rex
says. "Those boys told me how many horses they got on
and I couldn't believe it. They were *sooo* sore." It sounded
just like what Rex needed to jump start his career, and so

here he was.

That first morning Rex listened as John welcomed the students and explained how things would be run. He was especially impressed with John's philosophy on bronc riding. It was obvious as you listened to him that "can't" was not in his vocabulary. He stressed riding the horse, not the saddle, loosening up and getting the feet going, finding the horse's rhythm while lifting on the rein as opposed to getting in a strength bind and pulling on his head. "Remember, this is saddle bronc riding," he drilled into his student's heads, "not bronc saddle riding."

Rex was impressed right off with John's intuitive sense of where a cowboy's head was at and what he needed to get him going. "John can read people and read horses and he'll match up the right horse with the right cowboy so the cowboy can gain knowledge and gain confidence," he points out. "And that's a part of being an instructor that you can't teach . . . you either have it or you don't."

"God blessed me very much to go to John's school," Rex says today. "There's guys that can teach people how to ride broncs and then there's John. He's head and shoulders above all of them."

About that time Rex hooked up with Jim Sutton Sr. who headed up Sutton Rodeos. He was feeding stock, pulling gates and doing whatever he could around the Sutton place to learn the ropes and find a place in the rodeo world. By 1973 he was working for Jim as a pickup man at the rodeo school which proved that he had already earned a large measure of the boss's trust. Pickup men are as indispensable to a bronc rider as a bull fighter is to a bull rider: a good one can play the part of a safety net, a bad one can hang the bronc rider out to dry.

Rex has been a PRCA pickup man since 1972. In addition to the rodeo schools he has picked up at countless Sutton produced rodeos. He has picked up at high school rodeos in four states and at the Great Lakes Circuit Finals

Rodeo in the PRCA twice. Always a horseshoer like his father and brother, Rex eventually branched out into equine muscle conditioning, sharing his knowledge by offering clinics to the public. And through it all he felt the lure of the bronc riding.

In addition to working the school together, Rex would occasionally bump into John at a rodeo somewhere. He even had the privilege of traveling with him once or twice. So when he says, "I thought I was getting pretty good until John would come around, and I'm not even in his dust!" you know it's a well-considered voice of experience speaking. "I've seen him read a horse and get him to do just what he wanted . . . set up or whatever, so the horse would be worth more points. I've seen some weak horses that he would get to blow right there, and he could win on 'em. He has a talent to figure out what to do with a horse. I remember one time at the finals—I think it was number 50, Night Raid, of Sutton's he got on—they told John the horse takes an X and an X (the rein length measured with a fist with the thumb extended and another fist and thumb behind the saddle swells, ed.). He stretched the rein out behind the *cantle* and gave him X right there. The horse sure liked that long rein because John went eighty one points. And that was in the seventies! It'd be *ninety* one points today.

"I don't know if you know this or not," Rex says with a measure of awe in his voice. "But his students have won eight bronc riding championships. I don't know of anybody else that can say that. He's lost count of how many went to the finals."

South Dakota, where John's school was located, is a hot-bed of saddle bronc riding talent and has been for years. From the first recognized saddle bronc riding World Champion, Earl Thode, in 1929, through the great Casey Tibbs to the modern-era Etbauer brothers, South Dakotans have dominated the sport. In the 23 years between 1987 and 2009 twelve world titles were won by South Dakota cowboys—over half. Many of them came through the Sutton ranch and John's school. As Rex tells it: "There's cowboys around South Dakota that think the world of him because he's made their careers."

Rapid City, South Dakota's Black Hills Stock Show and Rodeo awards the James Sutton Sr. Memorial Trophy to the saddle bronc champion at that rodeo—with a few caveats: The award can only be won one time, and to qualify the recipient must have been born or reside in South Dakota. The award, a 14 inch sculpture, is a copy of a larger piece, a half life-sized bronze statue of John McBeth, James Sutton Senior's long-time friend, riding Half-Velvet, a Sutton horse and perennial NFR qualifier. It's fitting that John was honored to be the only non-South Dakotan to receive that award—and not for winning the bronc riding, but for his contributions to the sport of rodeo and the state of South Dakota.

"The best part for me being a dad," Rex says, reminiscing about raising his two boys Jace and Jade, also South Dakota bronc riders, "is having my boys at a high school rodeo—and here's John McBeth helping them out in the chutes."

Jace and Jade both went to John's schools on Rex's recommendation (if you can call an ultimatum a recommendation). Jace, the older brother by two years, attended in 2010. At the school the bronc riders gathered behind the chutes and laid out their gear for John's inspection. He moved down the line making sure their chaps, spurs and rein were of good quality and correct for the bronc riding. He looked over the saddles they'd brought and made sure their anchor and quarter binds were adjusted correctly for their size.

While looking over his gear, John asked Jace, "How many horses have you been on?"

"Two hundred and fifty," Jace told him.

John McBeth with the James Sutton Sr. Memorial Bronze at the Black Hills Stock Show and Rodeo in Rapid City, South Dakota. JJJ Photo.

"So, you're just starting to feel comfortable on the horses then," John stated as a matter-of-fact. "You're beginning to see your feet when you set them in the front end. The horse's rhythm and your spur stroke are becoming intuitive—where you don't have to think so much about when to charge the front end—you're starting to just do it."

Jace's jaw dropped—that's exactly where he was at. "Yessir," he said.

"What do you hope to accomplish at this school?" John asked, then listened, studying Jace's face.

"Well," Jace said, "I'm having trouble holding my feet on the markout. I've been pulling them too quick and I get behind the horse. Sometimes I miss them out altogether."

"Congratulations," John said with a grin. "You just solved half of that problem by understanding what the problem is." He moved on to the next student to repeat the procedure, armed with what he needed to know to start working on Jace.

Later on, when the broncs were run in the chutes and the students were collecting their gear to slap it on the horses, John told Jace to "Put your saddle on that little black in the last chute." He then moved off, matching up some of the other riders with the horses based upon what he knew about the stock and had gleaned from the riders.

Jace did as he was told, slipping his halter and saddle on the black. When he was ready to go, John appeared beside his chute gate and said, "He's gonna take a run at you and blow, Jace. So mark him out. Put a lock on that front end and hold 'em in there until he blows. Don't pull 'em out until he breaks or you'll be set up for a fall."

"Okay," Jace answered, and resolved to hold that mark-out like John said. As he slipped into his saddle he visualized setting his feet in the horse's neck as he left the chute. He thought about squeezing his feet into the front end, toes turned out as the bronc gassed 'em well out into the arena. He saw himself still locked in the front end as the bronc blew up and him in perfect position to weather the first jump.

It happened just like he had imagined it. He stuck the black in the neck as he left the chute. He squeezed his heels into the hollow over the point of the bronc's shoulders at the base of his neck; he squeezed with all his might as they raced to the middle of the arena; and he landed in his stirrups when the bronc set up—jumping in the air and kicking. The black came back to the turf on all fours with a jolt, recoiling to kick again. Jace released his lock on the front end and his feet snapped back with the momentum of the horse, raking the black down both sides. Jace jumped for the front end again and beat the horse to the punch, setting his feet just ahead of the bronc's kick in jump two. He was in time now, stroking the horse as he gathered himself and charging the front end as the black kicked, absorbing all the horse's momentum and his power through the stirrups.

The ride smoothed out as Jace took control over the bronc. As the horse kicked, Jace lifted his rein and his free hand together, jumping forward in his stirrups, setting himself under his swells. As the horse recoiled, coming to ground on all fours, pulling his feet in beneath him, cocking his whole body for another kick in the air, Jace did the same, recoiling his rein and his free hand in toward his body, recoiling his feet up under his hips. Then they extended together, the bronc stretching out as he kicked in the air, Jace stretching out with him, his arms straightening, his legs extending.

After the immeasurable time that a bronc ride lasts for the rider, which could be a few seconds, or the lifetime the memory lasts, John was hollering for the pickup men to go in and "Pick him up!" Jace came back to himself as his feet hit the ground.

"Did that feel better?" John asked during the debriefing phase of the ride.

"Yessir!" Jace beamed.

"It looked like you had a good hold of him when he blew."

"Yessir!"

"Did you notice how that set you up to spur when he broke?"

"Yeah, it seemed like he almost spurred himself that first jump."

"Exactly!" John enthused. "The action of the horse blows your feet out and all you have to do is reset 'em."

"Yessir, I felt that," Jace beamed.

"The same thing happens if they blow up right out of the chute and don't take that run, but I thought putting you on the black and getting you to concentrate on holding them in there was the best way of demonstrating that."

"I got it."

"So lock 'em in there until the bronc blows 'em out and helps you pick up his time."

"Yessir!"

"Okay, go get on twenty more. . . ."

"Yessir."

"And quit callin' me by my dad's name."

"Yess- . . . okay."

Jace couldn't wait to get his saddle on the next one. As much as he had learned on that last horse he figured he'd be *good* after twenty more.

His brother, Jade, also attended John's bronc school. After hearing Rex talk about it, where else would he go?

Like most young bronc riders learning to ride, Jade had a tendency to develop bad habits before good ones. For instance, it's wholly natural for anyone, when that bronc starts to pitch beneath you, to pull on your rein and lock your feet into the horse. After all, your first instinct is to pull yourself down and hang on. John laid a plan for Jade as he'd done for his brother before him.

So when Jade saddled up a big, strong, tall, long-necked paint horse at the school one day, and had his rein stretched out over the swells of his saddle taking a measure on it, John hopped up on his chute gate and asked, "What kind of rein are you giving him?"

"An average plus four fingers," Jade answered, indicating an average—a fist with the thumb extended behind the saddle swells—plus the width of four fingers added to that measurement.

"Give him that," John said, holding up his fist with the thumb extended.

Jade looked unsure. "That seems pretty short," he said, "on such a big long-necked bronc." He was holding the rein stretched over the swells in his fist with the thumb extended and pondering four more fingers of length—*or not*—when John reached down and took his hand and slid it back on the rein, and back . . . and back, until Jade had the rein stretched a hand with the thumb extended—behind the *cantleboard* of the saddle!

"Really?" Jade asked, searching John's face for a sign that he was kidding.

"Really," John said without a hint of a smile.

So Jade took his rein there and slipped into the saddle. He got his stirrups on his feet, took a good bite of the swells between his thighs and lifted the slack out of his rein, and found that his arm was almost too short. He had the rein lifted way above his head—it looked like he'd be riding with *two* free hands. With a mental shrug he placed his trust in John and nodded to the gate man.

The paint turned out and took his head, bucking with his nose down between his front feet. That set Jade's rein hand about shoulder high—about a John McBeth average. Unable to get much pull on the rein, Jade lifted it out in front of him and charged with his feet to get the bronc rode. He leaned back to get more out of his rein—putting an arch in his back, the cantle pushing him forward in his saddle, under his swells. That position, with his upper body leaned back, made it easier—almost automatic—to get his feet up in the front end. It felt good. He charged. He laid back further, lifted the rein, setting him back on the cantle and charged. It felt great. Jump after jump he was able to get his feet higher and higher in the bronc's neck. With the horse bucking with his head down, Jade was setting his feet right in the mane-line. Lifting his rein kept him from spurring over it and hanging a spur. He put on a classy ride.

When he was back on the ground with a grin on his face, John said, "See how feeding out that rein just naturally keeps you from pulling on it. It gets you out of the strength bind, loosens you up, takes your weight off your feet and lets them fly."

"It felt great!"

"You were riding the horse, not relying so much on your

equipment. Remember, it's the saddle bronc riding—not the bronc saddle riding."

Armed with evidence that a few words or a quick suggestion from John could advance a bronc rider's career by dozens of horses and months or years of effort, Jace and Jade keep in close touch with their mentor. They typically call John before or after every horse they get on for a McBeth debrief while they're rodeoing. Often a word from John can bring an issue into focus or solve a problem.

For example, Jace was having a problem with his saddle slipping back off the horse's withers, making it hard to reach the front end with his spurs and putting him back further on the horse, into the bronc's power. His friends watched it happen time after time with Jace's scores suffering and the issue eating into his confidence. People suggested he was pulling his saddle too tight or too loose, so he pulled it tighter or looser and the problem persisted. Finally, Jace was ready to accept the consensus opinion of his family and friends and admit that something was wrong with his saddle—thinking it must be defective. But he didn't want to change. A saddle is like a well worn glove or a pair of favorite boots—after awhile it just fits. Not to mention replacing a saddle is a large expense. So he described the problem and his frustration to John over the phone one day and John told him, "You're pulling your back cinch too tight. Watch a horse buck and you'll see that when they kick they arch their back. That causes their belly to stretch, their flanks move farther away from their withers. If you have your back cinch tight in the flank it pulls the saddle back as they buck"

"It makes sense when you think about it," Jace admitted.

"Plus," John added, "You don't need the back of the saddle strapped down tight. That just hooks you down solid against their power. If the back of the saddle eases up and down a bit it acts like a shock absorber, insulating you from the horse."

So Jace loosened up his back cinch. "Fit four fingers width-wise between the cinch and the horse with the cinch angled back toward the flank a little bit. . ." John told him, ". . . and that's about the correct amount of slack." Problem solved. No need to buy another saddle. No getting on another fifty or a hundred horses with the saddle slipping before finding the solution himself.

Back when John broke into rodeo the "Old-Timers" wouldn't tell a newcomer anything. "It just wasn't done," John says. "I don't know if it was just the reticent old cowboy way, or if they were afraid you would beat them the next week with the information they gave you. But it just wasn't done." So, where John lacked someone to show him the tricks of his trade, the younger generation today is blessed with a cell phone and a mentor on the speed dial. That's progress.

The friendship between John and the Blackwells continued to flourish. Rex and John became partners in a business venture unrelated to rodeo that profited both—and many others in the process. John kept tutoring the boys and they looked up to him with reverence. Today, Jace is having a great career competing in the National Intercollegiate Rodeo Association and Jade is pushing hard for the Saddle Bronc Riding Rookie of the Year in the PRCA. "I expect you'll see those boys show up in the standings one of these years," John said, referring to the world standings.

John keeps finding ways to give back to the sport that has treated him so well. He served as the Prairie Circuit Secretary for ten years, and organized the Circuit Finals Rodeo. He was instrumental in bringing in $150,000 dollars in sponsorship money, much of which ended up in the pockets of those most deserving, the competitors. Hadley Barrett, four-time PRCA Announcer of the Year and ProRodeo and National Cowboy Hall of Fame Inductee, who announced the rodeo many times during those years and was awarded the Prairie Circuit Announcer of the Year award at that rodeo in 1979, said it was the best circuit finals ever. "It was a miniature NFR," said Hadley. "At that time we had the best circuit finals we have ever had. I know that long before and long since we have not equaled that. John got a group of businessmen to underwrite it and he put the whole thing together, and we did it in Kansas Coliseum and it was a first class event . . . he was definitely the guy."

John McBeth on Kenny at the Prairie Circuit Finals Rodeo held in the Kansas Coliseum in Wichita, Kansas, 1979. John was the Prairie Circuit Secretary at the time and ". . . the guy . . ." that put the show together. Bern Gregory Rodeo Photographs, Dickinson Research Center, National Cowboy & Western Heritage Museum, Oklahoma City, Oklahoma.

John has also been an ambassador for the sport, helping with a Wild West Show and Rodeo production in Caracas, Venezuela, getting exposure for rodeo outside of America's borders. And after a long and varied career judging such rodeos as the High School National Finals, College National Finals and even the PRCA National Finals Rodeo on two occasions, he recently got involved with the National Little Britches Rodeo Association and judged their national finals, lending his experience to the education of the youngest generation of rodeo competitors.

So it was . . . prophetic . . . or spiritual . . . or justified—no—it was *perfect* when the call came in on John's cell phone, that he happened to be sitting in the Blackwell's living room with his close friends gathered around. "Uh, huh," he said into the receiver. "This is John McBeth." He listened for a moment with nothing showing on his face. Then, "Uh, huh . . . oh! No kidding! I'm honored . . . really honored. Thank you so much for the call."

He hung up the phone and the suspense hung in the air. John seemed at a loss for words for a second or two. Rex tried to read his face but couldn't.

"Well," John said, looking around the room at his good friends—the room where he'd always been welcomed and the friends who made him feel at home.

"It looks like they're putting me in the ProRodeo Hall of Fame."

A BAD DAY

I asked John if he ever had a bad day in rodeo because all of his stories were about success and I wanted a little bit of strife for the book. I guess when you're the world champ most of your days are good ones. Still, he had no trouble coming up with this tale.

Sometimes you do what you oughta; sometimes you do what you gotta; and it's not always clear which is which. So, when John's wife, Francie, told him that her ten-year high school reunion was coming up on Saturday night, he might be excused for confusing the two. You see, he was entered at Fort Smith, Arkansas, and he had Jake (the Bucking Horse of the Year in 1960 and 1965) drawn. Jake was notorious for being an eliminator, but John got along with him better than most. At the least, Jake was rank enough that any fella who rode him might be in the money, but if you were cowboy enough to fit a good ride on him—as John had done in the past—you could be looking at a big payday. So, with a family to feed, his entry fees paid, and Jake's name written beside his own on the judge's sheets, it's no wonder that John told Francie, "I gotta go to Fort Smith," even if he ought notta.

It was a cold couple of days that summer, inside the McBeth household at least, as Francie and John made separate preparations for Saturday night. Francie went through her closet and picked out what to wear, spoke with old friends over the phone deciding where to meet, and entertained memories of bygone days running on an endless loop through her mind. She understood the nature of the rodeo business—you only earn what you win and no days

136

off—but that didn't make going to the reunion alone any easier to take. It was a disappointment. Many in rodeo call rodeo wives rodeo-widows, and with good reason: They single-handedly keep the household running winter, spring, summer and fall, and from year to year. They cook and clean and see the kids off to school. They are the sole disciplinarian. There is no, "Wait until your dad gets home . . . ," because who knows when that'll happen. They pay the bills, tend the yard and garden, and even fix a broken pipe or leaking roof when they have to. They do it all alone, without a second opinion or a guiding hand, and they perform under the added burden of worry about their significant-other traveling thousands of miles by car and plane and competing daily in the arena. Francie accepted it as her duty to her family and husband. "That's just the way it is," she told herself, and set her jaw as John might do when calling for a bronc, and went about her business.

John was a bit distracted as well, trying to show Francie his concern over missing her reunion and offering her the support she deserved, all while making travel arrangements to Arkansas and refusing to second guess his decision. Typical for him, he grew quiet and introspective as the day approached, thinking of Jake and getting his head right for his ride.

Rain is sometimes considered a bad omen by sailors and race car drivers, and it didn't rain that Saturday night at Fort Smith . . . , it poured. This was before Fort Smith's arena had a roof on it. The arena was a muddy quagmire. It was raining so hard the lights had trouble penetrating through the waves of water splashing out of the sky. You couldn't see the arena fence from the bucking chutes. The judges chased the bucking stock as they disappeared into the tempest, slogging after them through the bog, squinting into the lashing rain trying to follow the action. It was like finding your way through a dense forest on a moonless night by match light.

John knew that riding Jake was an iffy proposition at best. He'd won big on him before, but he'd ridden him a few times for nothing as well. Weather affects animals, too, much as it does men. Sometimes a good horse, lacking trust in the footing, will refuse to buck. Sometimes a bad one, having had their fill of Mother Nature, will get spooked and buck like the devil incarnate. John considered these things as he saddled Jake. He laid his rain slicker over his saddle swells to keep the rosin dry, folded the lower part of his leggings up and tucked them into his waist band for the same reason. Cold rivulets ran down his spine. He decided to stick with plan A and do his usual little thing on Jake, in spite of the weather.

So when the big bronc broke out of the chute, charging into the arena with his head up, knifing through the downpour, setting his usual trap, John pulled his right foot out of his neck and ripped him down the right rib cage. Then he bounced that foot off the right quarter bind and stuck Jake in the ribs a second time on his way back to the front end. Predictably, Jake broke right there, took his head and cracked back to the left in a big explosion. He came around in a circle splashing through the quagmire. John pulled his feet out of the front end and started to spur. He leaned back on the cantleboard, lifted on his rein and charged back to the front end. Always noted for his broncy attitude, Jake was up to the challenge. He scorned the lashing waves of water, the mud and the cowboy who had stung him in his side, and, putting his head down, let his fury flow out through each kick.

John could see the fence looming up through the torrent. He knew Jake didn't. The bronc was bucking blindly through the gloom with his head down in the splashing muck. Just before Jake hit the fence full-bore, John stepped off, landing on his back in a huge puddle. Jake rebounded off the fence, toppling over backward onto the now empty saddle in the morass next to John. The mud was so deep it multiplied the effort required to move, and made the cowboy and the bronc appear in slow motion as they scrambled to their feet and went their separate ways.

John was soaked. He was mud from head to toe. Every piece of his gear was a mess. Because he had stepped off the horse before the wreck he did not get a reride. His trip was for nothing. He didn't win a dime. He was six or seven hours from home and suddenly consumed with a desire to be at the reunion with Francie, dry and warm, laughing among friends. It was enough to make a guy re-evaluate a gotta into an ought notta.

THE LUCK OF THE DRAW

*"If you want to make a living in this business you
can't just win on the good ones, when you're
supposed to. You've got to be able to win on the bad
ones, too."*

John McBeth

One fall at Huron, South Dakota, a friend of John's, who
shall remain nameless, drew a horse that was branded with
a 7-Bar and named Tornado. This friend of John's was a
pretty fair bronc rider—better than most. During the bronc
riding 7-Bar charged out of the chute and blew across the
arena more like a nor'easter than a tornado—fast and true
in a straight line. It looked like he was intent on running
clear off as he drew a bead on the roping chutes at the far
end of the pen. In the first few seconds of the trip the bronc
rider did everything he could to get the horse to break: he
spurred Tornado in the belly once, and then hollered
"BUCK!" in the horse's ear in time with a second belly
punch as he tried to jar the bronc out of Kentucky Derby
mode—all to no avail. Tornado just stretched his neck out
and gassed 'em across the arena. After about four seconds
the bronc rider gave in, resolving himself to his fate. He
quit trying to make the horse buck and set his feet in the
front end, settling down for the duration. He knew from
experience that if the horse did break this late in the ride he
couldn't earn enough points in the remaining few seconds
to win anything anyway. So he started hoping the horse
would run clear off and wishing for a reride.

About that time Tornado reached the end of the arena
and spun around like the wind he was named for, launching
his rider head first toward the calf roping chute. A loud
"CLANG!" could be heard throughout the premises as the

bronc rider's head came in contact with the metal bars of the roping chute. When the rider failed to get up some cowboys ran to his aid, only to find that he was physically all right but had his head stuck between the vertical bars of the roping chute gate. The rodeo was delayed for about ten minutes while a pry bar and jack were procured to extricate the bronc rider from his predicament. John crossed the arena to observe the proceedings and encourage his hard-headed friend who suffered more from embarrassment than physical harm.

"Looks like you got some scrapes on your face," John said after his friend's head was returned to his body's side of the gate.

"Probably wind burns," the man said with disgust. "From the velocity we were going."

John decided he wouldn't cross the street to get on a horse like that.

The next spring he entered Montgomery, Alabama. The rodeo was two go-rounds in the bronc riding to fill the five performances. He had entered alone and so drove the entire 900 miles down there by himself, wracking his brain over the first horse he'd drawn. "7-Bar, Tarnation . . . ," he thought. "There's something familiar about that. I must know him from some where. But where! I don't remember a horse called Tarnation for the life of me."

It wasn't until the whole 900 miles were behind him that he stood on the bottom rail of the bronc pen at the fairgrounds in Montgomery looking over the bronc herd and realized that 7-Bar Tarnation was the same 7-Bar Tornado he'd seen in Huron the preceding fall—a horse he had decided at the time that he wouldn't ". . . cross the street . . . ," to get on. He was 1500 miles from Huron at a rodeo with a different stock contractor; the horse had a different name, Tarnation instead of Tornado; only the brand was the same—7-Bar.

"How'd you come by that 7-Bar horse?" John asked the

stock contractor before the rodeo that day.

"I traded some bulls for a group of horses and he came as part of the deal," the man told him.

John just shook his head at his unavoidably bad luck and prepped his gear for his ride. "The luck of the draw," he mumbled to himself as he chapped up. He knew what was about to happen, and it came off pretty much as he expected. Try as he might, using his whole bag of tricks, he couldn't make Tarnation . . . or Tornado, break before he reached the end of the arena. He belly punched him, he spurred him in the neck, he hollered, he snatched at the rein and then threw back the slack. Nothing worked. Seven Bar ran the length of the arena before he got his act together.

"I knew it was coming," John says today. "He scotched and blew up and made a grand total of two jumps before the whistle. I am a whopping 39 points and no reride because he broke. Now, I'm hoping I've got a good one for my second horse. And thank heaven I did."

He placed in that second round and slipped in for a piece of the average, ". . . just on the strength of some other guys turning out, or not making the whistle, or whatever," he says, "as luck would have it."

After picking up his winnings, he asked the stock contractor if he'd be interested in selling that 7-Bar horse. The man looked at him kind of funny.

"I know you traded some bulls for him," John said. "How much do you think you've got in him?"

The man said, "Oh I don't know. A hundred and a quarter maybe."

John said, "I didn't win all that much money, but I've got a hundred and fifty dollars. I want to buy that horse."

"Why? I thought you didn't like him."

"I don't like that sucker. But maybe I can retire him and then I won't have to draw him again."

It was No-Sale.

UNTOLD STORIES

This story was gleaned from discussions with Blake McBeth (John's youngest son) and Blake's wife Shellie.

John told me that his son Blake was an energy broker—oil and gas. "There's only about twenty of them at his level in the country," he said, the pride sounding in his voice and showing on his face. I asked if he ever rode broncs like his older brother Bart did. "Nope," John said. "But he could flat hit a baseball."

Intrigued, I wanted to talk to Blake and see if he had any good John McBeth stories to tell. I also wanted to get a glimpse of John the dad, John the man, at home, away from rodeo and his public persona. To know the man would be to understand the champion. Of course, John-as-cowboy dominated our conversation when, eventually, we did talk.

"We went to a rodeo one day, my mom and dad and me," Blake said. "I was just a kid then, real young . . . maybe four or five years old. I really can't remember. But I was real little. I remember my dad pulling his gear out of the trunk of the car—his gear bag and bronc saddle. It was how he went to work, like other kids' fathers picking up a lunch pail or briefcase and heading for the office. It was something I saw him do hundreds of times. I guess I always took it for granted. He was always so calm, so in control. And I was no more interested in his line of work—the bronc riding—than those other kids were in their father's jobs, whether they were carpenters or lawyers or whatever. It was just what he did, what I knew, and it was familiar, not unusual or different at all for a young kid that'd been exposed to it all his life.

"So he made his way over to the chutes, and mom and I found seats in the grandstand. Watching rodeos, for me at that age, was about like watching somebody mow the grass: It really didn't hold my interest. I was too young. I didn't recognize more than a couple of the cowboys, didn't understand the nuances of the competition. The unpredictability of the outcome was over my head. It just seemed like everything always came off as planned—like a guy mowing the lawn.

"Sometimes my mom would sit with the wives of the other cowboys. Sometimes they'd have kids and we'd play together while the rodeo was going on in the background. We'd be running around or playing in the dirt under the grandstands. When dad got ready to ride she'd call me over so we could watch together.

"I remember that day in particular. She called me over to where she was sitting—I think us kids were being rowdy, getting out of hand and she kind of wanted to break it up as much as anything. I sat down beside her and she said, 'Watch your dad ride. He's next to go.' He had a horse that was fighting the chute and it took a long time for him to come out. We were waiting—it seemed like a long time—and my attention was starting to wane.

"'There he is,' she nudged me. 'Watch your dad.' I looked up into the arena in time to see the horse take a jump or two with dad sitting up there riding like always, and then suddenly, there was no one in the saddle. I was stunned. Where was dad? Then I saw him get up out of the dirt and dust himself off and put on his hat. I wondered what was going on. I was in shock. It felt like falling off your bike for the first time: It surprises you, and it hurts. I grew up a lot in that instant. I looked up into my mom's face. She looked concerned, too.

"'What now?' I said. She looked down at me with a wrinkled brow and asked, 'What?'

"'What do we do now?' I wanted to know.

"She must have seen how worried I was, because she said, 'It's all right honey. We just go get on another one.'

"'He can do that?' I asked, amazed. 'He can still ride?'

"'Of course he can,' she said, smiling at me. 'He just got bucked off.'

"I learned a lot that day."

Blake McBeth (left) with Clem McSpadden, opening ceremony Prairie Circuit Finals Rodeo, Wichita, Kansas, 1979. Bern Gregory Rodeo Photographs, Dickinson Research Center, National Cowboy & Western Heritage Museum, Oklahoma City, Oklahoma.

I knew that John had won the world when Blake was very young, too young to remember, but due to the longevity of John's career I supposed that Blake had seen him make some great rides. So I asked about that.

"I remember another rodeo mom and dad and I went to, years later it must have been," he told me. "It was an Old Timers rodeo. They always bring this 'easy' stock to the Old Timers rodeos, nothing rank or wild. They don't want to hurt any of the old guys and they want them to look good. Dad drew this big black bronc that fought the chute like crazy. I remember thinking it was unusual for the stock at those rodeos to show that kind of fight. I don't know if it was a new horse that the stock contractor didn't know very well, or if the horse just had a burr under his hide that day, but this horse was rank. He reared out of the chute and really blew up. Dad scored like 82 points I think it was, and won the bronc riding by fifteen—and it probably should have been more. I think second place was a 67 or something like that."

"Amazing!" I said. "He was still riding that well after all those years."

"He rode until he was forty-eight," Blake said. "And never rode like he *was* forty-eight."

"Tell me more," I prompted. "What was it like growing up with a world champion bronc rider for a father?"

"Well, the bronc rider part of it wasn't really all that important at home. We never really talked about it. It was like having a dad that did anything else. They pretty much leave the work at the office. I will say, though, that bronc riding was never pushed on me. I was raised to believe that I could succeed at whatever I chose to do and that choice was left up to me."

"And you were never that interested in the bronc riding?"

"No, I never really was. I liked football and baseball better. So that's what I played."

"Do you have a story that illustrates what kind of a dad or what kind of a person your father is?" I asked. "Outside of rodeo."

He thought for a moment, and then he said in very measured tones, "He's a much more tender-hearted man than he would like for you to believe. But maybe you should talk to my wife, Shellie," he added. "She may be able to give you some insight that I can't, being as close to him as I am. She may have noticed something I've missed."

Shellie echoed much of what Blake had said. "I've really been blessed to have him and Francie for my in-laws. We have a very special relationship," she assured me. "He's a big softie," she said of John. "So tender-hearted."

"Do you have a story that illustrates that?" I asked.

"I have some *great* stories about John!" she exclaimed. "But none that pertain to rodeo, and he'd kill me if I told you my stories," she laughed.

So, as so often happens, some of the best stories will go untold.

FATHER AND SON

Bart McBeth qualified for the Prairie Circuit Finals
rodeo sixteen times in his saddle bronc riding career.

The sun blazed red like a kiln fire on the eastern Kansas horizon. It peeked over the rim of the earth in striated lines shooting up into the rapidly brightening sky, turning it from black to blue. The fireball faded to orange at its extremities to portend the coming day: hot and dry. The father and son drove north through a world scalded in a bright orange glow that reflected off the pavement, the prairie and their faces. They experienced one of those "Omigawd!" moments, overcome by the beauty of their surroundings.

The father was John McBeth, the son was Bart.

"That's the nice part about leaving in the middle of the night," John said from the passenger's seat, "seeing the sunrise."

"Yep," Bart agreed, nodding from behind the wheel.

John was the former world champion saddle bronc rider now approaching the twilight of his career. Bart had bought his permit a month ago and was entered in his first pro rodeo. They were in Bart's car heading up I-35 toward Topeka. They'd got up before the crack of dawn and pulled out of Burden, Kansas, for the drive to the rodeo at Ponca, Nebraska.

There's no feeling in the world like going to a rodeo. Once entered, all you have to do to set your heart racing, your lungs puffing, is visualize setting your saddle down on the back of a big hairy bronc, remember the feel of that saddle beneath you as you slip down into the chute, and imagine the power that will hit you as he blows into the arena. Adrenalin can't tell the difference between your imaginings and the real thing. It courses through your veins, heightening your senses, energizing every fiber of your body. It can affect your digestion—alter your sleep. Your vision clears, your reflexes sharpen, even your sense of smell seems better. It makes a young cowboy feel invincible and an old cowboy feel like a young one.

A rodeo is a microcosm of life: It is hopes and dreams, victory and defeat, charted on a time-line three hours long. The pressure to perform is all on you; there's no "team" to cushion the blow of a poor performance, no coach to fall back on. It's a gamble as big as any in Vegas—betting your entry fees against all comers with no guarantee of any return. In the arena you are alone between those fences, risking your pride and ego, your reputation and your health. The obvious risk, the possible reward, infuse you with excitement that makes the day brighter, the air crisper, the sights, smells, and tastes stronger when you're going to a rodeo.

Bart was somewhat of a late bloomer on the rodeo circuit. He attended college on a cross country and track scholarship that monopolized his athletic efforts. But that spring he got out of school and said to John, "Hey dad, let's go to a couple of rodeos."

"Where you want to go?" John asked. He was working on a bronc saddle in the back of his store, The Cowboy Shop in Burden, Kansas, and Bart was helping, learning the trade.

"Ponca, Nebraska, and Clear Lake, South Dakota," Bart answered.

"Sounds good to me," John said. "You got your permit?"

"Yep."

"Well then, let's go."

So here they were, the old pro and the rookie, father and son.

There have been a lot of father/son combinations in the sports world. Take Al Unser Junior and his father for instance, race car drivers at the top echelon of that sport; or Bobby and Barry Bonds of baseball fame. There's Bobby and Brett Hull in hockey, Rick and Brent Barry in basketball, and even boxers Muhammad Ali and Laila if we relax our discussion to include daughters of sports greats. One of the most famous examples of the fruit falling close to the tree is the Manning brothers, Peyton and Eli, both professional quarterbacks following in the footsteps of their famous father, Archie, who starred for the New Orleans Saints. It has happened so many times in so many sports that everyone assumes the skill to succeed is innate, inherited, yet very few sons have been able to equal or surpass the accomplishments of an all-star father. Granted, a famous father may be able to open a few doors, make the right introductions, grease the skids to help jump start a career, but no father can hit the ball, shoot the shot or take the punch intended for his offspring's jaw. And there never was a bronc saddle built for two. So it weighed on Bart alone to win the thousand dollars required to fill his permit and become a full-fledged member of the fraternity of professional cowboys. Just a thousand dollars—that's all— won from the toughest professional bronc riders in the world. In fact, some of the money he needed—that he was betting he could take—was riding in the car alongside him deep in his father's pockets.

As they cruised along beneath the brightening sky, Bart was thinking about the time he'd attended his dad's bronc school. He'd suffered an inauspicious beginning to a rodeo career. He hadn't covered a single horse at the school— thrown by every one. Then, his education was cut short when he broke his arm bucking off a nasty one. Although the son of a bronc rider and a fixture around Kansas rodeos in the summer time, he hadn't grown up in the saddle like his dad had, or like many of the other students at his dad's school. They were ranch raised, he wasn't. Starting out, he would have fallen off a saddle horse—much less a bucker.

Although exposed to the bronc riding at an early age, Bart got a late start on his own career. Photo from the John McBeth Collection.

"Do you want to stop and get some breakfast?" John asked.

"Yep," Bart replied in a clipped-but-sure way that would remind you of his dad.

They pulled in to a truck stop, gassed up and hit the diner. After sliding into a booth and debating how much food to put in his jittery stomach, Bart laid his menu down on the table and looked across at his dad. He said, "I'm curious."

"Yeah. What about?"

"Do you get nervous?"

"More like excited," John answered. Then he had a second thought and amended his statement, "If you aren't a little bit nervous it's time to quit," he added, ". . . and you're just getting started."

"Well, I guess I'm ready then," Bart said.

"Trust me," John went on, "It'd be strange if you weren't a bit apprehensive. It's your first pro rodeo. But it's just like any other riding. The broncs buck the same here as they do in the practice arena. . . ." He made eye contact and added, ". . . but the cowboys spur more." He didn't smile until Bart smiled first. He'd been giving his son a strong dose of "Get your feet going. Charge! CHARGE!" since Bart decided to become a bronc rider, so his comment was a gentle nudge compared to some of the other exhortations he'd launched over the past year, and worthy of the smile. He had emphasized the importance "getting your feet going" played in the bronc riding. And he knew that Bart knew it. It was just a matter of "getting it done" being miles down the road from knowing what to do.

"What'd you draw, anyway?" John asked.

"Number fifty one, Stomper, at Ponca, and Empty Saddles at Clear Lake."

"Well, Stomper earned his name . . . ," John said and gave Bart a look. "He stomps across the pen hitting like a ton of bricks every jump. But he has no kick. He just stomps on his front feet and about knocks your teeth loose. He's not hard to ride if you can take the punishment but he is hard to score big on. He doesn't lift you up out of your saddle so you can really spur him," he said, as he unconsciously slipped down into the booth, reached out with his rein hand over the table, and put his free hand up. "You gotta do it all on your own." Bart was sipping at his water glass and looking out the window. John saw that he was listening, but he didn't know what kind of an impression he was making on him. "He's a good draw for you," he summed up. "If you can spur *him* you can spur any of 'em."

"What about Empty Saddles of Sutton's?" Bart asked.

"What was his name again . . . ?" John said and grinned.

"Shoot!" Bart exclaimed, "He's that rank one they always put in the eliminator pen at the finals isn't he?"

"I don't know . . ." John said, still smiling. "What was that name again . . . ?"

Later, after they had jumped back in the car and were headed up highway 75 toward Nebraska, Bart asked, "So what did you draw?"

"I don't know what I have at Ponca," John told him. "Some new horse I've never heard of. But I've got Half Velvet at Clear Lake."

"Half Velvet!" Bart cried. "That's the bronc in those pictures at home, isn't it? That series of pictures from your last ride at the NFR."

"Yep."

"And it's also the bronc you're on in that bronze they made of you for the Black Hills Rodeo in Rapid City."

"Yep."

Then after a pause where John watched Bart absorb the magnitude of finding himself in the big-time, he said, "Well, I guess we're drawn up in Clear Lake, but it's no time to worry about that now. We need to be concentrating on what we're doing in Ponca." And he went on to coach Bart on the length of rein to give Stomper; how far up on the bronc's withers to set his saddle; and where and how to position the back cinch.

They grabbed a hamburger for lunch at the fairgrounds in Ponca and went immediately to the stock pens to look over their draws. Stomper was a husky bay horse with a well-muscled neck. John's draw, Lady Luck, was a little black mare that nobody knew anything about. She was new to the herd . . . and the world, evidently.

When the performance started, the bareback riding was going smoothly and quickly. Bart noticed a big difference between the high school rodeos he'd been to and the pros: The way everything ran so efficiently here.

The bronc riders chapped up while the bareback riding

was going on and checked over their gear. A young bronc rider that John had never met before was sitting in his saddle nearby checking his stirrups, spurring back and forth on the ground—cantle-boarding to check the feel of his binds—when he noticed the world championship buckle hanging off John's belt.

"Say," he said, "If you don't mind my asking, what kind of saddle do you ride?"

"Well, I'll tell you," John said with an amused look on his face. "It's got a high cantle and pretty small swells, and it would probably scare the begeesus out of you."

"Well, shoot!" The young cowboy grinned after thinking for a second. "*This* one does that, too!"

In no time the bareback riding was over and the broncs were loaded in the chutes. John's bronc came eighth in line and there were only six chutes, so they'd have to buck some horses and make room to roll his horse forward into a chute. He'd likely be the eighth man to ride. Bart was ahead of him in chute four. If the contractor went by common convention—bucking from the last chute forward—then Bart would be the third rider to go. John verified that that was the case with the arena director and then came over to Bart's chute to help set him down on Stomper. He'd have plenty of time to pull his own saddle after Bart rode.

Bart pulled his front cinch when the bronc riding began. He pulled his back cinch when the bronc behind him bucked out of chute five, and then measured his rein. He gave Stomper the cantleboard as John suggested, although it seemed like an ungodly amount of rein to deal out.

"Trust me . . . ," John said. "And SPUR!"

Stomper was one of those broncs that acts . . . broncy. He stomped his feet as Bart mounted up, and rattled back and forth and front to rear in the box. He turned his head to glare at the bronc rider, and looked into the arena with wide eyes. He clearly knew the score.

He stomped into the arena when the chute gate opened. Then he stomped clear across the arena toward the grandstand on the opposite side, grunting every time his front feet thudded into the ground. He bucked with his head right down between his front hooves. Bart got his feet moving alright. But he was out of time, spurring to the cantle as Stomper hit and struggling to get his feet in front of the cinch when he did charge the front end. Stomper's lack of a kick made getting in time unintuitive. Bart took a severe jerking for eight seconds. He felt like he'd put in a full day's work as he swung to the ground off the pickup man's horse. He went a whopping 57 points, but he rode his first bronc at his first pro rodeo and was glad to get a score.

He was feeling pretty good about it overall as he hustled back to the chutes to help his dad set down. He held the black's head when John measured his rein. Lady Luck was twitchy, nervous and hostile to be around, but John avoided getting bradded in the chute. She stalled for a second when the gate swung open, then blew into the arena in a huge leap. John stuck her in the neck. When she hit the ground at the end of the chute gate she abruptly turned left and blew into the air again. John held his mark out for the second jump and then raked her hard on the third one. He was tapped off that quick. As soon as he pulled his feet out of his mark out he spurred in time, full stroke, and set his feet in the front end, toes turned out. The black had four big showy leaps in her where she left the ground off all four feet, and then she leveled out in a good strong jump and kick down the arena fence to the left.

John had a ball. Lady Luck had a lot of action. She kicked nice and bucked with her head up. She had a good even rhythm and not much power. John made a "rocking chair" ride on her.

When they headed out of the fairgrounds after the rodeo with Bart behind the wheel once more, John was winning the riding with 77 points.

"How'd that rein feel on ol' Stomper," he wanted to know.

"It felt a little bit long," Bart told him sincerely.

"That's because you were pulling on it instead of lifting," John countered. "You didn't jump up out of your saddle and charge the front end," he said, "and lean back, which would have made it feel more natural. You did a great job of getting your feet moving. Way to go there. You looked fairly loose for what that horse was putting you through. But you were out of time and not getting any front end. You'll have to work on that."

Bart felt a little bit deflated. He went 57 points, but he rode his first bronc at his first pro rodeo. He wished for more praise, less criticism.

They got a room that night and watched TV until they fell asleep shortly after dark. They weren't up in Clear Lake until the next night and it was only a three-hour drive, so they had time to catch up on the sleep they'd missed leaving Kansas that morning.

They drove in to Clear Lake about noon the next day and spoiled themselves with the luxury of a sit-down meal at the local café before heading out to the arena. They bumped into a lot of friends on the main street. South Dakota was always John's rodeo home away from home. The Suttons—John's partners in his rodeo school in Onida—were there contracting the stock. He ran into some former students of his and several long-time competitors that he knew well. It was like old-home-week.

One hundred and twenty centuries before the first rodeo was held in Clear Lake, a glacier cut "America's Most Natural Rodeo Bowl" into the South Dakota prairie on the Crystal Springs Ranch seven miles northeast of the town. Surrounded by three hills, the arena lies in the bottom of a natural bowl forming a spectacular amphitheater-like setting. Sheltered from the prairie winds and blessed with enhanced natural acoustics due to the unusual topography, the hillsides surrounding the arena contribute to an intimate interaction between cowboy and spectator. The slope of the hills eliminates the need for a grandstand or bleachers; the thousands in attendance bring a lawn chair to set up on the hillside, or throw down a blanket or tarp to sit on. The crowd is so close you can *feel* them from the arena floor; you can distinguish individual voices when they roar. The bucking stock seem to love the setting too, the crowd pressing down on them, echoing nervous excitement off the three hills. They always buck well in the Crystal Springs Ranch Arena.

South Dakota has always been known for its skilled bronc riders and the Sutton Rodeo Company for their good bucking stock. The combination made for a tough riding. Bart was as wired as he'd ever felt. He remembered an expression that six-time all-around champion of the world, Larry Mahan, always used: "This ain't no dress rehearsal. We are professionals and this is the Big-Time!" That's how he felt. In the big-time. But that was intimidating, too—being a professional, or at least competing on the pro level and having a rank one drawn to boot. He didn't really know what to expect. And of course his imagination, his subconscious, got his nerves all revved up. Once you've been on a few thousand of them things slow down for you and it gets easier. That wasn't the way it was on Bart's twenty-fourth bronc.

Empty Saddles was a big paint horse. Bart had to let his latigos out a long way to strap his cinch around the big bronc. He stood in front of his chute when the riding started and watched from ground level as horse after horse exploded into the arena and bucked with all their might, upholding the Sutton's reputation for rank saddle broncs. It was like they were competing with each other, each successive horse trying to top his predecessor, like they were part of a bucking contest—not a riding one. One bay kicked so high he got almost vertical. He jumped in the air and kicked with a vicious snap, dropping his front end out from under a bronc rider. He sucked back when he hit the ground and the guy was dashboarded—hard. And they kept getting ranker. Up close they were sleek, large, muscled, athletic, determined and devious. It was the rankest pen of broncs Bart had ever seen. Not to be outdone the bronc riders came with their hammers cocked too, man after man stuck it on his mount with only a few exceptions, and the buck-offs there were—were stupendous.

John walked up and stood beside Bart at his chute gate and they watched a couple of horses buck together. "You ready to go?" he asked.

"Yep," Bart replied in that set-jawed, McBeth way he'd inherited.

"How you feeling?" John asked, looking him over.

"You were right, dad," Bart said, ignoring the question.

"About what?"

"They do spur more than at the school."

They both grinned at that.

"Where are you at, dad?" Bart asked, looking down the line of chutes for Half Velvet.

"Four behind you; they're holding me for last."

When there were two broncs ahead of him, Bart jumped up on the chute gate and pulled his latigos. The bronc was a notorious chute fighter and was showing all the signs of throwing a fit. He was goosey about being cinched and rattled back and forth in the box. John saw that Bart already had a helper on the back of his chute to hold the bronc's head while he measured his rein, so he backed off to watch. With one bronc to go before him Bart pulled his back cinch. Empty Saddles kicked the back of the chute a vicious lick as he did so. When the flank man hopped up on the back of the chute to adjust the flank strap, Bart stretched his rein out over the swells of his saddle to measure it. His helper lined the horse's neck and head out straight, with one hand on the bronc's nose and the other on his neck. Suddenly, the bronc reached up and bit at him— narrowly missing biting him square in the chest. The guy instinctively struck out in self-defense, swatting the horse between the ears. The bronc was stunned; he was used to getting away with it. Bart was stunned; he'd never seen anybody antagonize a chute fighter quite like that before. The flank man was stunned, but he was the first to recover. "You'd better get out of here in a hurry," he growled, "before he kills us all!"

Bart pulled the rein again. His helper held the horse tight—and at a full arm's length—while he took his measurement. John, in the meantime, had moved in close thinking he might have to hold the bronc's head after all. When Bart slipped into his saddle, John growled, "Stick him right here . . . ," and he gestured toward the horse's neck with his hand formed into a blade shape like a karate chop, ". . . and stick him every jump!"

Bart put the stirrups on his feet, gripped the swells with both hands and pulled himself down in his saddle. When he lifted the slack out of his rein, Empty Saddles—the old pro—reacted to the movement and started in the chute, throwing his head and hopping up in anticipation. By then Bart was nodding for the gate and they flew into the arena.

The bronc was nasty. He reared out and then bolted, taking two strides running before he blew up. Then he jumped left and right and left and right, changing leads every jump. No two jumps were the same. He'd roll his body one way and then the other depending on which side he was kicking to. He was walking on his front end at the same time which made his timing erratic. In short, he was horrible to ride.

Bart marked him out cleanly when he reared out of the chute. He held his feet in the front end through the short run until the horse blew up and committed himself. He spurred him three jumps after that, mostly out of time, searching for the bronc's rhythm that just wasn't there. Finally, he dillied to the left when he should have dallied to the right and the bronc's side to side action sent him flying. Empty saddles.

He picked himself up out of the dirt, grabbed his hat and headed back toward the chutes. He was happy with the way he spurred the horse out and came charging, but was disgusted with the result. Shrugging off his disappointment he made his way over to his dad's chute to see if he could help out. John had watched him ride, but didn't have time to dwell on what he'd seen. He had a helper on the back of his chute, so Bart found his way out of the arena and stood along the fence to watch him ride. He was unbuckling his chaps when the cowboy next to him looked over and said, "Don't feel too bad. I've seen him do that to a lot of good bronc riders."

"Well, he didn't do it to one today," Bart answered—disgusted.

Half Velvet bucked under several different names throughout an all-star career in response to different promotional campaigns, being called Indian Sign, Coors Lite and One-Eyed Skoal in addition to Half Velvet at various times. John had ridden him on numerous occasions and he was one of his favorite horses, consistently carrying him to the pay window. Half Velvet was the last bronc John got on at his eleventh and final National Finals Rodeo in 1978. He and John were the models for the James Sutton Memorial Bronze.

Half Velvet always bucked the same way. He got in the air with a big kick and stretched out, his front feet off the ground. He held his head up when he bucked, his long mane and tail flying. John always rode him the same way, too, exactly as he was immortalized in metal. It's debatable whether John ever drew a horse he liked to ride more than Half Velvet or ever had more fun riding than on that day in the Crystal Springs Ranch Arena. Five years into his second retirement, surrounded by his good friends, his son, and a knowledgeable crowd of raucous and appreciative rodeo folks, he beat a great bronc to the punch every jump, setting his feet in perfect time to make a classic bronc ride.

As the pickup man set him back on the ground, the roar of the crowd echoing around that little amphitheater was deafening. The people cheered on and on. John felt self-conscious about the appreciation being heaped on him so heavily and at such close quarters. He tipped his hat to acknowledge the compliment he was being paid, something he rarely ever did out of sheer modesty, he was that moved. He was eighty five points—the same score he had on the horse back in 1978 at that last NFR. It's debatable which ride was more fulfilling and, ironically, more disappointing at the same time—he won second place both times.

After picking up his check, and with Bart behind the wheel of the car once more, they headed back to Ponca where John had another check waiting for him. He'd won the bronc riding there. Later, rolling out of Ponca onto the open road, John pulled both checks out of his pocket and holding them up with a satisfied air, added them up. He turned to Bart with an amused look on his face and said, "I believe I filled my permit this weekend."

Epilogue

Today Bart says, "I never got on very many practice horses. I bought my permit (in 1983) and I'd enter a pro rodeo and go get drilled and do it again the next week." His career built momentum as it progressed. As he gained in experience he kept getting better. He qualified for

Notice the family resemblance? That's John McBeth (Top) on Deacon Brown at Chicago, Illinois, in 1969, and son Bart some twenty odd years later at Ponoka, Alberta. Top photo by Bern Gregory Rodeo Photographs, Dickinson Research Center, National Cowboy & Western Heritage Museum. Bottom photo by Dave Jennings.

sixteen Prairie Circuit Finals rodeos. He went to the *National* Circuit Finals. From a fella that had not ridden a whole bunch before, there emerged a national-class bronc rider that was a threat to win every time out.

Bart won his card in 1987. He married his wife Eunice in 1988 and they started a family a few years later. He went the hardest he ever did in 1990. He had mouths to feed and although for Bart, rodeo paid for itself—and then some!—it never paid the whole bill. But he kept going, and he kept winning. He came home from a "World's Toughest Bulls and Broncs" rodeo one time in a car with three other guys and they had just won $14,000 between them. And Bart had a big chunk of that. So rodeo contributed to his bottom line and with the support of his wife and family, he got to go.

Bart was always humble about having a famous father. Maybe it was because at the pro rodeos he was hauled to as far back as he can remember most everybody there was famous themselves or had a famous father in the rodeo world. Maybe it was because trying to measure up to his dad's accomplishments was humbling. Maybe it was because he's simply humble by nature. He still says things like, "I bucked off about two dozen head before I got my first one rode . . . ," and he laughs. When asked about his sixteen appearances at the Prairie Circuit Finals rodeo he doesn't have a lot to say, but then quips, ". . . and in all those times I never did win it . . . ," and genuinely laughs again. But those who rode broncs back in the day when Bart was competing easily ignore the self-deprecating facade. They remember the frequency with which his name appeared in the rodeo results printed in the *Prorodeo Sports News*; they remember the bronc rides he made and the scores he consistently racked up on his way to those sixteen circuit finals qualifications; and they remember all the times he took their fees home in his pocket.

John says, "Bart was very talented—and capable. He just never went hard enough to hit it big."

Bart McBeth in the second go-round at Cheyenne Frontier Days in 1993. He said about this ride that, ". . . nobody knew the horse . . . sometimes you have to rely on your own assumptions and experience as to what rein, or what will work on a particular horse. Sometimes it works and sometimes it does not. It worked this time and I remember it fondly." He placed in the short-go and average at the "Daddy of 'em All." Photo by Dave Jennings.

MONKEYSHINES

Larry Clayman, a third generation bullfighter and lifelong animal trainer, had a part in the movie J.W. Coop (he played a rodeo clown). He was featured on ABC's Wide World of Sports and appeared in an episode of The Streets of San Francisco.

I'll tell you a story about the time a couple of friends of ours came to our local rodeo here in Burden. Larry Clayman was a bullfighter and rodeo clown. He was working the Burden rodeo fighting bulls, and entertaining the crowd. He also had a specialty act he performed between events with the other friend of ours, Todo. Todo was a chimpanzee. Larry had raised him like a child from the time he was a baby. Todo took baths, he ate at the table—and bussed his own dishes—he even used the bathroom and wiped and flushed. He could do everything a person could except talk. He lived in a cage in the back of Larry's truck when they were on the road. The cage was never locked, but when Larry had to go in somewhere or he needed Todo to go to bed, he'd tell him, "Get up there in your cage, now," and Todo would do it. Larry and Todo were buddies.

Todo was a big hit at the Burden rodeo on Saturday afternoon. He had a cowboy hat on, and chaps and a leather vest and boots. He strutted into the arena like a cowboy out of the old westerns on his way to a shootout. Of course chimpanzees have a kind of bow-legged walk naturally. The crowd loved it. He was an instant celebrity.

That night there was a big dance on the tennis courts beside the fairgrounds. The courts were lighted and had a nice surface for dancing and there was a great turnout.

Todo and Friends. From left: Larry Clayman, Paddy, Todo and Squirrely Shirley. Foxie Photo.

Francie and I were there and we danced a little and visited with friends. I noticed one of the locals there, a fellow named Bob Bagley, who lived in a house right by there, up against the tennis courts and the fairgrounds. Bob was an oil field pumper and he liked his beer. His wife was there, too, and you could tell Bob was in high spirits because he was dancing up a storm. I guess Bob had an excuse for blowing off some steam. He typically worked a six-day week and that Saturday had been no exception. He told me he'd hated missing the rodeo that afternoon and asked me about what had gone on, but he was pretty well lit and with the music and the commotion we didn't talk much.

The next morning Larry Clayman came down to the Cowboy Shop where I was working on a saddle. I told him I'd been over at the concession stand that morning, getting a cup of coffee and some biscuits, and I'd seen Todo. The seniors had set up a food stand under the grandstand there at the fairgrounds and I guess when Todo smelled the food he crawled out of his cage in the back of Larry's truck and went down there looking for something to eat. While I was sitting there enjoying my coffee some of the kids got to playing with him and messing around with him, and one big kid of about high school age got out his rope and tossed a loop over Todo's head.

"What'd he do?" Larry wanted to know.

Well, I told him that Todo had one hand inside the loop where it was around his neck and the other one on the tail of that rope, and darned if he didn't pull that kid over on his face!

We had a good laugh at that.

"People don't understand how strong a chimpanzee is," Larry said. Then he asked if the kid was okay.

I told him the boy was all right, but those kids all took off after Todo when he threw off the loop and ran into the floral hall over by there. This was a big building, probably thirty or forty yards long down the center aisle, where the 4-H and FFA had set up their exhibits of flowers and vegetables and all the stuff they'd grown. I hollered at those kids as they ran in the door, but they didn't hear me. So I ran down the side of the building figuring I'd catch 'em when they came out the other end. I didn't think they could catch Todo but I wanted to make sure—for their own good.

I told Larry that Todo came tearing out of that door in the lead. He had something in his hand. I didn't know what it was, but he'd obviously picked it up in the hall—he didn't have anything when he went in through the other door. Well, before I could call to him or anything, he took off at a dead run across the field by there, and as he was making his escape, he reached up and took a big bite out of whatever it was he was holding.

"Well, I mean to tell you!" I told Larry. "He *immediately* spit it out, threw it down, and ran even faster, going, 'Blubula, blubula, bluh, blub, poot, patooie,' as he went!"

I told Larry that those kids came charging out of the building right then, and I collared the big one. He had a scrape on his nose that was oozing a little blood. I asked him what was going on—like I didn't know.

"He grabbed something on his way out the door!" the kid said, "and stole it!"

I walked over to where I'd seen Todo throw down his booty and picked it up. It was a big red onion with a bite out of it! Larry and I had a good laugh about that.

A few minutes later some of the local boys came drifting into the shop, like they would do sometimes, to hang around and talk about nothing much. None of them recognized Larry from the rodeo because he wasn't in his clown makeup. They thought he was just another cowboy. They were followed a minute later by Bob Bagley, the oil field pumper. Bob sure didn't know who Larry was, because he'd missed the rodeo altogether.

Well, Bob came right into the middle of the group and he looked real upset. Now you've gotta understand that Bob talks real slow, and he talks through his teeth, so you have to really listen to understand what he's saying.

"Yer never gonna guess wha' happent to me!" he said.

Nobody said anything. They just looked at him. So I bit. "No, we probably won't, Bob," I said. "What happened?"

He said, "I went to that dance las' night and I had a little too much of that beer." He threw a sheepish look at the group, but nobody argued with him. "When I got home I passed out on the couch. And when I woke up this mornin' I could hear water runnin' in my bathroom. Now, I know that mama got up and went to work 'bout eight o'clock, so I hadda wonder, 'who's runnin' th' water in my bathroom?'"

He looked around at us and saw that he had our

Todo practicing good hygiene. Here getting a bucket-bath at the rodeo from Larry Clayman. Photo from the Larry and Renee Clayman Collection.

attention. He went on.

"So I get up off the couch and I've got a turrible

headache. It tuk me a second but I got my bearings and walked over and pushed open th' bathroom door, and you ain't *never* gonna b'lieve what I seen. . . ." He stopped and looked around at the boys again.

"What'd you see, Bob?" I asked.

"I seen a dang monkey! . . . standin' up on *my* sink, brushin' his teeth with *my* toothbrush!" He had a faraway look on his face, like he still couldn't believe his own eyes. The boys were quiet for a second, and then all hell broke loose as they cracked up.

Over the noise, I said, "Bob! You had too much to drink!"

"I know! I know!" he agreed. "I went back in and set down in my recliner right quick an' shut both my eyes real tight."

"What happened then?"

He said, "It got real quiet. Too quiet. It got me to worryin'. So I got to thinkin' maybe I better open up my eyes an' see what's goin' on." He paused and looked around at the fellas again, like he was afraid nobody'd believe him. "So, I opened up one eye and you ain't never gonna guess what I saw. . . ." Nobody said a word. "I saw another eyeball that weren't a foot away!"

"What'd you do then?"

"I just tightened up right quick! I didn't know what was goin' on! I didn't know what to do, so I shut my eyes real tight. And then a minute later I heard the door slam so I got up and locked it." He had a pleading look on his face when he added, "I've just gotta tell somebody. There's a damn monkey out there somewhere!"

Larry Clayman was laying on the floor of my shop he was laughing so hard. I thought he was gonna bust a gut.

ONE DEFINING MOMENT

*"Tell John I said that Francie should have gone into
the Hall of Fame with him."*
Tom Reeves

The kid was born a cowboy. He'd been in the saddle
since he could walk. His dad, Dean, raised quarter horses
on the Cheyenne River Indian Reservation in Eagle Butte,
South Dakota, and there were always colts to be ridden. He
remembered that as a young boy he could hear some of
them stomping and kicking down their stalls from the
house they were so wild. He cowboyed up at a young age.

He and Dean saddled up Old Gray one day. He was a
fairly gentle 1500 pound Percheron they used for pulling,
but when you tossed a bronc saddle on Old Gray and
spurred him a little he morphed into a classic jump and kick
nineteen or twenty point bronc! Tom weighed about a
hundred pounds. Old Gray won. He bucked Tom off on
his head and put the hurt on him. Tom told his dad, "I'm
not getting on him again, until I've been to that school."

That school, of course, was John McBeth's rodeo school
over in nearby Onida. Tom came to study the bronc riding.
Riding broncs was a lot different than riding colts—which
he had down cold. It was obvious he had tons of talent, but
he rode the broncs like he rode the colts. He was "ranch-
riding" everything he got on. He'd pull on his rein and
stick his feet in the belly and go. When he did start to spur
he was behind and slow, not crisp, in his "stroke." He was
kind of messing around, too, not taking the whole deal as
seriously as he should. He was fourteen years old.

Now there's a kind and gentle side to everything—but
this ain't it. This was Bronc School, where everyone, no

matter what their skill level or experience, gets tested—
that's the point. Tom was getting by on skill alone, going
along in that cloud of teenage bliss, when he ran into a
medium-sized, average looking, red dunn horse aptly called
Contrary and branded X27. Tom knew of the horse. He
was an old Bud Annis horse. Bud was an Indian stock
contractor and had sold the horse to Jim Sutton who was
supplying the stock for the school.

Contrary was a bad dude in the chute. He had a
reputation for throwing a fit. He'd flip, so they typically
tied him in. When he came in the chute John said, ". . .
don't tie him in." So Tom saddled him up and climbed on.
Contrary flipped and mashed him good. His spur got hung
on a chute rail and the spur strap broke. Tom clambered off
the bronc and went to fix his equipment. It took about 30
minutes. When he came back over to the chute he saw
Contrary standing right where he had left him, still saddled,
no tie rope.

He asked if he could put a neck rope on him and John
said, "Nope." So now the bronc riding had his undivided
attention. He was being tested. Tom slipped into his
saddle as fast and smooth as he could, trying to get out
clean, but at the first rattle of the gate Contrary smoked him
on the latch post again. When he reared up, Tom spurred
him out good and held on through the mashing. When the
bronc broke into a good jump and kick out in the arena
Tom rose up in his saddle and ripped him every jump. His
feet were snapping off the cantleboard and jumping to the
mane.

A cheer rose from the bucking chutes as the other
students caught the thrill.

"Give it to him, Tom!" John hollered. "Charge!"

But the horse and rider heard nothing. They were
locked in that perfect zone—that place where athletes and
inventors go: where instinct rules, impulse takes over,
desire is animate, and genius is unfettered; that place where

second sight exists, inspiration runs rampant, and mortals find immortality. They were the living embodiment of the old saw about the horse that couldn't be rode and the cowboy that couldn't be throwed. John yelled, "Pick him up, boys!" when he figured it had gone on long enough. Still, Contrary bucked hard clear to the pickup man, and Tom, drenched in the ecstasy of conquest, lifted up the bronc with his rein and charged, and kept charging, immersed in smooth chaos. The pickup men intruded to break up the action. That was the first bronc Tom rode right.

More than one cowboy who saw his ride that day and followed his success through the years to come said that was the defining moment in Tom's career. From then on he was, "On his way . . . ," as John himself said. "That ride was pivotal in his career. That ride made him. After that he drilled holes in everything he got on." He took to the bronc riding like an eagle to an updraft.

He went home from the school and got ready for the high school state finals rodeo. The day before the finals started he and Dean put the saddle on Old Gray one more time. Tom spurred him for six seconds before the big bronc got him. So, they saddled him up again the next morning before leaving for the rodeo. Tom gave it to Old Gray good.

That year at the state finals—his freshman year—Tom made the high marked bronc ride of the rodeo. The following year he was the National High School Saddle Bronc Champion as a fifteen year old sophomore. When he was a junior he did all right, but slipped a little bit. He went to the finals with some friends and started ". . . having too much fun," in his own words. He didn't place. His dad had noticed a tendency to have too much fun with his friends living on the rez, too. It was a tough situation. Tom attended a boarding school on the reservation fifty miles from home. He would ride six miles on horseback to a neighboring ranch and catch the bus to school. Then he would spend all week away from home and his parent's influence. On Friday the bus would drop him off six miles down the road and he'd make the long ride home for the weekend. His dad was worried that Tom was falling into some bad habits spending all that time away from the ranch in the company of the other kids. Dean had developed a great relationship with John so he gave him a call.

"Hey John," he said. "I'm worried about Tom running with some of these kids around here. He has a lot of talent and I'd hate to see him get side-tracked. He's wanted to be a bronc rider since he could crawl, and I want to see him give himself the chance by putting in the effort."

"That's a problem with any young kid these days," John sympathized, "wherever they live."

"What would you suggest I do?" Dean asked.

"Send him down here," John said. "We'll straighten him out."

So Tom spent his senior year of high school in Burden, Kansas, living with the McBeths and graduated from Burden High. He became close friends with John's sons, Bart and Blake. Bart was a year ahead of Tom in school and was leaving for college. So when Bart moved out of his room, Tom moved in. Blake was several years younger than Tom and became like a little brother to him, and like a little brother he took a lot of razzing whenever the three boys got together. But as so often happens with younger siblings, his survival instinct kicked in and he was soon giving as good as he got. John's wife, Francie, treated Tom like her own son and he felt right at home. John was his mentor and the bronc rider he emulated. Even at that young age Tom knew what an opportunity he'd been given and put out the effort to succeed. He went back to the High School National Finals that year and won his second championship.

He shunned the usual route for a bronc rider and avoided

amateur rodeo altogether. John signed for his PRCA permit when he was fifteen and he jumped straight to the pros. Although John was in his semi-retirement, he hauled the kid down the road some, showing him the ropes in pro saddle bronc riding. Tom would drive all night, often struggling in the bronc riding by day, while John, who was in his forties by this time, would catch up on his rest from the passenger's seat while saying things like, "I'm about through doing this . . . ," while riding well and winning consistently.

Tom Reeves (Left) with John McBeth at John's home. Photo from the John McBeth Collection.

Through John, Tom met many of the great stock contractors and rodeo producers in the game: Bennie Beutler, Harry Vold, Bob Barnes and Dell Hall. Despite his young age and lack of amateur experience he was ready, although when he and John showed up at one mid-western rodeo where Tom had drawn the bucking horse of the year, the stock contractor wouldn't let him saddle the bronc—didn't even want him to touch the horse. Tom had to wait, stewing and brewing, under the disapproving eye of the contractor for John to ride his bronc and come back over to the chutes and saddle his horse for him. Tom was pretty worked up over it and let it be known.

"That's not really right," John told the contractor as he saddled the bronc. The contractor was a good friend of his and a person he held in high regard but, still, it wasn't right.

"I don't want any *kid* messing with my best horse," the guy said.

"He's got his card, so that should be good enough," John replied and they left it at that.

Tom didn't buy for a minute that the contractor thought he was incapable of saddling the horse. He figured the guy was afraid that his prized possession was about to have it hoed out of him by an under-aged teen—a lot of people drew that conclusion when he pulled into a rodeo with John. He thought the fellow was trying to get into his head, distract him. And it may have worked. Tom threw some serious licks, letting the bronc feel the challenge and the contractor see his worst fear coming to life, before he bucked off short of the whistle. However, he may have accomplished more than he realized that day as he hauled his gear bag and saddle back to the car, shaking his head and mumbling about the way he'd been treated. That stock contractor remembered his name and never again doubted his skill—and never again used that old trick.

That was what John meant to Tom in those formative years. He helped him get going. He always kept a cool head in any situation. He set an example for Tom to follow. And that meant everything.

Tom qualified for his first National Finals Rodeo at the age of twenty one. He went to the NFR eighteen years in a row from 1985-2002. He repeatedly finished in the top handful of saddle bronc riders in the world and that consistency became a hallmark of his career. He reached the pinnacle of rodeo competition in 2001 when he was awarded the gold buckle as the World Champion Saddle Bronc Rider. Tom went on to be inducted into the ProRodeo Hall of Fame, win a silver medallion while serving as captain of the United States' championship team at the 2002 Olympic Command Performance Rodeo held in Farmington, Utah, and receive the ProRodeo Hall of Fame Mentoring Award in 2007 for his ". . . dedicated leadership in serving youth as a treasured mentor and positive role model."

He coached Ranger College in Ranger, Texas, to the 2007 National Intercollegiate Rodeo Association Championship in only his second year as their coach after the school had been without a rodeo team for the previous twenty-three years. One day he called John on the phone and said, "I don't know if I ever thanked you for the things you said to me when I was growing up or not. But, I'll say it now, thank you. In coaching these kids I find myself saying the same things to them that you said to me. I can hear you saying the words as I'm using them."

While it took a talented individual years of work and tons of effort to build such a resume, and undoubtedly contributions large and small came from a myriad of different people and places along the way, it may be that it all turned on a ride one afternoon in one defining moment.

SCIENCE PROJECT

"I never remember John rubbing it in that he won.
He was a very gracious winner."

Derek Clark

Derek Clark is a fourth generation rodeo cowboy. His great grandfather and grandfather are enshrined in the Rodeo Historical Society of the National Cowboy and Western Heritage Museum. His great grandfather, Monroe Veach, founded Veach Saddlery in Trenton, Missouri in 1919. A trick rider and roper himself, he understood the requirements for a good saddle. He began producing the premier Trick Riding saddle in the industry and later teamed up with Fred Lowry, the six-time world champion steer roper, to develop the Fred Lowry Roper, setting the standard in roping saddles and earning Monroe the title of Master Saddle Maker.

Monroe's eldest daughter, Imogene, Derek's grandmother, married Charley Beals. Charley competed in all three rough-stock events as a member of the old Cowboys Turtle Association. He won the bull riding at Houston in 1943 and 1948, the bareback riding at Tulsa in 1947, and the saddle bronc riding and all-around titles at Wichita in 1948. He and Imogene opened a second Veach Saddlery in Tulsa, Oklahoma, and maintained the family tradition of producing quality leather goods. Charley built the bareback rigging that carried his name and was used by every world champion bareback rider from 1946 to 1970. Back in the day, when you heard the words "Charley Beals," they were invariably followed by the words "bareback rigging." Those words went everywhere together like the front and back end of a horse—as in:

"He's got a Charley Beals bareback rigging," or, "He's riding a Charley Beals bareback rigging," or, "*I want* a Charley Beals bareback rigging."

As a young boy Derek puttered around his grandpa's shop doing whatever he could to help out. He learned to love the smell of tanned leather. It was the smell of family and home.

Charley Beals was inducted into the Rodeo Historical Society in 2010. His wife, Imogene Veach Beals, was the Tad Lucas Award winner there in 2001. The Tad Lucas Award ". . . recognizes an outstanding Western woman who is a champion in her field of work, and demonstrates the same creative spirit, zeal and Western values that (Tad) Lucas lived throughout her life."

Derek's father, Duke Clark, was a steerwrestler, and rode saddle broncs and bulls. He trains horses and is a successful cowboy in his own right. So, it's hard to imagine a better situation for a kid who wanted to rodeo. Derek appreciates the leg up his family's background and his ranch upbringing gave to his own career. "I was lucky even before I met John McBeth," he says.

That meeting came about in 1980 at the summer rodeo in Kansas City when Derek was nineteen. He'd already won the Oklahoma State High School Saddle Bronc Championship and made the finals in an amateur association in the bronc riding despite having very few horses under his belt. He'd started riding broncs and bulls at the pro level and so far the bull riding had been subsidizing his bronc riding education. With his ranch background and burly—one hundred and ninety pound—physique, he was getting the horses covered, but wasn't winning anything. John approached him at the rodeo that day and introduced himself. Derek knew who he was—John was a good friend of his grandfather, Charley Beals, and a friend of the family—but Derek didn't know him that well, personally. John suggested they go to some rodeos together, and Derek—like any prospective young rodeo cowboy staring at the chance of a lifetime—accepted.

"What was I gonna do?" Derek says. "When a former world champ offers to let you throw in with him, you do it."

John gave Derek directions to his home in Burden, Kansas, got Derek's card number so he could enter them both, and they agreed to meet at his house in a couple of days.

Derek moved into the basement at the McBeth home. The furnishings were spare.

"In later years they finished the basement and it was fixed up real nice," Derek says. "But when I moved in, there was just me and four walls in that basement."

John's wife, Francie, took the situation in stride like she'd always yearned for a third son, grown well beyond the "cute" stage, tracking arena dirt through her home. Without a hitch she set another plate at the table and tossed another potato in the pot.

"Francie's the greatest lady who ever lived," Derek vows. "She cooked my meals and did my laundry and put up with my coming and going and accepted me right off as one of the family." Derek attended John and Francie's 50th wedding anniversary a few years ago and showed his support at John's induction into the ProRodeo Hall of Fame in 2010 and the National Cowboy and Western Heritage Museum in 2013.

The McBeth boys, Bart and Blake, were quick to accept him. Bart was close to his age, and soon enough they'd go to a few rodeos together. Blake was younger, too young to go with them, and maybe that's why he blazed his own trail. He might have felt like he would be following the crowd to tag along behind them and echo what they'd already done. He took the grit instilled in him by being the youngest and applied it to his own life path.

"He ended up with the best job of any of us," Derek

observes.

At that time John was working to build his business, The Cowboy Shop.

"Everything John did was toward his business," Derek says. "He was rodeoing at that time to supplement his income and support his family. I never saw John McBeth not taking care of business."

Derek tried to help out. He was making knots and hondos in the ropes that John sold. It was tedious work, and repetitious, and boring. He was rarely at the shop before noon. He wanted to go rodeoing.

John would have them entered when it was time to hit the road. They'd take off in his blue van. That led them one August day to Kankakee, Illinois. Derek had drawn the infamous Ingemar Red—the scourge, the terror.

John didn't tell Derek what a mean-nasty Ingemar was. How he would maliciously, and intelligently—and by design—try to kill you in the chute. Derek was just a young kid at the time, and he didn't want to give him too much to think about. They tied the bronc in. They tailed him and they *blindfolded* him—that's something you rarely ever see. But in Ingemar's case it was SOP—Standard Operating Procedure. Derek got the idea. He'd never seen such drastic measures employed before just to mount a bronc. John told him to do everything just like he'd explained it and he'd get him rode.

"I ain't worried about gettin' him rode," Derek said. "I'm worried about him killin' me before I get the chance."

But he was game. That's one reason John had approached him that day in Kansas City—he was an incredibly tough competitor.

"He had an unbelievable amount of try," John says. "That was probably his greatest attribute."

Ingemar was wired. He'd spasm with every touch, kicking the back of the chute and jerking at the head rope. He was snorting like a bull at a bull fight below his blindfold. His attitude was clearly anti-cowboy and he was pissed off.

"So, I climbed in there," Derek remembers. "And John said to me, 'Don't worry, because I'm taking all the chances, because I'm running the head rope and if I let go you're dead.' Now, I didn't understand that at the time, but it got funnier and funnier over the years."

With John's help Derek got out clean. The bronc vented his frustration at his inability to hurt the cowboy in the chute by, ". . . damn sure trying to buck me off in the arena."

Derek got him rode but he didn't win anything, and maybe he wasn't supposed to. He was bigger and stronger than your typical bronc rider. He carried a 5'10", 190 pound frame as opposed to the more typical jockey-like 5'6", 140 pounds of most rough-stock riders. He'd been riding an old Hamley "Association" saddle passed down through his family from his grandfather to his father and finally to him. It was too small. It was almost impossible to spur cramped in that old Hamley. He just couldn't get the extension clear to the front end like he needed to.

As Derek says, "They turned him loose and I rode him. But true to form it wasn't very pretty . . . at all." But he took a big step that day. He got by Ingemar Red. "And more than that . . . ," John says. "He didn't just 'get by him,' he did it his way!"

Back in the blue van and headed for the next one, John was coaching Derek up—like he always did, for everybody. He talked about loosening up in the saddle, "getting out of the strength bind," and riding the horse, not the saddle. He talked about lifting on the rein instead of pulling. "John was a master of his rein and his feet," Derek says. "They can say all they want about all these other bronc riders, but they couldn't hold a candle to him—in my opinion."

But now John was faced with an unusual situation. He was tasked with coaching a student who had very different attributes than he had. As bronc riders they were polar opposites: Derek was big, John wasn't; Derek's main attribute was his strength, John's was timing and balance. John has been heard to remark, "There's very few people alive that can pull a horse up, pull themselves forward in the saddle, and still have the strength to lay back and get their feet into the neck." He was considering Derek's unusual size and strength and his unorthodox riding style when he turned to him that day in the blue van outside of Kankakee and quipped, "I guess you'll be my Science Project." He was committing to coaching a talent that couldn't ride the way he rode. Believing that there was more than one way to ride a bronc he was already looking outside of convention for things that would help Derek ride his own way, develop his own style. He must have sensed that in this partnership he stood to learn as much as Derek—after all, he'd admitted it was *his* experiment.

John drove for a while, and started telling rodeo stories to pass the miles. He told great rodeo stories then as now, and Derek was a nineteen year old sponge. He was a fourth generation cowboy so he'd heard more than a few rodeo yarns in his short time, but he hadn't heard McBeth's stories. As John told him about horses here and horses there, Derek sat back and listened, overcome by the turn of fate that had put him exactly where he wanted to be. The miles and the hours flew by as they took turns swapping tales. Then—all at once—in a way that Derek would come to associate with John, the older man abruptly pulled onto the shoulder of the road in the middle of nowhere and announced, "I'm played out. You're going to have to take it. Just drive as far as you can. And," he added, "we don't have a lot of time to spare, so put your foot in it."

Derek took the wheel and drove on through the night. Hours later, as the sun was coming up and light was starting to filter into the van, John suddenly sat bolt upright, immediately awake.

He said, "Where are we?"

Derek told him.

"How many miles to go?"

"About a hundred and fifty," Derek said.

"How fast you going?" John asked just as the van floated over a high spot in the road and they were weightless for a second.

"Doin' ninety, got 'er floored," the answer.

"Well, we got 'er made now time-wise. So slow this son of a bitch down."

"You told me to hurry."

"One thing you're gonna have to learn is when to speed up and when to slow down . . . just like in the bronc riding," John said. "Now let up. We got plenty of time."

That day at the rodeo, as so often happened in Derek's experience, he was yawning and tired. He noticed that John looked rested and alert.

"Why're you always so tired?" John asked.

"Oh . . . I don't know," Derek said. He was learning a lot about traveling the rodeo road just by paying attention.

During that first year Derek's bull riding was still financing his bronc riding. John enjoyed his bull riding as much (maybe more) than Derek did. "He loved to pull my rope," Derek says. He was entering the bull riding everywhere they went—unless John would forget to enter him in the bull riding, which happened once in a while. "And I've never forgiven him for that!" Derek adds, laughing. "I don't think he forgot at all, I think he figured we wouldn't have time to get to wherever we were going next if we hung around for the bull riding."

Derek lived in the McBeth household from that July, 1980, meeting in Kansas City until the following spring of 1981. It was during the winter of 1980-81 that John designed Derek a new saddle. He made a tree with a longer seat, lower cantle, and vertical swells that fit Derek's size and build. He had John Willemsma, the best saddle maker in his shop and a leather craft artist-in-the-making, do the actual build.

"Not only did he teach me how to win, but he built me a saddle to win in," says Derek.

It was that spring that he finally started winning a little bit here and there in the bronc riding. At a rodeo in Austin, Texas, that summer he got on one, ". . . and everything John had been telling me just clicked," he says. "I never really enjoyed riding bulls but it was something I could do, and it paid my way so I could travel with John. But I really enjoyed—not *riding* bucking horses—but *spurring* bucking horses." As he got better at it his passion focused on the bronc riding. Contrary to the bull riding, when you're riding a good bronc right you're not really working all that hard. The rhythm, the weightlessness, the feeling of flight as you vault into the air, like on some crazy amusement park ride, is exhilarating. About this time Derek discovered he was a bronc rider at heart.

He went down the road the rest of that year on his own, finding success in the bronc riding, and rarely got to stop in at the McBeth's. Then in July of 1982 John called and wanted Derek to haul a new kid along with him. The kid had a real shot at winning the saddle bronc riding Rookie of the Year in the PRCA, ". . . but he needs to go to more rodeos than I can go to," John told Derek. The kid's name was Tom Reeves. Like Derek before him, Tom had been bunking at the McBeth's. He'd moved into Bart's room the previous fall when Bart went away to college on a cross country and track scholarship. Tom spent his senior year of high school soaking up bronc riding tips from John, and won the National High School Saddle Bronc Championship for the second time that summer.

When Derek showed up at John's house to pick Tom up, John had a big run all planned out for them. "I've always questioned that run Mr. McBeth mapped out for us," Derek laughs. They went to Shawnee, Oklahoma, to start it off, then to Spooner, Wisconsin, and then back to Shawnee for the second go-round. Then they drove up to St. Paul, Minnesota, and over to Madison, Wisconsin. It was a long hard trip. They didn't know each other—they had never before met. Tom, by nature, was very quiet, and conversation was hard to come by. The payoff for all their effort came when Tom won St. Paul and Madison—a couple of big rodeos.

"All the top guys were coming up to me and asking, 'Where the hell did he come from?'" Derek says. "They weren't asking me where I came from; they wanted to know where Tom came from. He was that good, that young. I told them, 'John told me to bring him.' They said, 'Well, tell John to cut that shit out!'" Derek started wondering why he had brought him, himself, when Tom was winning his entry fees.

"Tommy Reeves was an NFR caliber bronc rider even at that point in time," Derek remembers. "He rode better than guys that made the NFR. He drew NFR horses at the National High School Finals that summer and embarrassed 'em. He was that outstanding. He already had the form that took him to the title later on in his career."

John mentored them. They were getting the riding part down cold as evidenced by their growing success, but by entering them, John was showing them how to do more than win a bronc riding; he was teaching them how to make a living rodeoing. He stressed that riding correctly is the easy part. Entering, traveling, getting there and back out is the hard part. His philosophy was that you don't have to hit all the big ones, travel huge distances and compete against the toughs every day, and rely on drawing a great horse to make a living. When everybody with a bronc saddle is headed out to a big run on the west coast, sometimes it makes more sense to stay close to your home base, limit your expenses, and enter where you're sure to win—on whatever you draw. You can pay for your entire local run—fees and all—for the price of a plane ticket to the west coast. It makes economic sense.

Derek credits John with teaching him how to enter, how to set up runs to get to the most rodeos for the least expense and have the best chance of cashing in. He taught him finer things that didn't relate to the old days when his dad and granddad were riding. John had created a science to entering and travel and Derek learned it from him.

"I'm very adamant on how good he was . . . ," Derek affirms, ". . . about how to enter and where to go, taking advantage of situations. But, sometimes when you do that they accuse you of 'Ducking Off.' That's what they call it, 'Ducking Off,' when you go where the toughs aren't and you get some easy wins. But then I went up to the north country where all the top guys were entered and beat them at Bremerton, Kennewick and Ellensburg, Washington. I won Denver and Cheyenne, and then they didn't have much to say."

John used to do the same thing. He'd show up at Houston, Fort Worth, or El Paso where everybody who was anybody in the bronc riding world was entered, and take their money. So much for ducking anybody.

"John taught me a lot of things," Derek says. "But the most important thing he taught me was how to win."

John always said, "Win something every time out, no matter what you draw. Get a check, even if it's a third or fourth." Consistently getting a check keeps you positive. You never get down in the dumps. He instilled that philosophy in his younger partners.

Derek and Tommy both made the Prairie Circuit Finals Rodeo that year along with John. They rodeoed together the rest of '82 and Tommy won second in the rookie standings. Derek got off to a hot start in '83 winning at Denver. He had a good year and made his first NFR. They drifted apart after that. Derek attended school at Texas Tech and won the College National Championship in the

Prairie Circuit Finals Rodeo 1982. From left: John McBeth, Charley Beals, Derek Clark, Tom Reeves, Bart McBeth. Photo from the Derek Clark Collection.

saddle bronc riding in '84. Tom went to Oklahoma Panhandle State University.

Bart was rodeoing by that time, and over the years he and Derek went to some rodeos together. Derek was the only one of the bunch who hadn't attended John's saddle bronc school. Bart used to kid him about it, saying, "You weren't smart enough to go to the three day school, you had to go to the year long one!" But the one-year training program paid big dividends for Derek. "John not only taught me what he knew, but he added on the thing that I could do," Derek says, "ride with power."

Derek returned to the NFR in 1985 and racked up 15 NFR qualifications for his career—the fifth highest total in the history of the sport. His best year was in 1990 when he finished second in the world. "It was all because of my sterling personality that I didn't win the world," he says with tongue in cheek, referring to his propensity to speak his mind.

John was Derek's mentor and friend throughout his

Derek Clark aboard the 1982 Bucking Horse of the Year, Buckskin Velvet, at the '83 NFR. Brenda Allen photo.

career, helping him whenever and however he could. In later years when Derek conducted a rodeo school of his own he talked to John about it. John told him to apply the principles he'd learned, the principles they both believed in, and then he added, "Anybody can put on a school, but not many can teach one."

"How do you think I'll do?" Derek asked.

"I'll tell you after you do one," John answered, in definitive McBeth style.

"Look at the students he's taught," Derek points out, referring to John's record as a saddle bronc instructor. "Just between me, Tommy and Billy Etbauer we have over fifty NFR qualifications." The total goes even higher if you add in Dan and Robert Etbauer, Tom Miller, Marty Jandreau and Larry Jordan, NFR bronc riders all. Three of his students, Robert and Billy Etbauer, and Tom Reeves, have eight world titles among them.

In 1999, with his competitive career winding down,

Derek Clark credits John McBeth with the longevity of his career. He splits second and third aboard Ram Power in the 6th go-round at the 1989 NFR (Top). Still riding and winning at Lovington, NM in 1996 (Bottom). Both Photos by Dave Jennings.

Derek was elected vice-chairman of the board of directors in the PRCA. He retired from competition in 2000. Looking to improve the association by bringing more money into the sport for the contestants, Derek became chairman of the board, and served in that capacity until 2005 when an injury precluded him from fulfilling his duties and forced his resignation.

Looking back over the years and remembering the day he hooked up with John at Kansas City, he says, "I was the luckiest kid in the world. And I still feel that way. He was the greatest thing that ever happened to me."

Trying to sum up his career in a few words, he says, "Without John it wouldn't of happened . . . no, none of it."

Then he adds with a wistful sigh, remembering the way it was, "I could hold onto their heads and slow 'em down. I could pull them up and still spur. And that's the reason I got to go play. I was his Science Project."

PERFECT SCORE

Everybody in the rodeo world will recognize Hadley Barrett. He's the friend with the pleasing voice. He's been the face of rodeo behind the voice at thousands of rodeos over the years. He's in the ProRodeo Hall of Fame, the National Cowboy Hall of Fame, and has been the Professional Rodeo Cowboys Association Announcer of the Year four times. It's interesting that often our favorite stories happened back in our formative years, even for those who have accomplished so much.

When Hadley Barrett started out in rodeo he got on broncs and bulls. Later on, but still early in his career, he was doing whatever he could to stay in rodeo and do something useful, so he was running scores at the National Finals Rodeo. Yeah, running scores at the NFR, standing in the arena at the NFR, watching each animal buck past—at ground level—right in front of him. Then he would go to each of the two judges in turn and get their scores—one to twenty five points for the animal and one to twenty five for the cowboy. He'd tally the scores up on a little slate he carried for the purpose, and flash the total score up to the announcer so he could announce it to the crowd.

The closest thing comparable to being down on the turf, in the arena, at the NFR, might be standing on the sideline at a Super Bowl watching the players run and pass and hit at close quarters; or being ringside at a championship boxing match, the slap of glove leather ringing in your ears as sweat sprays through the ropes; or the thrill might be matched if you were front row at the Kentucky Derby as the field thunders past—*if* you could hop over the fence to feel the hooves pound the turf, the wind off the pack. Hadley could feel the pounding hooves through the soles of his boots. He could hear the animal grunts and the swishing of chap leather. He smelled the dirt and the rosin and the sweat. Amid all the excitement it would have been easy to get distracted from his task.

At the NFR you see a lot of good scores. With the top bucking stock and the best cowboys in the world the scores are consistently high, enough so that a lesser man might run out of fingers and toes to count on and find himself mathematically challenged by the job. Not so with Hadley. He was a quick study and fell into a comfortable routine in no time.

In spite of the quality of the competitors—both two and four-legged—not one standing world record in the rough stock events was set at the NFR. Not one. It stands to reason if you think about it, with over 600 pro rodeos held each year and hundreds of horses and bulls bucking out thousands of times, the odds are strictly against one of the 150 rides per event at the NFR being the best ever. For example, the only perfect score ever recorded in a rough stock event was in the bull riding at Central Point, Oregon, back in 1991, when Wade Leslie and the Growney Brothers bull Wolfman combined for a perfect 100 points. That feat hasn't been equaled in all the years since. The highest marked bull ride made at the NFR was a 96 by Cody Hancock in 2001. The NFR saddle bronc record was set in 2003 when Billy Etbauer racked up 93 points on Kesler Championship Rodeo's Cool Alley Dip and was only equaled when Billy and Cool Alley came back for a repeat in 2004. It proves how rare perfection is in the rodeo arena and how reluctant rodeo judges are to proclaim a ride unsurpassable.

Perhaps the most important attribute of a rough stock judge is consistency. If one cowboy and one animal are marked a certain way then every animal and every rider should be judged on the same scale. Some judges may mark higher or lower than another—just as some baseball umpires have bigger or smaller strike zones over the plate—but as long as they are consistent they afford everybody an equal opportunity. Most judges are reluctant to give a perfect score, fearing that another contestant may top that performance leaving no way to award him sole possession of first place. It's undoubtedly why there have never been perfect scores in the bareback or saddle bronc riding and only one in the bull riding—that natural, conservative reaction to hold something back, just in case the superlative comes along to top the merely spectacular.

That's not to disparage the two rodeo judges that marked Wade Leslie's 100 point bull ride. When interviewed later they both affirmed their initial judgment—that Wade and Wolfman were perfect on that day, and merited every point.

So put yourself in Hadley's boots, down on the arena floor during the saddle bronc riding. Horse after horse turned out of the chutes and cracked 'em like defiant top-of-the-line renegades, and cowboy after cowboy came spurring and riding like the world class athletes they were. Hadley put his math skills to use and totaled up some pretty impressive scores. Back in that day a nineteen or twenty point bronc and a nineteen or twenty point ride was big-time; an eighty point total would have won most rounds at the NFR. So imagine Hadley's consternation after John McBeth's ride, when he approached the first judge, Ivan Daines, to get his scores and Ivan told him he'd marked John a twenty five. Hadley stopped for a second, stunned. In his rodeo career he'd never heard of a twenty five point ride. He flashed back on the ride he'd just watched. John had marked the horse out strong and spurred the second jump, setting his feet in the neck, toes turned out. And every jump thereafter was a duplicate—a quick snatch of his feet to the cantle and a sharp set of his heels into the mane. There was not a bobble or a twitch, his balance was perfect, his timing precise. He never missed a spur stroke or hung his feet in the cantle or cinch. Hadley didn't remember seeing even a slight glitch in the ride worthy of even a one point deduction. Still, he had to ask.

"A twenty five?" he said to Ivan.

"Yep," Ivan replied, moving away from Hadley, already settled in his mind with the score and positioning himself to watch the next ride.

Ivan Daines knew his stuff, there was no doubt. He had won the National Intercollegiate Rodeo Association Saddle Bronc Championship in 1966. He won the saddle bronc riding average at the NFR in 1970. He had already qualified for the NFR on numerous occasions and would go on to a total of six NFR appearances in a career that would culminate with his induction into the Canadian Professional Rodeo Hall of Fame. He says today that he, ". . . always used the full range of points from one to twenty-five on every ride and every horse." There were no scores that were off-limits or taboo to use. When he saw a perfect animal or a perfect ride he would, ". . . mark it a twenty five, and if another ride came along that was that good it'd be a twenty five, too."

Hadley wasn't surprised when the other judge marked John's ride a twenty three, but he wondered where the two point deduction came from—he hadn't seen it. He figured maybe the judge was being conservative, holding back a few points in case the superlative came along to top the spectacular. It was the only twenty five point ride Hadley ever saw.

GREATEST GO-ROUND

This story was written just as John told it to me.
Thad Beery

I'll tell you about the greatest round of bronc riding I ever saw. To put it in perspective, however, you have to know that I regularly entered a hundred and fifty or more rodeos a year throughout my career. I entered about thirty or forty rodeos a year in my "semi-retirement" and I rode broncs until I was forty-eight years old. Now when I say ". . . the greatest round of bronc riding I ever *saw*" that includes all the rodeos I attended when I wasn't up that day—maybe I was up the day before or the day after, or maybe I watched an afternoon perf and wasn't up until that night. It includes all the rodeos I judged, all the rodeos I went to after I quit riding, and even all the rodeos I've watched on TV. So we're talking about thousands of perfs I've either been a part of, or watched, in one way or another. And I was privileged, now that I think about it— privileged is the right word—to have been a part of the greatest go-round I ever saw.

It was at the NFR in the late '60's. It makes sense it would be at the NFR. You've got the best bronc riders in the world and the best pen of broncs—cherry-picked from among all the stock contractors in pro rodeo—matched up against each other. It doesn't get any better than that. Yet, of all the rounds I've seen at the NFR, this round stands out in my mind for its . . . excellence.

Bill Smith had a mare that I can't remember the name of . . . I wish I could, but it's been almost fifty years ago. . . . Anyway, this mare was temperamental, and her owner was telling Bill before the rodeo that he had to saddle her just so and he had to measure his rein just so, and he had to do *everything* just so to get the mare to really do her thing—to get the best out of her. Well, the guy's going on and on, and pretty soon Bill just tells the guy, "*You* saddle her up, and *you* measure the rein, and I'll just take her right there." So that's what they did. And Bill made what may have been the greatest bronc ride I ever saw. Now Bill made a lot of great rides—I saw plenty of 'em—but I don't believe I ever saw anybody spur a horse sharper than Bill did that mare. And whether it was that the owner set the saddle just right or measured the rein where the mare was most comfortable I don't know, but she bucked, lights out, like the world beater that night.

In fact, just to show you how good that ride was, consider that Roy Rodewald, a cowboy's cowboy and a great bronc rider in his own right, split second and third on Descent. Now, you know that Descent went on to win six of those silver halters they give to the bucking horse of the year. SIX of 'em. More than any other bronc—ever. And Roy sure stuck a ride on Descent that night, too, like you just didn't ever see happen to that big yella gelding. Yet with Descent at the top of his form and Roy making, probably, the ride of his life, they split second.

They tied in the round with Larry Mahan, the greatest all-around hand of that era. He had Hyrum Special. Now if you put a ride on Hyrum Special, you're supposed to win the bronc riding just about anywhere you go, whenever you go there. Just goes to show how good that round was.

Well, I was feeling pretty bad when I sneaked in for fourth place on Sage Hen. She was a great mare and I'd won a lot of money on her. In fact she was probably my favorite horse to draw in the whole world, and the one I'd have picked before-hand if they'd have given me my choice. Yet, all I placed was fourth. I was kind of hanging my head walking out of the arena, but then it dawned on me that fourth was all I could do because of how everybody

In the "Greatest Go-Round" Descent exits the chute and puts a big move on Roy Rodewald (Top). He circles around to the left and really catches some air (Bottom). Bern Gregory Rodeo Photographs, Dickinson Research Center, National Cowboy & Western Heritage Museum, Oklahoma City, Oklahoma.

Still circling Descent lays his ears back as Roy sticks it on him (Top). The bronc comes clear around to the left corner of the arena where he ends up spinning (Bottom).   Bern Gregory Rodeo Photographs, Dickinson Research Center, National Cowboy & Western Heritage Museum, Oklahoma City, Oklahoma.

else was drawn up. That was the most intense go-round I ever saw.

John McBeth aboard Sage Hen during the "Greatest Go-Round" at the National Finals Rodeo Oklahoma City, Oklahoma, 1967. Bern Gregory Rodeo Photographs, Dickinson Research Center, National Cowboy & Western Heritage Museum, Oklahoma City, Oklahoma.

OLD TIMERS

Some of the names have been changed. But rest assured, it happened!

Trey Thomas was a bronc rider from the old school. That would be the School of Hard Knocks, back before rodeo had real schools. He grew up working dawn to dark on the family ranch, feeding cattle in the wintertime, branding and doctoring in the spring, and putting up hay in the summer. By the time he was twelve years old he'd spent long days and weeks in the saddle on round-up in the fall, forty miles from home.

About that time he started breaking horses around home and for some of the neighboring ranchers. He soon earned a reputation as a hard man to unseat, which was a double compliment since he was really still a boy. Long before he dropped out of school Trey knew he wanted to be a bronc rider, so by the time other kids his age were going to the prom he was headed down the road earning his keep with his saddle. It took him awhile to be accepted by the old timers who dominated the rodeo circuit in those days, but in time he proved his mettle and became one of the boys. He learned to drink and he learned to fight (although not all that well since he was pretty small), but he never took to cussing; it just didn't fit his personality. He was quiet and soft spoken. If he saw a bull charging headlong down an alleyway about to steamroll an unsuspecting cowboy he might say something like, "Um . . . say fella . . . the bull. . . ." And if he got real excited he might even point, ". . . the bull. . . ."

Since fighting and cussing weren't for him, Trey took to drinking and riding broncs and excelled at both. He placed consistently, even went to the NFR a couple of times, and he got married and raised a family in the meantime. He rode broncs well into his fifties and reached the point where he looked better on the horses than off—his bowed legs fit around the horses like a cinch, but appeared spindly and wobbly when he walked. It was at about that time in his career that John McBeth ran into him at a multiple go-round event out in Kansas. It was a blazing hot July day.

"Hey, Trey, good to see you," John said as they shook hands. "Long time no see."

"Hi . . . John . . . ," Trey acknowledged in his soft voice, displaying his patented friendly grin.

"I missed you during the first two rounds," John said. "I'm working a couple other rodeos at the same time as this one and just got back."

Trey smiled.

"How are you doin' so far?" John wanted to know. "What's your average?"

"Oh . . . ," Trey said slowly. "It used to be about a pint . . . but I guess it's up to about a quart now."

They laughed.

"Would you like to try a little?" Trey offered, pulling a bottle of Annie Green Springs wine out of his gear bag and *twisting* off the top.

"No, No. I'm not tough enough," John said, eyeing the hot wine on the hot day.

Trey took three or four big gulps, twisted the cap back on the bottle, put the bottle back in his gear bag and smiled.

They had drawn the best horses in the pen that day and went one-two in that third and final round with John out in front. And that's the way they finished in the average as well, John winning first and Trey second.

After all the years and all the broncs Trey's spurring lick had slowed down some, but it was his walk that showed his age. He walked like every bone in his body had been broken at least twice—and some hadn't healed right.

"There goes the genuine article," John thought, as Trey hauled his saddle from behind the chutes and across the parking lot to his old pickup.

It was several years later when their paths crossed again. It was at an Old Timers Rodeo in Colorado. John dropped his saddle and gear bag behind the chutes, next to where Trey sat on his saddle, leaning back on a post of the stock pen.

"Hey Trey, how you doing?" he said.

"Okay, John . . . yourself?"

"Doing alright," John answered. "Say, do you know these horses?"

"No . . . not too well."

"What'd you draw?"

"Oh . . . I got Flashy . . . a little appaloosa."

"Is he a good'n?"

"Oh . . . they say he's alright," Trey said, smiling.

"What's Dark Angel?" John asked. "Do you know him?"

"Don't believe I do . . . ," Trey answered, searching his memory.

The rodeo was being produced by Edward Staley, a stock contractor that specialized in amateur rodeos, with an occasional college or high school or Old Timers rodeo thrown in on the side. As a result, being pros, neither John nor Trey was familiar with the bronc string.

A little while later they were both chapped up and rosining their swells when Edward Staley walked behind the chutes with a load of flank straps draped over his shoulder.

Trey pointed him out to John and said, "That's the man . . . ask him."

As Edward passed by where they sat, John said, "Excuse me. If you've got a second could you tell me a little bit about Dark Angel?"

Edward stopped and looked them over where they sat in

their saddles on the ground. He gave a curt nod of recognition to Trey and looked John up and down before answering.

"Oh, she's a good little black mare," he said. "Jumps and kicks straight away—nice to ride." Then appraising them both once more with a look a man might give to a three-legged dog, he said, "Don't worry, she doesn't have a dishonest bone in her body." Then in a condescending tone, "I didn't bring anything rank this weekend . . . I don't want to hurt you *old* fellas."

When Trey Thomas laughed so hard he rolled off his saddle into the dirt, Edward got a curious look on his face and wondered what he'd said that was so hilarious. Trey laughed like he spoke—quietly. But his face turned red, his sides convulsed, his eyes watered and he couldn't get his breath. Some of the other cowboys, who had no idea what was going on, laughed just watching the fit Trey was having. John just smiled, happy that Trey was enjoying himself.

Edward waited, watching Trey try to compose himself. He still had a curious look on his face, waiting for an explanation of the joke. When Trey finally got his breath back and wiped his eyes dry, he looked up at Edward, and sputtered between a couple remaining spasms of laughter, "You don't know who he is . . . do you?" pointing at John.

"Nope," Edward said, and looked John up and down once more. Then he adjusted the load of flanks he carried over his shoulder, shrugged off his embarrassment and turned and walked away.

Later, after the rodeo was over, after John and Trey went one—two in the bronc riding, just like the last time they'd met, Edward came by and shook hands with them both, introducing himself to McBeth.

"John McBeth, huh," he said. "I've sure heard of you, but I didn't recognize ya one bit. And I'm still glad I didn't bring any ranker horses, after all. You didn't need any more horse to win today, and I don't need my best ones shined up."

They smiled all around.

TV COWBOYS

"A rodeo cowboy should be able to succeed in just about any job. Anybody who can make a living rodeoing has got to do well at whatever they choose to do."
Cotton Rosser talking about John McBeth

The National Finals Rodeo telecasts from the Myriad Convention Center in Oklahoma City had been going smoothly all week. Hadley Barrett was the anchor man stationed at the desk on what the TV production crew called the podium. From his elevated position he had a full view of the arena, the bucking chutes and most of the 12,000 spectator seats. The only obstructions in his line of vision were the TV cameras and lighting stands on the platform in front of him.

Hadley didn't man the desk alone. He was joined by a different rodeo personality—a dignitary—each day. It might be a former champion, a member of the PRCA executive board, or a movie star or recording artist, sharing impressions from live spectator to TV audience.

The third face of the broadcast team was the "man on the ground," John McBeth. John was followed everywhere he went by a mobile camera crew. They were filming while he patrolled the grounds, conducting on-the-spot interviews of contestants as they completed their rides or runs. He had a thing in his ear called an IFB, an Interruptible Feedback device that provided for what amounted to *one-way* communication between the director and the on-air talent. It allowed John to hear the audio broadcast as it was fed-back to him from a technician in the television production truck outside the building. It kept

Hadley Barrett (Left) and John McBeth (Right) bracket Randy Corley who became an integral member of the "TV Cowboys" in later years. Photo from the John McBeth Collection.

him abreast of where in the telecast they were at all times. He could hear Hadley and his guest star calling the action up on the podium. When it came time for one of John's segments in the program—professional analysis or contestant interview—he heard his own introduction as Hadley turned the television feed over to him.

John's earpiece used a "mix-minus" program that ensured that he could hear everything in the broadcast *except* his own voice or that of the person he was interviewing. This was due to the physics of audio transmission where his own words would be delayed upon their return from the truck, causing a distracting "echo" effect resonating from the IFB, or in the worst case, an audio feedback—screeching and howling—transmitted through his microphone. The mix-minus "filtered" the input from John's mike out of the feedback to avoid the problem. The only damnable part of the device was that it could be *interrupted*—hijacked by a director's intercom microphone—and then all John could hear were the boss' instructions.

Everything went along fine for nine days. Nine perfs. Hadley emceed the show, introducing each event and his co-star, adding tidbits of his personal knowledge about the proceedings and personnel as he described the action. The co-star would elaborate between rides, providing insight into their own expertise. John followed up, recapping the action from his perspective "on the ground." He elicited first-hand accounts from the contestants, delivered in the heat of battle, or nearly so, and complemented the interviews with his own observations. There was no time pressure—the show was being taped. If you did make a goof it could be edited later. An interview question could even be re-recorded if need be. There were no commercial breaks in the "tape," they would be edited in later. There was just the constant flow of rodeo action. It was very laid back. It was a day at the rodeo.

Everybody had the routine down by the last day, the tenth round. Then the game changed. The format of the show was altered from the "Record-a-Rodeo" format of the first nine rounds to a cut-and-edited production version of a tape-delayed telecast complete with commercial breaks. Tape-delayed in this instance meant that the tape was on the airwaves while the rodeo was still happening live, with only about an hour's delay in the start of the telecast from the start of the rodeo. Suddenly there were time constraints imposed on *everything*: The roughly three-hour rodeo was condensed into a two-hour telecast. Also, a sizeable portion of the already limited air time was spent in commercial break, necessitating rigid editing of each event. Some rides and runs couldn't be shown at all. You could say they fell on the cutting room floor, although they were actually deleted through the video tape recorder in the truck. Interviews, human interest pieces, event history and background and all the other side-stories that had been a part of the telecasts all week long suddenly imposed on the time available to televise the arena action and had to be run slam-bang like a city-hall press conference.

The director sat before a wall of video monitors in the mobile production control room or "production truck" parked out back of the arena. He watched video feeds from all the various input sources for the telecast, including video cameras, video recorders, graphics and slow-motion replay machines. The wall of monitors also had a preview monitor showing the next source to be broadcast and a program monitor showing the feed going out to the airwaves on the video tape recorder. The director had the responsibility of boss, and the power of god—or at least a dictator. He was the brains of the production. Everything was filtered through him like a nerve center. He saw everything on the monitors. He heard everything through his headset. He had the capability to talk to anyone on the team, announcers, cameramen, engineers, through their IFBs, and use them like his own eyes and ears. He cut that rodeo apart in real-time, as it happened, and molded an abridged version of reality for public consumption. If a ride wasn't especially thrilling he cut it. He had to. He chopped that rodeo down to its bare essence, and then he filled it back out, splicing in commercials as he went. He was manipulating all aspects of the show through that accursed IFB, the Inflexible Feedback. So what happened early on in the performance, after the bareback riding was over and the steer wrestling had begun, sounded like this:

IFB: *"JOHN, WE'RE COMING TO YOU IN TEN SECONDS TO INTERVIEW THE BAREBACK WINNER AND THE WORLD CHAMP."*

John had to find the winner. He was the second bareback rider out in the perf and John hadn't seen him for about fifteen minutes. He had been preoccupied watching the action in the arena. He couldn't afford to look away and risk missing the winning ride. He'd caught the world champ after he rode and kept him close at hand, but he didn't know who would win the go-round until the riding was over—about two minutes ago—and then the guy had disappeared.

IFB: *". . . he's had a great year, Hadley. He came into the finals in . . . um . . . about third place and really rode well. Tonight, he really put it on old Buckshot and put an exclamation point on his season's championship."*

John spotted the go-round winner and yelled over to him to ". . . get over here!" He gestured to the champ who was standing by.

IFB: *"FIVE SECONDS."*

IFB: *". . . agree. He seemed to get stronger as the year went on, and stronger as these finals went on, too. And we've got John McBeth standing by with today's go-round winner and the new world champion bareback rider, down on the arena floor: John!"*

"Thanks, Hadley. I'm here with today's winner . . ."

IFB: *"ONE MINUTE, JOHN."*

"Tell me about Baldy Sox. He looked real strong."

"Yep, he was. I've had him before, and I knew I better be gettin' some drag and settin' my feet or he'd darn sure give me a jerking. But if you can beat him to the ground he's a good one to ride. I'm glad I drew him . . . especially in the last round. It's a good way to go out."

IFB: *"WRAP HIM UP, JOHN."*

". . . came into the finals ranked fifth in the world and you were able to improve on that ranking, so you rode well this week."

"Well, thank you . . . I drew pretty well and that always . . ."

IFB: *"MOVE ON TO THE CHAMP, JOHN."*

"Thanks . . . and congratulations!"

John shifted the microphone over to the world champion.

"Well, champ! It didn't . . ."

IFB: *"THIRTY SECONDS, JOHN."*

". . . were taking the conservative route here tonight in spite of your lead in the standings."

"No, I really don't think you can do that. You've just . . ."

IFB: "TIME FOR ONE MORE QUESTION, JOHN."

". . . your all on every one or . . ."

IFB: "A SHORT ONE."

". . . bucked off."

"Well, this is your third title. Was it the best one?"

IFB: "TEN SECONDS."

". . . it's hard to say. The first one was sure special. . . you know. . . because it's the first one. But later on . . ."

IFB: "CUT HIM OFF."

". . . don't know if you can get back to that level, you know."

IFB: "CUT HIM OFF."

"I got hurt and then . . ."

IFB: "CUT HIM OFF, NOW!"

". . . several years. . . Back in . . ."

"Well, you had a great year *this* year, champ. Congratulations. Hadley back up to you!"

IFB: "Thanks John. And now a word from the folks who pay the bills."

During the commercial break, the guest host, who was an ex-rough-stock rider, was poring over the PRCA Media Guide trying to get the lowdown on the team ropers—who he was very unfamiliar with—for the upcoming event.

"I'm not prepared for this," he told Hadley. "I don't know how much these guys have won, or where they're ranked . . . or even who's winning the finals!"

"Don't you sweat it," Hadley told him. "You're the guest host. I'll introduce the contestants and interject the statistics. You just talk about their performance—add a little color." That worked pretty well, but the fella heard himself saying the same thing over and over again as he described the action. They were *all* good ropers. He found that he lacked personal insight into the cowboy's careers, the year they'd had, and their performance at the finals that Hadley had only gained through hours and hours—and even years—of study and preparation.

When it was time for the bronc riding, John was on the back of the bucking chutes concentrating on the action when his IFB interrupted his train of thought.

IFB: "JOHN, WE'RE COMING TO YOU IN FIVE SECONDS FOR AN OVERVIEW OF THE BRONC RIDING. GIVE A SHORT INTRO."

John had no idea that was going to happen. He hadn't been told that he'd be introducing the event. He had to think fast.

IFB: ". . . now down to John McBeth at the bucking chutes."

"Thanks Hadley. . . . I'll tell you we've got a great pen . . ."

IFB: "FIFTEEN SECONDS."

". . . out today. The bucking horse of the year is in this bunch, and the best horse from last year will also be going out. Typically, they'll buck the best horses in the last performance at the NFR and today is no exception."

IFB: "FIVE SECONDS."

"With the world championship still undecided and this great pen of broncs, it should be quite a riding contest, Hadley."

IFB: "Thanks, John . . ."

John was surprised at the lack of lead time the director gave him on that deal. He decided he better leave his hammer cocked. And it was a good thing.

IFB: "WE'RE COMING TO YOU IN TWO MINUTES FOR THE TEAM ROPING INTERVIEW, JOHN."

At least that was expected. He knew he'd be interviewing the winning team.

IFB: "WE'LL ALSO BE COMING TO YOU WHEN THE BUCKING HORSE OF THE YEAR COMES OUT,

JOHN. WE WANT YOUR TAKE ON HIM."

That *could* work out, John thought—if the horse didn't buck while he was interviewing the team ropers. He positioned himself strategically, where he could see the action in the arena while he did his interview just in case.

IFB: "FIVE SECONDS, JOHN."

IFB: "... now down to John McBeth who has the team roping world champions standing by."

"Thanks Hadley. Congratulations on your second championship, you guys . . . but tell me Bob, you're the header on this team, how did you rope so well all week after hurting your hand in the first round?"

IFB: "ONE MINUTE, JOHN."

". . . gotta cowboy up and go out there and do it, you know. This is the NFR and it's what you worked for all year . . . to get here, so you just put it behind you and rope."

"Well, you roped good enough to win the hat trick—the last go-round, the NFR average, and the world. . . ."

John noticed that—sure enough—the bucking horse of the year was the next to go in the arena. He tried to watch the action over the fence while not missing a beat in the interview.

"So this is the second year in a row for you two to win the world title roping together. Was this one easier than last year?"

John held the mike up to the heeler for his face time.

"They're never easy. But I think roping together for as long as we have been is making it a little easier."

IFB: "THIRTY SECONDS, JOHN."

". . . of know what the other guy is going to do in a given situation. And we know each other's horse better, so maybe it's a little easier for that reason. And then traveling together gets easier, too. We're pretty compatible."

The bucking horse of the year blew out big, took a nasty swoop to the left, and skipped a jump, throwing off the rider's timing and catching him in the cantle. Then he took his head and really started to buck down along the chutes to the left. John was concentrating on the bronc *and* his interview when. . . .

IFB: "FIFTEEN SECONDS, JOHN. TIME FOR ONE MORE SHORT QUESTION."

"Well, you guys are both pretty young and in good health. . . ."

John watched the bronc buck into the corner of the arena while he framed his last question. The horse kind of got lost for a second like he couldn't decide which way to come off the fence. He stalled for a jump and threw the rider's timing off again.

". . . so does that mean you're going to be a threat to win the world for quite a few years to come?"

That made them smile. They were both a little bit embarrassed with a farm boy kind of modesty.

"Well, we sure hope so. It'll depend on if we can stay healthy."

IFB: "FIVE SECONDS!"

"Thank you guys and good luck down the road. Hadley!"

IFB: "Thanks, John."

IFB: "GO BACK TO JOHN FOR HIS TAKE ON THE RIDE, HADLEY."

IFB: "COMING BACK TO YOU FOR YOUR ANALYSIS ON THE RIDE, JOHN."

IFB: "While we were away the horse we were all waiting to see bucked out, John. We'll run the replay. Were you able to see it from your position?"

IFB: "FIFTEEN SECONDS, JOHN."

"I did Hadley, and I'll tell you the old bronc did not have his day today. He did a nasty little shuffle out of the box and then kind of got hung up in the corner over there and confused himself about where to go. The cowboy put a good ride on him . . . as good as I think he could have, but it probably wasn't enough horse today."

IFB: "I agree, John, he had a bad trip for him."

The Infernal Feedback kept the announcers off balance through the rest of the telecast. John came to view the device in the same way that he saw a lot of the broncs he'd ridden: Just as he was getting his act together, finding a comfort zone, the IFB would throw a hitch into his rhythm—"do a nasty little shuffle out of the box"—and he'd have to hustle to catch back up again. Good thing he was used to being in the limelight and performing under pressure.

Of course numerous interruptions occurred during the calf roping, the barrel race and the bull riding. The Interruptible Feedback certainly had a mind of its own and seemed married to Murphy's Law—it tended to not interrupt unless you were busy doing something . . . interruptible. As soon as one or the other of the broadcast team would start talking it would stir to life and inflexibly, inexorably, raise its incessant head and shower him with its Insatiable Feedback. So it was not surprising that when the telecast ended the three members of the broadcast team heaved a sigh of relief as they removed the IFBs from their ears. Lesser men might have proceeded out to the truck and stuck their Insufferable Feedback where it could do no further harm—and called it the Invisible Feedback.

THE LAST RIDE

" 'The difference between supreme confidence and
arrogance is this far,' John said, holding up his
thumb and first finger to show me the distance—and I
swear his fingers were touching."
Thad Beery

It's often been debated whether champions are born or they're made. I've been to eleven NFR's, am proud to count more than a few champions among my friends, and I can't even say for sure. Genetics plays a big part. You've got to have the strength, the balance, and an innate sense of timing to excel in the rodeo game. Yet, I know of at least one champion that claims to have been born a klutz.

In my own case I was never a great athlete. I never excelled at running or jumping or any of the "ball" sports back in my home town, but I wasn't clumsy or slow either. My dad, Harold, was a bull of a man. He wasn't very tall, but he was about that wide, too. I'm sure I inherited some of his strength. He was a cowboy, too, a roper and bulldogger, and you know it takes a lot of power to stop a steer and throw them to the ground with your bare hands.

My mom, Lorene, was a farm wife and mother. Enough said. The strength and endurance required to raise a passel of kids during those years, on the Kansas prairie, is legendary, so I sure had the genetics to excel. One rodeo publication said of me that I was a man with, ". . . superlative natural athletic ability . . ." who lacked the height or weight to qualify for the "major sports," but they may have been stretching it. Unless I come back in a super-sized version we'll never know.

You see a lot of rough-stock cowboys—especially in

these modern times—getting by on athletic ability alone. You know the type I mean, the urban cowboy with no background in riding horses or working stock. They have the lithe, athletic body of a gymnast and view the stock they've drawn like the thoughtless, soul-less apparatus found in the gym. They're successful all right—some of them hugely so—but over-reliant on their innate ability, and out of touch with the thinking, breathing and plotting mind of their adversary.

I grew up in an environment where understanding what was in an animal's mind was essential. You watched the animal, saw what they were doing and tried to get inside their head to understand why they were doing it, what they were thinking, and if you could do that—get in tune with the animal—then you were on your way to controlling their behavior, guiding them to do what *you* wanted them to do.

That was back about 1950. The U. S. Cavalry was being decommissioned as the Army was fully mechanizing; the tank, truck and Jeep were replacing the last of the horses and mules. As a result there were trainloads of horses moving across Kansas and being sold at auction. The military had had a big horse breeding program where they raised much of their own stock and many of these horses were a result of that effort, so often they were young and untrained and unbroken. My dad saw an opportunity there and started buying up carloads of those horses for about ten dollars a head. I was just a young kid then, but was quickly put to work riding the horses in a round-pen on the farm at home with a surcingle and Running W. The Running W would hobble the horse's front feet so they couldn't really buck. We didn't have a saddle at the time. My dad would drive the horses around in a circle in the pen with me on their back, getting them used to being ridden and moving out with someone aboard. Whenever dad would see that things were about to get rough—the horse showing signs of getting juicy—he would holler at me to jump off. So I had done the flying dismount—made popular by more than one saddle bronc rider showing off in the arena—hundreds of times before I even knew it was flashy.

That was how I learned to ride the horse—not the gear; to watch the horse for signs of behavior; was he going to buck, or stall, or bolt for the fence and try to jump it? After awhile I could get inside a horse's head and feel what they felt. I got good at predicting their behavior, the moves they would make. It got to where I'd move before they would—to where they were going—and be there when they arrived, still on top of them. It wasn't a matter of gripping a saddle or pulling on a rein, reacting after the fact to the horse's action and getting drug along with them by sheer strength. It was thinking ahead, leading in the dance, so to speak. Hadley Barrett, a very well-known hall of fame cowboy and a good friend of mine, once said, "It wouldn't be fair to the other bronc riders to say that John was smarter than they were, but sometimes it looked that way." Now, I know it wasn't smarts, and Hadley was right to qualify his statement. Experience, especially experience like I had—riding those horses by the hundreds at a young age, virtually devoid of gear, bareback—made me horse smart.

I owe a heck of a lot to my dad, too. He passed on a lot of the experience he had to me, told me what to look out for and what would likely happen in certain situations. Later on, we got a Veach roping saddle and used it to train the horses with, making the job a little bit easier. My dad strictly prohibited me from riding the horses when he wasn't around, though, and since I'd decided I might want to be a cowboy by this time, I had to improvise. We had a dairy with a bunch of Holstein cows that we milked. As a result, some of the best practice I ever had was riding our milk cows in that old saddle while dad wasn't around—he never said I couldn't ride the cows. You can learn an awful lot about staying in a saddle from the snaky moves some of those old ladies put on. In fact, there are some people in and around rodeo who have witnessed a wild cow riding that are of the opinion that they can be every bit as rank as the bulls. I learned a lot from those cows about staying off of the rein and not relying on it too much. There are some very undependable heads on those old cows.

I guess you could say that my saddle-cow riding career came to a halt one day when I rode one old black and white we called Sway-Back. She took one good jump out of the barn and I fell off. I slid my foot, still in the stirrup, over the seat and hung my heel in the gullet of the saddle. There I hung upside down off the side of her for about an hour, unable to get loose. She walked around the barnyard chewing her cud, occasionally looking back at me hanging there helpless. I learned a lesson about obeying my dad that day before I was able to finally get myself free, but the real lesson came from the fear that the old girl would take a rest and lay down on me before I got off.

Getting back to the question of whether cowboys are born or they're made: I guess I'd have to vote for both. How else to account for a thirty-two year rodeo career where I ranked among the elite in the sport and never was laid up because of an injury. You've got to have the genetics to perform athletically and have the endurance to succeed, but at the same time the environment you live in is crucial. Studies have shown that reaction times between even world-class athletes and non-athletes are not that much different. No matter who you are, it takes about the same amount of time for the eye to interpret what it sees and signal the brain, and for the brain to send a signal down the spinal cord to enervate the muscles. Instead, the differences in people's performance levels are determined by the laser quick interpretation the expert draws from a given situation. That boils down to training and practice— the environment. In fact, there is a thing called the 10,000-hour rule (also known as the ten-year rule) that postulates that 10,000 hours of practice (or ten years) are required and adequate to make anyone an expert at anything. That's not to say that I, or any other bronc rider, have spent 10,000 hours aboard a buckin' horse, but that we've probably spent that amount of time mentally practicing, thinking about it, going over and over different scenarios in our mind, training our brain to "see" the next jump the bronc will make almost before it happens.

How else to explain an old cowboy of forty-eight traveling down to Yukon, Oklahoma, with a body growing stiff and refusing to bounce back from soreness like it used to, reflexes that were slowing down, vision that was growing blurry—requiring reading glasses to study the judge's sheets—scoring 81 points on his last bronc ride? It had to be practice and experience giving a foresight bordering on precognition. Knowing what the horse was going to do almost before he did. Of course, that will to win has to be there, as strong and all-consuming as it ever was.

I know this because on that day I saw every move that bronc would make before I even got out of the car at the rodeo. I had drawn Red River of Rumford's, a little sorrel mare. I knew her well, having been on her before and having seen her buck several times, besides. She would come around in a circle to the right. You could lift her up and get more hang time if you rode her right. I spurred her every jump, over and over again, on an endless loop running through my mind all the way from Kansas to Oklahoma—until my legs got tired just sitting in the car. And as for the will to win? I am still rankled all these years later that I came in second.

HALL OF FAME

*"Nobody gets this far in the sport without having a
lot of people to thank."*

John McBeth

Have you ever wanted to be a fly on the wall at a big
event among famous people? Where the glitterati—the
movers and shakers of an industry, those truly
accomplished, with household names in their profession—
gather in a social setting to rub elbows with one another
and carry on conversations mined from the highest
echelons of their business. Where you could buzz around,
all but unnoticed, and flit in and out among this group or
that group of celebrities as they meet and mingle working
the room, reacquainting themselves with old friends and
striking up conversations with iconic characters from other
eras who even they may know only by reputation. You
could observe their interpersonal relationships, listen in on
their private conversations, and hear their old war stories.
Well, you're looking at the fly; and I'll tell you it was
everything you'd hope it would be.

I was privileged to be a guest of John McBeth at the
National Cowboy and Western Heritage Museum induction
ceremony for the Rodeo Historical Society held at the hall
of fame in Oklahoma City in the fall of 2013. John was
being inducted into the biggest hall of fame a cowboy can
aspire to. He was already in the ProRodeo Hall of Fame—
an incredible honor—as well as the Kansas Cowboy Hall of
Fame at the Boot Hill Museum in Dodge City—what else
can you say—Dodge City! Yet, this was the pinnacle. No
other way to look at it. The scope of the Western Heritage
Museum encompasses everyone who has made a

contribution to the American West: frontiersmen, mountain men, Native Americans, ranch cowboys, movie cowboys, rodeo cowboys, western artists, and others, with no restrictions.

I arrived at the hall for the two-day event. The ceremonies featured a Friday evening Champions Dinner with both silent and live auctions to help support the Rodeo Historical Society, followed by a Saturday luncheon—The Reride Rendezvous—with a story-telling contest, culminating with the Saturday night main event where the rodeo inductees took center stage at the podium to deliver their acceptance speeches.

When I first spotted John at the museum, he was in the company of a tall cowboy with a bona fide-rancher look to him—jeans, old boots and a well-worn hat. An official of the hall was escorting them through a metal security door that had an access pad and electronic lock into one of several huge display rooms at the facility. I buzzed up behind them like the inquisitive fly I was, intending to follow them through the door which was quickly swinging shut. I was a little late to arrive and reached out as the door was closing in my face.

"Don't touch that door!" a stern voice warned me. I desisted—the door clanked shut. A security guard approached and said, "I'll get you in there, but if you touch that door you'll be surrounded by security guards in seconds."

"This is sounding good," I thought to myself as the guard punched a code into the keypad and jerked the door open. "McBeth is already opening doors for me."

We entered a big exhibit hall where displays were being set up for an upcoming western art show. I caught up with John and said "howdy," and was introduced to his old friend and ex-employee, John Willemsma, "Long John" Willemsma, according to McBeth. Long John told me that he had made saddles, ". . . a lot of bronc saddles . . . ," back in the day, for McBeth's "The Cowboy Store" in Burden, Kansas. "I used to build a bronc saddle a week," he said with pride. In his words you could see the work shop, the tools, both men at the work bench building bronc saddles, stock saddles, roping saddles and chaps, the smell of leather in the air, the saddle trees stacked in a back corner. At the time, many of the toughs wanted Cowboy Store equipment and used their boots and saddles and leggings, Derek Clark, a fifteen-time NFR qualifier in the bronc riding being one of the more notable.

McBeth had hired Long John when he was nineteen years old and straight out of tech school, giving him his first experience in the "art" of saddle making. I say art because Willemsma had a saddle—along with an array of other objects—being set up for display in the art show at the hall scheduled to take place two weeks hence. The three of us were admiring Willemsma's latest work, a hand-tooled saddle with pure silver hand-laid conchos and one-piece hand-carved wooden stirrups. Not the sort of a saddle you would ever toss down in the dirt.

As I listened, they launched into a discussion about the finer points of braiding a rawhide round-braided six-plait saddle string, tasseled on the end with some horse hair and fancy knot work that was set over an engraved silver concho on Willemsma's latest creation—too much for my little fly's brain. It evidently is counter-intuitive that the bevel on the leather strands goes up in your hands instead of down while braiding the saddle string. Not really understanding the concept of the bevel or the finer points of braiding in general, my interest was drawn to Long John's next display, a custom leather guitar case. It was tooled in an intricate floral design with a woven-rope pattern stamped into the leather around the lid and main body of the case.

Did you draw this pattern out on paper before you started tooling it," I asked.

John McBeth explaining some of the finer points of leather working to customers at The Cowboy Shop, circa 1990. Photo from the John McBeth Collection.

"Yes," John answered. "I draw it all out on paper to scale."

"That seems to be where the artist part of the whole deal comes in," I observed. He agreed.

"So, what's that saddle worth," I asked, my attention drawn back to the saddle, my curiosity overcoming my natural inclination to avoid being nosey.

"Thirty eight thousand," Willemsma was quick to say, not missing a beat or batting an eye.

"How many hours do you have in it?" I asked him, my interest, again, overcoming my usual good manners.

"Hundreds."

Then he and McBeth launched into a discussion about who had metal-worked the conchos and who had braided the saddle strings and who had carved the stirrups for the saddle. Long John was quick to credit the other artisans that had built the various accessories he had incorporated into his saddle.

"Don't touch that door!" I was warned again as we made our way back out into the hallway. We were let out by a guard with a key code. Security is tight at the cowboy hall of fame—what with $38,000 saddles and all.

As we wandered out into the huge atrium of the hall, John bumped into a cowboy he knew from the past and struck up a conversation. I was introduced to Vernon "Dude" Smith, a bulldogger and rough-stock competitor who rodeoed in the generation before McBeth, their careers overlapping by only a few years. After a few minutes of reminiscing over old bronc rides—where no lies were told—Dude said that one time he went a whole year without being bucked off. Trust me; he had the buckle to prove it.

"I once went *three* years without being bucked off," John put in. "Then I went to the finals that year and bucked off my first three broncs in a row—boom, boom, boom . . . just like that. The next day . . ." he said. "I pinned my number on upside down . . . so the people in the grandstand would know who I was!"

Dude talked about some of the great fighters in rodeo from back in the day, when—if you were a cowboy— fighting was an occupation second only to rodeoing, and your reputation was built on both. Dude knew the guys who had whipped everybody. Some of the tough guys had built up such a reputation that nobody would fight them anymore—they'd pretty much just give them their own way. One time, Dude got fed up and knocked out one of the toughs. 'Nuff said.

John told a story about his high school days. The science teacher put his desk in the middle of a group of football players that were in the class—front row center. The teacher was also the football coach and John was a good student, so he had some idea why he was put there. One day he was late getting to school because the milk truck that picked up the milk from their family's dairy was late making the pick up. John was responsible for milking the cows *and* getting the milk shipped. So he arrived late for class, still in his "work" boots replete with cow-pie packed heels.

As he slipped into his usual seat in the front row of the classroom, the 250 pound offensive tackle next to him yammered, "I smell a farmer!" and gave John a disgusted look, turning up his nose.

"I had to stand on the seat of my desk to hit him in the mouth," John said. "It was the only way I could reach," he laughed. "Then, as he was about to pile-drive me, the 220 pound fullback on the other side of me jerks me out of the way and says to the guy, 'He's a frisky little shit . . . ain't he?'"

Francie was at the museum with John. It was obvious right off the bat why she had a thirty year award-winning career with the Mary Kay Cosmetics company and rose to the position of National Sales Director. She can work a room. She makes everyone feel right at home—wherever they are. Somehow, she is friends with people even *before* she meets them. So when they meet for the first time they are already simpatico. She is stylish and sage, and intuitive and regal, and empathetic and . . . cute . . . and everything you would think of if you thought of a rodeo champion's wife, and more. In a very candid moment she told me that John, ". . . is worried about his speech. . . ."

"He'll do fine," I said, already aware of John's ability as a public speaker.

"He's worried about losing it. . . ." she explained. "He's emotional about it. He'll be glad when he's made it through the speech part."

I hadn't considered that. John—unsure—was a new concept in my experience. But her comment brought to mind something their son Blake had said to me in an interview for this book. "He's a much more tender-hearted man than he would like for you to believe," he had told me.

John and Francie McBeth at the National Cowboy & Western Heritage Museum for John's 2013 induction into the Rodeo Historical Society. Photo by ownbeyphotography.com.

"He'll do fine," I repeated to Francie—more out of habit than conviction considering what she'd said.

At the Champions Dinner that night the special honorees receiving the Ben Johnson and Tad Lucas Memorial Awards were recognized along with the All-Around Champion of the World. A silent auction was held in conjunction with the ceremony. That's an auction where bids are entered on a bid sheet attached to each item. Bids are entered by bidder number, not name, so the auction retains a strong element of anonymity. Before dinner, everybody mingled around the two dozen or so tables set up at one end of the auditorium where all the items up for bid were on display. There were a couple hundred items at least. There were boots and hats and shirts and buckles and BIG buckles, and western portraits and rodeo artifacts— NFR jackets, rodeo photos and even photo albums of old champions from places like Madison Square Garden and the Cow Palace. And of all the items on display, the thing that caught the eye more than any other was a 2' by 3' black and white of John McBeth on KO Sundown of Kesler's. Nicely framed.

"That was in the second go-round at Houston . . . ," John said as the two of us stood in front of the picture. "I placed in the first go-round too, so I won some money there."

The picture is perfect. If you're a bronc rider—of any era—this picture is gonna hurt good. Sundown is flat "Gettin' It." John's spurring him in the mane with his toes cranked full out and his heels cocked down. He's lifting on his rein and sighting down his arm like it was a gun barrel. He has a cocky twist to his hand and wrist, an arch in his back and a "set" to his neck. Just looking at that picture would lift the heart of any old bronc rider. Every fiber of Sundown and of John is extended in perfect athletic harmony—they are each at the top of their form and elevate each other.

I watched through the rest of that night and the next day when the silent auction drew to a close—and that picture of John and Sundown held sway near the top bid of the auction.

There was also a live auction held during dinner—for the big bucks. The most memorable item up for bid—of all the high-dollar jewelry, artwork, and stud fees offered—was the trick roping package put up for bid by Gene McLaughlin, the master. Gene was being inducted into the hall for his calf roping, steer wrestling and trick roping prowess. The package consisted of two trick ropes and a half hour lesson tutored by Gene on how to use them. The bidding went up and up on the floor. The battle for the roping lessons was centered between two tables near the front of the hall. As the money escalated higher and higher, everybody in the crowd was craning their neck trying to see who it was that kept pushing the price. Finally, the auctioneer dropped the hammer and proclaimed the package "SOLD!" The winning bidder's name was announced and to everyone's surprise it was Paul Tierney's wife. Ironically, Paul was being inducted into the hall himself, for winning the 1980 World All-Around Championship. He also won the Calf Roping Championship that year on the way to his all-around title, so he's a guy that handles a rope fairly well to say the least. So, it was pretty funny that he would be taking a lesson from Gene—or that his wife would think he would need one. The room rippled with laughter. The lesson was set up for noon the next day and the public was invited. It would be held in the atrium of the Hall following the Reride Rendezvous luncheon.

One of the highlights that evening was when Tater Decker, the Ben Johnson Memorial Award winner, took the stage to give his acceptance speech. Tater, who is pushing ninety years old, had a long and illustrious rodeo career. He has won virtually every major rodeo in the country at one time or another—including Madison Square Garden, Fort Worth, Houston, Denver and Cheyenne—and takes a backseat to no other competitor. He paid a strong tribute to

Ben Johnson, the award's namesake, and the only person to win both a World Championship in rodeo and an Oscar in Hollywood—who he knew personally—saying, "Everything came easy to Ben, he was so talented." He wound up his tribute to Ben, which was supposed to be a tribute to Tater, by saying of Ben, "He was a cowboy's cowboy, and that's what I wanna be."

If you were that fly on the wall that night you'd have found that these cowboys never had it so good. The host hotel was a nine-pillow establishment. Nine pillows!

After a good night's sleep I piled in the car with John and Francie to head back over to the hall for the Reride Rendezvous—a luncheon combined with a membership meeting for the Rodeo Historical Society topped off with a story-telling session. Francie jumped in the back seat as I approached, making me somewhat uncomfortable as I slipped into the front, feeling like "ladies first" should apply—that, and it was her car.

The lunch was excellent, the meeting was just that, and the stories were over the top. John told one about a roper that was judging a rodeo. He didn't really know his way around the bucking chutes, so during the bronc riding the boys told him to "get in close" so he could see the mark-out better. A bronc knocked the chute gate open on the way out, swinging it back and laying the roper out flat on the ground in the process. Then, while everybody's attention was focused on the poor guy getting up, the bronc had made a tight little circle in the arena and was coming back around to hit the gate a second time and flatten the guy again. Everybody laughed at John's chagrin that the judge had been laid out the whole time and hadn't even seen the ride.

The prize-winning story was told by Gary Leffew. Gary and his father lived down six miles of crappy road where they had a ranch and raised bucking bulls. In addition to winning the 1970 World Championship bull riding title,

Gary runs one of the oldest and most notable bull-riding schools. One day one of their neighbor's breeding bulls got in with their herd of bucking bulls, and according to Gary, "If you're a bull and you're in my pasture . . . you're getting bucked!" Turned out the breeding bull was a great "beginner" bull, perfect for getting novice bull-riders a start. So Gary and his dad bucked the neighbor's bull and even started calling him "Neighbor."

When the neighbor eventually came over to take his bull home he found that he could no longer handle him: He'd been converted into a rodeo bull.

"I'm gonna have to take him to the sale and get rid of him," he lamented.

Gary thought he was a pretty good bull, so he bought him on the spot and saved the guy a trip to the sale barn. They put Neighbor in with their herd and all was happy, for awhile.

Then, one day Gary and his father were driving home down that six miles of crappy road and as they were going past a different neighbor's place—a fella that had just moved in that they'd never met before—they noticed one of their bulls that had been missing for several weeks was in the guy's corral eating hay with his horses.

According to Gary, his dad said, "Let's go home and get Neighbor. We'll put him in the stock trailer and go get that bull. We'll unload Neighbor in the corral and load both bulls back up together. I'll bet ol' Neighbor will just lead that other bull right in the trailer."

So they went home and loaded Neighbor up and went back over there and backed their trailer right into the guy's corral to unload their bull. They never said anything to the guy about what they were doing, they just did it.

"When we let Neighbor out of the trailer he got into a fight with the bull we were trying to get in," Gary said. "And the two of them busted through the corral fence and were fighting in the brush over on the hill beside the guy's house. Well, my dad was snapping that buggy whip he always used for working bulls and yelling 'Dammit Neighbor! I'm gonna kick your ass! You son of a &%#*@ you better get out here right now. I'm gonna kick the #&)* outta you, Neighbor, when I get my hands on you.'"

About that time, Gary noticed the neighbor peeking out his window at all the commotion, and then suddenly he ducked away from the window altogether and didn't reappear. Gary was laughing so hard he was no help at all and his dad had to load both bulls. On the way home in the truck Gary was still laughing and his father said, "What's with you, boy? You were no help at all. What're you laughing about anyway?" Gary told him and his dad laughed so hard he had to pull over to the side of the road.

"The worst part," Gary said, "was that we never did go over and explain to the guy what was going on. Within the week he had packed up and moved."

Gene McLaughlin giving Paul Tierney a roping lesson: now there's a sight. It was like watching the skillful Joe Montana throw a football around with the strong-armed John Elway. Gene spun loops big and small, stepped in and out of his spinning rope and walked loops up his back and over his shoulder; Paul could probably throw a loop through a brick wall. It'll be left up to the reader to decide which champion portrayed Montana and which Elway in their exhibition.

The weekend's ceremonies culminated with the Saturday evening gala event where the 2013 Rodeo Hall of Fame Inductees took the stage to accept their awards and deliver their acceptance speeches. The over-riding theme that ran through all the anecdotes, the laughter and the tears as the class of 2013 said their thank-yous, was that it was never about fame or fortune for these very accomplished people, but was for the love of the sport that they did what they did. They felt blessed to have been able to make a living doing what they loved and never stopped loving what they were doing. For example, Bill "Goodtimes" Feddersen took the mike and related a story about a roper friend of his who was once asked if he'd ever made a living rodeoing. "Nope," his friend replied. "I had to live off of what I made."

Only the infirmities of age had ever slowed these cowboys down. Quail Dobbs, the award winning barrel man and bullfighter and the ultimate rodeo funny man was unable to accept his award in person because of his health. Quail was released from the hospital a couple of days before the ceremony and told his family to, "Pack my bags. I've gotta get to Oklahoma City. . . ." His family was forced to say, "No, you're not," for his own good. The incomparable Etbauer brothers, Robert, Billy and Dan, who had dominated the sport of saddle bronc riding for over two decades and won a total of seven world championships between them were finally forced to call it a day. Gene McLaughlin who was finding it harder and harder to jump through loops as he neared ninety and John McBeth, the bronc rider who was still hanging up eighty point plus scores at the age of forty eight when he decided to "Spend some more time at home . . ." had finally slowed down as well.

John summed up what everyone had been thinking and talking about all evening when during his speech he spoke of the support a cowboy needs. "You don't get to this podium all by yourself," he said. "There's a lot of thanks that has to be given. I think I'd like to start with the person or persons who nominated me . . . this is an unbelievable honor. Thank you." The hall was filled with resounding applause.

"There's also a special thanks I need to make note of . . ." he continued, ". . . friends. They've been supporting me during and after an active rodeo career . . . and there's so many of them here tonight, and I thank you. . . ."

John McBeth at the podium delivering his induction speech. Photo by ownbeyphotography.com.

When he said, "This next one's a little touchy . . . ," I remembered what Francie had told me, and I smiled. "I

Where all the great cowboys go—The National Cowboy & Western Heritage Museum. Photo by ownbeyphotography.com.

want to thank everybody who came to those schools," he said in a scratchy voice, like something was caught in his throat. "You've made me very, very proud. Not only have you collectively won every major rodeo in North America. Just those few in this room have qualified for over fifty years of NFR. And there's nine world champions—nine gold buckles—in this room from those schools. There are seven in saddle bronc riding alone. And that doesn't include one in calf roping and one all-around title. You know when you teach concentration and focus and build confidence in these students they seem to win in every event. I had a letter from Derek Clark today who . . . qualified for the NFR fifteen times. I'd also like to recognize the Etbauers. They were great students. And Paul Tierney, he's the calf roper and the all-around. And one of the greatest things about him is that he rode broncs, too!" There was soft laughter at that as John added, "Not many people know that anymore." He continued, "And my son Bart—we don't get to do that very often. And family. . . . You know, I couldn't have done this, I couldn't of gotten to this spot without their support and encouragement, it just wouldn't of happened. Francie, would you stand please!" And Francie stood to rousing applause. "My son Bart and his family." Applause. "My son Blake and his family." Applause. "These guys stepped up from boys to men when I had to be gone rodeoing. It was their duty to help keep the responsibility at home, help their mother. Thank you.

"This is a very humbling experience. I remember the first time I saw this place. It was in 1965, the first year I qualified for the finals. . . . I am just as much in awe today as I was then. Can you imagine a whole museum dedicated to rodeo cowboys, ranch cowboys, singing cowboys, movie cowboys, all kinds of cowboys? And I think it was then that I decided that I just didn't have a clue how big the role of cowboy really was.

"I'm honored to be here tonight. But I want to tell you that as I stand here, the real glory and the real honor goes to

God almighty. He put me in the places that I needed to be at the times I needed to be there to make this happen.

"There was one other time that was really noteworthy in my career. My son Bart and I both qualified for and competed at the Circuit Finals together. That's the only time in my life that I really realized I was riding for second. Thank you."

The McBeth family. Back row left to right, Blake McBeth, Blake's daughter Baylie, John McBeth, Francie McBeth, Bart McBeth. Front row left to right, Bart's son Brandon, Blake's daughters Blaire and Breton, Blake's wife Shellie, Bart's daughter Mackenzie and his wife Eunice. Photo from the John McBeth Collection.

GLOSSARY OF RODEO TERMS

Anchor Binds: Small strap threaded through the bars of the saddle tree. Attach to the inner side of the stirrup leathers of a bronc saddle (the weight bearing side) so that they are fixed or "anchored" and the stirrups can't change length by slipping around the bars of the tree.

Arena: The fenced area where rodeo events are held. No standardized dimensions or shape. Usually an oblong circle roughly 150' by 200'.

Average: The average score over all go-rounds in a multi-go-round rodeo. The cowboy with the most points or the lowest time over all go-rounds is said to "win the average." Although generally both the go-rounds and the average pay money, the average pays better; that's where the big money is.

Bareback Riding: Riding bucking horses with a single handhold attached onto a leather strap or surcingle cinched down on the horse's withers. See Bareback Rigging.

Bareback Rigging: The leather strap used by a rider in the bareback riding. Equipped with D-rings, latigos and a cinch for strapping it down on a horse's withers. Has a single hand hold of hard rawhide fashioned for right or left hand use attached on the top.

Barrel Man: The rodeo clown that lives and hides in the barrel during the bull riding. He will use his barrel for protection for himself and the bull rider, the other clowns and bull fighters.

Barrel Racing: (Slang, Can Chasing.) Women's timed

rodeo event where a mounted contestant traverses a cloverleaf pattern around three barrels set in an equilateral triangle in the arena.

Bars: The lateral supports for a saddle tree. They lie along each side of the horse's back and spread the saddle's weight out over a large area. The bars are attached at the front with the saddle fork; at the rear with the cantle board.

Binds: See anchor binds, quarter binds.

Bradded: Mashed by a horse rearing over backward in the chute. A metaphor derived from a small nail (a brad) being driven in by a BIG hammer.

Bronc: A wild horse. Also, a bucking horse in today's rodeo. Only called a bronco (with the O sound) in old movies and discussions about Ford's SUV . . . or a football team.

Bronc Rein: See Hack Rein.

Bronc Saddle: A saddle specially built for riding broncs in rodeo competition. Designed along the lines of an Association Saddle approved for use by the rodeo association rules. Typically has no saddle horn, big swells, tall cantle board, and is equipped with anchor and quarter binds for stirrup leather adjustment.

Buck: The jump and kick action of a horse or bull attempting to throw their rider.

Bucking Chute: A chute sized to fit a single bull or horse. The animal has limited room to move fore and aft or side to side and cannot turn around.

Buck Rein: See Hack Rein.

Bull Fighter: The rodeo clown who works to get the bull away from the bull rider when he gets off or gets bucked off. Keeps the bull rider safe. May also turn a bull back by getting the bull's attention while he is bucking so he will buck better and be worth more points.

Bull Riding: Rodeo event where a bull is ridden by means of a loose rope (a bull rope) pulled taut around the girth of the bull.

Bull Rope: Tightly braided (plaited) grass rope with an integrated hand hold and a looped end used for riding bulls.

Bulldogger: See steerwrestler.

Bulldogging: See steerwrestling.

Buzzer: See Whistle.

Calf Roping: Timed event where a calf is roped from horse back, flanked to the ground and tied by three legs.

Cantle: The rear part of a saddle's seat that curves up and wraps around the rider.

Cantle Board: 1. Essentially, the same as cantle. It is the thin board that rises up at the rear of a saddle seat and wraps around the rider. 2. A saddle bronc rider in the part of his spurring stroke where his feet travel back to the rear of the saddle is said to be cantle-boarding.

Champion: See World Champion and PRCA Champion.

Chaps: Pronounced "Shaps" (never "Chaps" with the Ch

sound like chair). The leather leggings worn over pants or jeans by a cowboy to protect the legs.

Charge: Charging, or Charging the front end. Vigorously spurring to the front end in the bareback or saddle bronc riding. Charging the front end, i.e. setting the feet over the breaks of the horse's shoulders, into his neck, and gripping the horse between the cowboy's heels is how to get a bronc rode and the way to score big points to win a riding (witness the old cowboy's adage, "The money's in the mane!" Usage: "He's a good one son, so you'd better come charging."

Chute: See Bucking Chute and Roping Chute.

Concho: Curved, often decorative, medallion tied into saddle strings as a retainer for the saddle skirt.

Covered: Riding the animal to the whistle is to get him covered.

Cowboys Turtle Association: The original "pro rodeo" association formed in 1936. Aptly named because the cowboys were slow to form an association and were afraid to stick their necks out to get what they wanted. Renamed the Rodeo Cowboys Association in 1945, and renamed again to the Professional Rodeo Cowboys Association in 1975.

Crow Hop: A weak buck that resembles the bird hopping from place to place.

Dally: Wrapping the tail of the lariat around the saddle horn to make a catch in the team roping.

Dashboarded: Being bucked off over the animal's front

end, especially in the saddle bronc riding.

Draw: Method for assigning stock to contestants in a rodeo. The rodeo judges randomly draw an animal's number out of a hat for each contestant, then post the draw sheet (usually in the rodeo office) showing what each cowboy has drawn. Makes the competition as fair as possible. The source of the old adage about "The Luck of the Draw." This phrase addresses the fact that some animals are better than others for the contestants and the draw plays a large part in a contestant's probability for success.

D-ring: The D shaped ring on a saddle that attaches to the cinch via latigo straps.

Eliminator: A rank draw that is not the nice one to get on. Frequently "eliminates" the rider from the competition by bucking them off.

Entry Fees: A rodeo contestant pays an entry fee to compete. A portion (the majority) of the entry fees are added to the purse along with the added money (sponsorship money) to constitute the total purse.

Fees: See Entry Fees.

Filled his Permit: See Permit.

Finals: Slang term for the National Finals Rodeo, or NFR. The last rodeo held in a given year where the top fifteen money winners in each event qualify to compete.

Flank: Short for flank strap. See Flank Strap.

Flank Man: Stands on the back of the chute and sets and

adjusts the flank strap on a bronc or bull. Pulls the strap snug as a bucking horse exits the chute.

Flank Strap: A sheepskin covered strap that attaches like a belt around the flank of a bucking horse encouraging them to kick when they buck. Also, a soft rope serving the same purpose in the case of a bucking bull.

Flying Dismount: A saddle bronc rider can time a jump out of the stirrups (and off the horse) with the bucking of the horse to launch himself in the air in a dramatic high-flying fashion. When performed correctly the rider is vaulted out of his saddle with the impetus of the horse's buck and lands on his feet at a safe distance away from the bronc.

Fork: The front of a saddle where the saddle horn is mounted on a western saddle. It attaches the bars (the sides) of the saddle tree together.

Gate Man: Two gate men operate a bucking chute gate, one to "jerk" the latch and the other to pull the gate open with a rope.

Get you at the gate: If the judges "got you at the gate" you missed the horse out. See miss out and mark out.

Go-Round: All contestants in a given event competing one time. Often multiple go-rounds are required to fill the schedule at a given rodeo held over multiple days and numerous performances. The go-rounds pay money as does the average. The go-round payouts are sometimes called "day moneys." Also see Short-Go.

Grand Entry: A parade of mounted contestants and dignitaries follows our flag in a serpentine pattern around the arena at the start of the rodeo. The colors are presented followed by our national anthem.

Gullet: The area underneath the fork on a saddle and between the swells. Forms the void over a horse's withers.

Hack Rein: The round loosely braided grass or poly rein used by a bronc rider. Usually five or six feet long. Also called a Bronc Rein or Buck Rein. The "measure" of the rein—or the point where the rider grips the rein—is critical: too long and the rein provides no leverage, too short and the horse can pull the rider off balance with the rein. Methods for measuring the rein differ from rider to rider but typically an eye-line is taken by pulling the rein up over the back of the bronc's head and marking the rein at the top of the eye on the other side of the head. This measurement is averaged with a mane-line measured on the rein where the mane ends at the base of the neck. The average of these two marks is then again averaged with a measurement taken as a fist with the thumb extended behind the swells of the saddle. Sometimes broncs take more or less rein than this average or "av" and can be said to take just a fist behind the swells (shorter) or an av plus one or two or three fingers, etc. (longer).

Half-Knot: The knot a cowboy ties in a bareback rig or bronc saddle latigo. The latigo is run through one side of the D-ring and tucked under the top run of latigo coming up from the cinch. (In contrast to a full-knot where it is also run back through the other side of the D and pulled down through the loop formed in the latigo like tying a necktie.

Halter: Leather straps forming a head stall for leading or restraining a horse. Used in the bronc riding to attach the rein.

Header: See Team Roping.

Heeler: See Team Roping.

Hobble Cinches: To connect the front and back cinches with a small strap. The back cinch is hobbled, i.e. it cannot move back toward the horse's flank.

Hock: The joint just above the fetlock in the rear leg of a horse or cow. Analogous to the ankle in man.

Hondo: The loop in the end of a lariat that the rope passes through.

Judges: There are two judges in rodeo. They score the rough-stock events and qualify and time the timed events.

Jump and Kick: The typical motion a bucking horse executes when they buck. They jump in the air and then kick while their weight is off their feet.

Lariat: Also lasso. A loop of rope thrown around a target and tightened by pulling.

Latigo: Not a river in Mexico as has been suggested (in jest) but rather the leather straps threaded through the D-rings on the saddle and the cinch ring, used for pulling (cinching) the saddle down tight.

Leggings: Cowboy slang for chaps. See chaps.

Luck of the Draw: See Draw.

Mark Out: In the bareback and saddle bronc riding the rider is required to have his feet in contact with the horse above the break of the shoulders when the horse's front feet first touch the ground upon leaving the chute or the rider is disqualified.

Miss Out: Usually "missed him out." A failure to mark the horse out. Results in a disqualification. See Mark Out.

National Finals Rodeo: The final rodeo of the year where the top fifteen money winners in each event qualify to compete.

Neck Rope: A rope looped around an animal's neck to help control them in the chute.

NFR: See National Finals Rodeo.

Out Gate: The gate by which cowboys and bucking stock exit the arena.

Perf: Short for performance.

Performance: One performance of a rodeo. A rodeo may have one or a few or several performances held over a day a week or a couple of week's duration depending upon the particular rodeo.

Permit: An amateur cowboy can buy a permit from the PRCA to enter and compete in some pro rodeos (usually the smaller ones). He must win $1,000 dollars at PRCA rodeos to "fill" his permit. He then has the option to buy his PRCA membership card and turn pro.

Pickup Horse: The big, strong, fast, fearless and athletic saddle horse used by the pickup men.

Pickup Man: Or men. Two mounted riders whose job is to remove the cowboy from the bucking horse at the conclusion of the ride in the saddle bronc and bareback riding. They work as a team to remove (pickup) the rider off the back of his mount after he has completed his ride. They generally ride in on both sides of the bucking horse to bottle him up between them, so the rider can dismount the bronc onto the back of one of the pickup horses. They also remove the flank strap from the bucking horse via an integrated "quick-release" mechanism.

PRCA: Professional Rodeo Cowboys Association. The preeminent rodeo association in the world.

PRCA Champion: In the period 1976-1978 the top money winner for the year was crowned PRCA champion; the winner of the NFR was the world champion.

Pulling Gates: Refers to the two cowboys who open the chute gates during the rough stock events. The latch man releases the gate latch and the second man pulls the gate open with a rope tied to the latch end of the gate.

Purse: The total of the sponsor's contribution to an event's purse (the added money) and the contestant's entry fees.

Qualified Ride: In the rough-stock events you must stay aboard for eight seconds riding with one hand and not touching yourself, your equipment or the animal with your free hand. In the bareback and saddle bronc riding you also must mark the horse out of the chute to qualify.

Quarter Binds: They enable the rider to spur without losing (blowing) a stirrup. Small straps (similar to the anchor binds) affixed to the saddle tree near the base of the swells. They retain the inner stirrup leather causing it to fold or bend at the swell as the rider spurs back (cantle boards) to keep the distance from the swell to the stirrup constant regardless of the position of the foot.

RCA: Rodeo Cowboys Association. The name was changed to the Professional Rodeo Cowboys Association in 1975.

Rear Out: Refers to the way some horses will stand up on their rear feet while leaving the bucking chute when the chute gate is opened.

Rein: See Hack Rein.

Reride: If an animal "fouls" the rider on the chute or chute gate, or falls down, or fails to buck satisfactorily in the eyes of the two rodeo judges, denying the rider a fair chance at the money, they have the discretion to award the rider a reride on another animal.

Rodeo Clown: The generic term encompasses bull fighters and rodeo clowns in general. The specific term describes the funny man doing acts and entertaining the crowd, not necessarily a bull fighter.

Rodeo Producer: The person or company hired to produce a rodeo. Responsible for all facets of the production from hiring contract help (rodeo secretary, contract acts, clowns, judges, chute help, pickup men, announcer, and any others), to contracting stock, and acting as liaison with the rodeo association sanctioning body. Often works with a local rodeo committee who manage facilities, advertising, required permits, provide the purse and other ancillary support. Often the Rodeo Producer and Stock Contractor are the same entity.

Rodeo Secretary: Works for the rodeo producer or stock contractor managing the entry list, timing events, recording scores and making the payout.

Roll: Running the bucking stock ahead in the bucking chutes to fill empty chutes. Called "rollin' 'em up" for the chute gates on the front and rear of the chutes that roll open.

Roping Chute: A chute in the end of the arena from which a calf or steer is released for roping or steerwrestling.

Rosin: Dry rosin powder used to make the equipment tacky and easy to grip in the rough-stock events.

Rough-Stock: The bucking stock at a rodeo: bareback horses, saddle broncs and bulls.

Rough-Stock Events: One of two classes of events in rodeo. The rough-stock events, bareback, saddle bronc riding and bull riding, are scored by judges. The other class is timed events. See timed events.

Round Pen: A corral or pen with no corners for an animal to get trapped or hung up in. Useful when training/breaking horses.

Run Off: When an animal fails to buck.

Run Way: The passage from stock pens to bucking chutes.

Running W: Consists of several parts. A surcingle with two rings attached to it near the D-rings, two leather ankle hobbles, and a long rope. The rope is tied to the ring on the right side of the surcingle and threaded through a ring on the right ankle hobble of the horse. From there the rope runs through a ring on the center of the cinch, between the horse's front legs, and is threaded back through the ring on the left hobble. From the left hobble the rope is run through the ring on the left side of the surcingle and out to a cowboy who can stand well away from the horse as he works him around in a counter clockwise direction. (The rope would be routed in the opposite way to work the horse in the clockwise direction.) If the horse bucks, kicks or otherwise gets out of hand the trainer can pull on the rope, severely restricting the animal's mobility (i.e. hobbling his front feet).

Saddle Bronc Riding: Riding bucking horses with a bronc (or association) saddle. Often just called the "bronc riding."

Saddle Tree: The frame of the saddle. Usually wood or fiberglass. Two bars run along the horse's back and connect the fork (or swells—the front of the saddle) with the cantle (the back of the saddle). The bars are designed to conform to the horse's back for comfort and safety.

Score: In rodeo rough-stock events the highest possible score is 100 points. The score is split between two judges, one on each side of the animal, and each with 50 points maximum to award, twenty-five points for the animal and twenty five for the rider.

Short-Go: The final go-round in a multiple go-round rodeo where the top ten or twelve (typically) contestants in the average qualify for one more chance to compete for the championship of the event. Not all multiple go-round rodeos have a short-go or short-round, some just pay off the average of all go-rounds.

Short Stroked: Refers to a truncated or abbreviated spurring stroke. For example a bronc rider may just spur back to the cinch area before "charging" back to the front end when trying to catch up with a horse if he's behind in his timing. Often this is noticeable as the horse first leaves the chute when the cowboy is trying to pick up the bronc's timing.

Slap: Slapping or touching the animal with the free hand in the rough-stock events results in disqualification, i.e. a score of zero.

Spur: 1. A U-shaped metal device with a dulled rowel wheel attached to its business end worn on the heel of a rider. Used to goad, impel, or encourage an animal to greater effort. 2. The act of spurring.

Steerwrestler: Also called a bulldogger. A contestant in the steerwrestling event. See Steerwrestling.

Steerwrestling: Rodeo event where a mounted cowboy chases a longhorn steer into the arena and jumps from his horse onto the steer's shoulders. He grabs the steer by the horns, digs in his heels and brings the steer to a stop. He then puts a hold on the steer's horns and using them for leverage wrestles the steer to the ground. Also known as bulldogging.

Stirrup Leather: Adjustable leather straps hung over the bars of the saddle tree and carrying the stirrups.

Stock Contractor: The person or company that contracts to provide the animals for a rodeo production. They provide calves for roping, steers for roping and steerwrestling, bucking horses for the bareback and saddle bronc riding and bulls for the bull riding.

Stripping Chute: After his performance, a bucking

animal, bronc or bull, is run out of the arena into the stripping chute where the bareback rig or bronc saddle is removed. A bull's flank is removed in the stripping chute as well.

Surcingle: A leather strap like a bareback rigging that is cinched around the horse and strapped on behind the withers. Has rings on the side about where the D rings on a saddle or bareback rig would be and has another ring right in the center of the cinch between the horse's front legs.

Swells: The front part of a saddle that connects the bars of the saddle tree. The swells on a bronc saddle are large and typically undercut to provide better grip on a rank one. Because the swells protrude in front of the rider's seat the cowboy is able to grip the swells between his thighs providing the only really solid hold a bronc rider has on the horse.

Tapped Off: Spurring in time with the bucking of the horse and doing everything right.

Team Roping: Rodeo event where a long-horned steer (typically a Corriente) is roped around the horns or head by the header who then dallies his rope while the heeler ropes the steer's two hind legs, although one hind leg is legal but suffers a time penalty.

Timed Events: The rodeo events that are timed by the clock rather than judged, including calf roping, steer wrestling, team roping, the women's barrel race, and in some venues steer roping. The quickest time wins the event. Also see Rough-Stock Events.

Tree: See Saddle Tree.

Turn Out: When a bronc rider doesn't show up to compete on his stock the animal is "turned out" of the chute without a rider and returned to the bronc pen. Sometimes a bronc rider will turn out a horse he doesn't want to get on because there's little chance of winning on the animal. Sometimes he can't make it to the rodeo in time to compete and has to turn out. Whenever a cowboy turns out—in any event—he pays a turnout fine as a disincentive for doing it again.

Turtle Association: See Cowboys Turtle Association.

Whistle: A whistle or buzzer is used to signal the end of an eight second qualified ride in the rough-stock events.

Wood: Slang term used by a bronc rider for his saddle. Derived from the fact that back in the day bronc saddles had wooden trees—in fact many still do, although fiberglass has become very popular in saddle construction as it is light and strong.

World Champion: The cowboy that wins the most in a given event over the course of a full year. The exceptions to this were a couple of times in the past when the rule was changed so that the world champion was the winner of the National Finals Rodeo alone. In those years the overall winner for the year was called the PRCA Champion and the winner of the NFR was the World Champion. The system was quickly restored so that the top money winner for the year was again crowned world champion.

BIBLIOGRAPHY

1. CHAMPIONSHIP RUN
   a. McBeth, John. Personal interview. 7 Apr. 2013.
   b. PRCA. "2012 Media Guide-Records & Statistics."
      Scribd.com. Scribd, Inc., 2014. Web. 7 Apr. 2014.
   c. PRCA. "2012 Media Guide Wrangler NFR Records
      and History." scribd.com. Scribd, Inc., 2014. Web.
      7 May 2013.
   d. ProRodeo Hall of Fame. "Clem McSpadden, Rodeo
      Notable, Inducted 1990." prorodeohalloffame.com.
      ProRodeo Hall of Fame, 2014. Web. 7 May 2013.
   e. *Rodeo Sports News Championship Edition*, Volume
      23, Number 3, Rodeo Cowboys Association, Inc.,
      January 1975. Print.

2. STATUE IN BRONZE
   a. McBeth, John. Personal interview. 7 Apr. 2013.

3. TOPSY TURVY
   a. McBeth, John. Personal interview. 7 Apr. 2013.

4. TWENTY SEVEN HEAD
   a. McBeth, John. Telephone interviews. 23 Nov. 2013,
      20 Feb. 2014.
   b. Buchman, Frank. "World Champion Cowboy John
      McBeth Remains Closely Tied to Sport of Rodeo –
      For The Love of Horses." ruralmessenger.com.
      Rural Messenger, 13 June 2013. Web. 7 Jan. 2014.
   c. Pierron, G. Joseph. "Gerald Roberts, Rodeo
      Cowboy." kshs.org. Kansas Historical
      Society, Kansapedia. Nov. 2012. Web. 7 Jan. 2014.
   d. ProRodeo Hall of Fame. "Gerald Roberts, All-
      Around, Inducted 1990." prorodeohalloffame.com.
      ProRodeo Hall of Fame, 2014. Web. 7 Jan. 2014.

e. Hauser, Shannan. "Gerald Roberts." geraldroberts.com. 2000-2011. Web. 7 Jan. 2014.
f. Flint Hills Rodeo Association, Inc. "Rodeo Honors for the Emmett Roberts Family." flinthillsrodeo.com/history.htm. Flint Hills Rodeo Association, Inc., 2012. Web. 7 Jan. 2014.

5. FINDING OUT
a. McBeth, John. Personal interview. 7 Apr. 2013.

6. TICKET TO RIDE
a. McBeth, John. Personal interview. 7 Apr. 2013.
b. Boothill Museum, Inc. "Cowboy Hall of Fame: Carvel 'Kurly' Hebb." boothill.org. Boot Hill Museum, Inc., 2014. Web. 10 June 2013.
c. ProRodeo Hall of Fame. "Bill Linderman, All-Around, Inducted 1979." prorodeohalloffame.com. ProRodeo Hall of Fame, 2014. Web. 10 June 2013.

7. TURK
a. McBeth, John. Personal interview. 7 Apr. 2013.
b. Montana Cowboy Hall Of Fame and Western Heritage Center. "2013 Hall of Fame Inductees, District 7, James Thurkel 'Turk' Greenough." montanacowboyfame.org. Montana Cowboy Hall Of Fame and Western Heritage Center, 2013. Web. 12 May 2013.
c. Wikipedia contributors. "Pretty Boy Floyd." Wikipedia, The Free Encyclopedia. Wikipedia, The Free Encyclopedia, 13 May 2014. Web. 12 May 2013.

8. YOU BE THE JUDGE
a. McBeth, John. Personal interview. 7 Apr. 2013.

9. PEER PRESSURE
   a. McBeth, John. Personal interview. 7 Apr. 2013.

10. FRIENDS IN HIGH PLACES
   a. McBeth, John. Telephone interview. 26 Jan. 2014.
   b. Bob Tallman:
   1) Wikipedia contributors. "Bob Tallman." Wikipedia, The Free Encyclopedia. Wikipedia, The Free Encyclopedia, 24 Jan. 2014. Web. 26 Feb. 2014.
   2) National Cowboy & Western Heritage Museum. "Events, Rodeo, Inductees, Bob Tallman." nationalcowboymuseum.org. National Cowboy & Western Heritage Museum, 2014. Web. 26 Feb. 2014.
   3) Rodeo Country Radio. "Bob Tallman to Step Down from Announcing Wrangler National Finals Rodeo…Tallman Withdraws Name from WNFR Consideration." rodeocountryradio.com. Rodeo Country Radio, 29 Apr. 2013. Web. 26 Feb. 2014.
   4) ProRodeo Hall of Fame. "Bob Tallman, Contract Personnel, Inducted 2004." prorodeohalloffame.com. ProRodeo Hall of Fame, 2014. Web. 26 Feb. 2014.
   c. Mac Baldrige:
   1) ProRodeo Hall of Fame. "Malcolm 'Mac' Baldrige, Rodeo Notable, Inducted 1988." prorodeohalloffame.com. ProRodeo Hall of Fame, 2014. Web. 24 Feb. 2014.
   2) National Cowboy & Western Heritage Museum. "Hall of Great Westerners, Inductees, Macolm Baldrige." nationalcowboymuseum.org. National Cowboy & Western Heritage Museum, 2014. Web. 24 Feb. 2014.
   d. Cotton Rosser:
   1) Flying U Rodeo Company. "Cotton Rosser." flyingurodeo.com. Flying U Rodeo Company, 2010.

Web. 24 Feb. 2014.

2) ProRodeo Hall of Fame. "Cotton Rosser, Stock Contractor, Inducted 1995." prorodeohalloffame.com. ProRodeo Hall of Fame, 2014. Web. 24 Feb. 2014.

e. Rodeo Schedule: *Rodeo Sports News Championship Edition*, Volume 23, Number 3, Rodeo Cowboys Association, Inc., January 1975. Print.

f. Wikipedia contributors. "British Aerospace 125." Wikipedia, The Free Encyclopedia. Wikipedia, The Free Encyclopedia, 4 May 2014. Web. 26 Feb. 2014.

11. MISDIRECTION

a. McBeth, John. Telephone interview. 20 Feb. 2014.

b. Rodeo Schedule: *Rodeo Sports News Championship Edition*, Volume 23, Number 3, Rodeo Cowboys Association, Inc., January 1975. Print.

12. GOING FOR TWO

a. McBeth, John. Personal interview. 7 Apr. 2013.

b. NFR scoreboard and stocklist: *Rodeo Sports News Championship Edition*, Volume 23, Number 3, Rodeo Cowboys Association, Inc., January 1975, P. 38 and 107. Print.

13. PINK CADILLAC

a. McBeth, Francie. Telephone interview. 22 July 2013.

14. GRUNDY ON A MONDY

a. McBeth, John. Telephone interview. 26 Jan. 2014.

b. Barnes PRCA Rodeo Company. barnesprcarodeo.com. Barnes PRCA Rodeo, 2014. Web. 13 Mar. 2014.

15. JESSE JAMES
   a. McBeth, John. Personal interview. 7 Apr. 2013.
   b. Barrett, Hadley. Telephone interview. 1 July 2013.
   c. PRCA. "Stock of the Year, 1956-2011." scribd.com.
      Scribd, Inc., 2014. Web. 3 June 2014.
   d. Beery, Thad. Personal experience riding Jesse James,
      1974, Colby, Kansas.

16. INTERNATIONAL COWBOY
   a. McBeth, John. Telephone interview. 16 June 2013
   b. Tirelli, Roland "Butch." Telephone Interviews. 1
      July 2013, 3 Aug. 2013, 9 Aug. 2013, 20 Sept.
      2013.
   c. *Rodeo Sports News,* "RCA Cowboys Rodeo In
      Venezuela," Vol. 26, No. 9, 22 Mar. 1978. Print.
   d. Leipold, Judith, *Straight from the Horse's Mouth, A
      Biography of Hub Hubbell.* Sarasota: Peppertree
      Press, 2013. Print.
   e. Wikipedia contributors. "Wild West
      Shows." Wikipedia, The Free Encyclopedia.
      Wikipedia, The Free Encyclopedia, 28 May. 2013.
      Web. 15 July 2013.

17. HIGH ROLL
   a. McBeth, John. Personal interview. 7 Apr. 2013.
   b. "Saddle Bronc." *Prorodeo Sports News* 1979
      Championship Edition: P. 19. Print.
   c. "NFR Qualified Stock." *Prorodeo Sports News* 1979
      Championship Edition: P. 68. Print.

18. ALL-AROUND COWBOY
   a. McBeth, John. Personal interview. 7 Apr. 2013.
   b. Sutton, Jim. Telephone interview. 1 July 2013.
   c. "Jim Sutton." gojacks.com. South Dakota State
      University, 29 Oct. 2009. Web. 23 Apr. 2013.
   d. "Jim Sutton." sdshof.com. South Dakota Sports Hall

of Fame. Web. 23 Apr. 2013.

e. Journal Staff. "Top South Dakota bronc rider. . . ." rapidcityjournal.com. Rapid City Journal, 22 Jan. 2013. Web. 23 Apr. 2013.

19. LOW 'N' SLOW
a. McBeth, John. Telephone Interview. 26 Jan. 2014.

20. McMENTOR
a. McBeth, John. Telephone Interview. 5 May 2013.
b. Barrett, Hadley. Telephone interview. 1 July 2013.
c. Blackwell, Jade. Telephone Interview. 11 June 2013.
d. Blackwell, Rex. Telephone Interview. 12 June 2013.
e. Blackwell, Jace. Telephone Interview. 12 June 2013.
f. Laughlin, Mike. "Rex Blackwell, The Man Who Rubs Horses." cowboyshowcase.com. Web. 22 June 2013.
g. "About Rex Blackwell, Equine Specialist." zoominfo.com. Zoom Information, 2 Dec. 2004. Web. 22 June 2013.

21. A BAD DAY
a. McBeth, John. Telephone interview. 14 June 2013.
b. McBeth, Francie. Telephone interview. 22 July 2013.

22. THE LUCK OF THE DRAW
a. McBeth, John. Personal interview. 7 Apr. 2013.

23. UNTOLD STORIES
a. McBeth, Blake. Telephone interview. 5 Sept. 2013.
b. McBeth, Shellie. Telephone interview. 28 Oct. 2013.

24. FATHER AND SON
a. McBeth, Bart. Telephone interviews. 16 Dec. 2013, 19 Apr. 2014.
b. Clark, Derek. Telephone interview. 1 Apr. 2014.

c. Crystal Springs Rodeo. "CS Rodeo History."
crystalspringsrodeo.com. Crystal Springs Rodeo,
2013. Web. 14 Jan. 2014.

25. MONKEYSHINES
a. McBeth, John. Telephone interview. 26 Jan. 2014.
b. Grosswiler, Ed. "Bull Sense Keeps Clown Alive."
news.google.com. The Nevada Daily Mail, 23 Aug.
1969. Web. 20 Feb. 2014.
c. Bass, Shermakaye. "XL Cover Story: South by Wild
West." mo.austin360.com. Cox Media Group, 3
Mar. 2005. Web. 20 Feb. 2014.

26. ONE DEFINING MOMENT
a. Reeves, Tom. Telephone interviews. 23 Jan. 2014,
20 Feb. 2014, 4 Mar. 2014.
b. "Pro-rodeo - Saddle Bronc World Champions, 1929-
2009." worldofrodeo.com. World of Rodeo. Web.
28 Jan. 2014.
c. Renaud, Roseanna. "Rodeo Star Has Roots In Eagle
Butte." lakotacountrytimes.com. Lakota Country
Times, 2010. Web. 28 Jan. 2014.
d. ProRodeo Hall of Fame. "Tom Reeves, Saddle Bronc
Riding, Inducted 2008." prorodeohalloffame.com.
Professional Rodeo Cowboys Association, 2008.
Web. 28 Jan. 2014.

27. SCIENCE PROJECT
a. Clark, Derek. Telephone interviews. 13 Mar. 2014,
1 Apr. 2014.
b. "PRCA Media Guide-Wrangler National Finals
Rodeo, Records, History." scribd.com. PRCA,
2012. Web. 28 Apr. 2014.
c. "Rodeo Historical Society Announces Inductees into
National Cowboy & Western Heritage Museum
Rodeo Hall of Fame." nationalcowboymuseum.net.

National Cowboy & Western Heritage Museum, 9 Aug. 2010. Web. 28 Apr. 2014.

d. Woerner, Gail Hughbanks. "Goin' Down The Road." rodeoattitude.com. Rodeo Attitude, 2005. Web. 28 Apr. 2014.

e. "CNFR History: Saddle bronc riding champions." trib.com. Casper Star-Tribune, 8 June 2012. Web. 28 Apr. 2014.

f. "Monroe Veach-Veach Saddle Company History." vintagegunleather.com. Vintage Gun Leather, 2005. Web. 28 Apr. 2014.

g. Lenepah, Thelma Garpner. "Kate Lowry's Men: Horses, Ropes and Rodeo." newspapers.com. Miami Daily News-Record, 30 Dec. 1956. Web. 28 Apr. 2014.

28. PERFECT SCORE
a. McBeth, John. Telephone interview. 20 Feb. 2014.
b. Daines, Ivan. Telephone interview. 2 Mar. 2014.
c. Barrett, Hadley. Telephone interviews. 1 July 2013, 23 Mar. 2014.

29. GREATEST GO-ROUND
a. McBeth, John. Telephone interview. 15 May 2013.
b. Clark, Derek. Telephone interview. 9 May 2014.

30. OLD TIMERS
a. McBeth, John. Personal interview. 7 Apr. 2013.

31. TV COWBOYS
a. McBeth, John. Telephone interview. 26 Jan. 2014.
b. Barrett, Hadley. Telephone interview. 23 Mar. 2014.
c. Wikipedia contributors. "National Finals Rodeo." Wikipedia, The Free Encyclopedia. Wikipedia, The Free Encyclopedia, 4 Mar. 2014. Web. 3 Apr. 2014.
d. Wikipedia contributors. "Cox Convention

Center." Wikipedia, The Free Encyclopedia.
Wikipedia, The Free Encyclopedia, 16 Jan. 2014.
Web. 3 Apr. 2014.

e. Wikipedia contributors. "Interruptible
foldback." Wikipedia, The Free Encyclopedia.
Wikipedia, The Free Encyclopedia, 10 Feb. 2014.
Web. 3 Apr. 2014.

f. Wikipedia contributors. "Mix-Minus." Wikipedia,
The Free Encyclopedia. Wikipedia, The Free
Encyclopedia, 10 July 2013. Web. 3 Apr. 2014.

g. Wikipedia contributors. "Production
truck." Wikipedia, The Free Encyclopedia.
Wikipedia, The Free Encyclopedia, 10 Mar. 2014.
Web. 3 Apr. 2014.

h. Wikipedia contributors. "Outside
broadcasting." Wikipedia, The Free Encyclopedia.
Wikipedia, The Free Encyclopedia, 16 Feb. 2014.
Web. 3 Apr. 2014.

i. Staff Writers. "National Rodeo Has Area TV
Coverage." newspapers.com. The Belleville
Telescope, 24 Nov. 1983. Web. 1 Apr. 2014.

32. THE LAST RIDE
a. McBeth, John. Telephone interview. 8 Aug. 2013.

33. HALL OF FAME
a. Beery, Thad. Personal experience. Attended hall
inductions. 27, 28 Sep. 2013.

ABOUT THE AUTHOR

Thad Beery lives in Stockport, Ohio, with his wife, Lynne. He was born and raised in the west where he began entering Little Britches rodeos at the age of fifteen, progressing from there through the ranks of high school and amateur rodeos to intercollegiate competition. His career culminated with ten years of riding saddle broncs on the professional circuit. He has competed against world champions at some of the biggest and most well-known rodeos and strapped his saddle on many national finals horses as well as one bucking horse of the year. His first book "The Rodeo Road" caught the attention of John McBeth and led to this collaborative effort with the former world champion saddle bronc rider.

John McBeth and Thad Beery, 2013.

The author is online at:
http://www.facebook.com/ThadBeeryAuthor